A Lawyer's Guide to

Filing Long-Term Disability Claims and Appeals

A Lawyer's Guide to
Filing Long-Term Disability Claims and Appeals

ALLAN CHECKOWAY

Cover design by Amanda Fry/ABA Design.

Printed in the United States of America.

23 22 21 20 19   5 4 3 2 1

Library of Congress Cataloging-in-Publication Data

Names: Checkoway, Allan B.
Title: A lawyer's guide to filing long-term disability claims and appeals / Allan Checkoway, RHU.
Description: Chicago : American Bar Association, 2019. | Includes index.
Identifiers: LCCN 2019003762 (print) | LCCN 2019004080 (ebook) | ISBN 9781641052962 (epub) | ISBN 9781641052955 (softcover)
Subjects: LCSH: Disability insurance—Law and legislation—United States.
Classification: LCC KF1178.D5 (ebook) | LCC KF1178.D5 C48 2019 (print) | DDC 344.7302/18—dc23
LC record available at https://lccn.loc.gov/2019003762

Discounts are available for books ordered in bulk. Special consideration is given to state bars, CLE programs, and other bar-related organizations. Inquire at Book Publishing, ABA Publishing, American Bar Association, 321 N. Clark Street, Chicago, Illinois 60654-7598.

www.shopABA.org

Contents

Dedication

First came Jen, my oldest daughter, and then Jess arrived three years later. That was over four decades ago. From our first moment together until now in my last quarter of life, my lovable, loving daughters have remained my greatest source of gratitude and inspiration.

Author's Note

Over the course of my career, I have focused exclusively on disability insurance and have assisted a multitude of people with their claims. Although I myself have never suffered a lingering long-term disability, I have experienced a short-term total disability that had the potential to continue for much longer. This relatively brief but harrowing experience allowed me to know firsthand the psychological aspects of filing a disability claim while contending with a physical challenge.

People often ask if they require an attorney to help them file a disability claim. Technically, the answer is no. Everyone has the right to file their own disability claim directly with the insurer. Nevertheless, an attorney can greatly help with the process and protect their client. If I ever again face a disability, I myself would undoubtedly seek out an experienced attorney for the following reasons:

- Regardless of whether a claimant is filing a claim with the Social Security Administration, the Department of Veterans Affairs, or a private insurer, the disability claims process entails numerous obstacles that can reduce the likelihood of collecting benefits.
- The claimant's overall state of health is one factor that points to the importance of having legal representation. Medical research tells us that a multitude of medical conditions serious enough to cause a total disability might also have a secondary disability—depression. Medical professionals tell

us that avoiding stress is imperative in dealing with depression, and personally filing a disability claim is undoubtedly stressful.

- To file a disability claim on one's own, a claimant must deal directly with the insurer, and while waiting to hear from the insurer, bills will pile up, virtually guaranteeing a level of stress detrimental to one's well-being. In fact, studies show that disability claim applicants report an extreme level of stress, affecting their overall health. The ultimate effects of stress and depression only add to the setbacks of a primary physical disability.

These stresses, and the need to collect, can make it extremely difficult for a claimant to remain objective. Claimants often justly feel they have their own and their family's financial security on the line. "Breadwinners" especially feel the burden of this uncertainty, and the potential loss of their breadwinner status creates unanticipated anxieties of its own.

Another reason for claimants to work with an attorney is that filing a claim is very personal. Dealing with strangers in a disability claim department can feel like an invasion of privacy and thus be alienating, embarrassing, and onerous. This is especially true when a claimant senses that a stranger is questioning the legitimacy of the disability, the claimant's honesty, or the doctor's determination of a disability.

Claimants may also be at a disadvantage when filing their disability claim without an attorney because of their long-term relationship with their physician. Given the deep trust that often attends the claimant–physician relationship, many unthinkingly defer to the physician's judgment, feeling disinclined to question their doctor. Sadly, this type of relationship can easily hinder a successful claim. When working with a physician directly, the claimant must ensure that the doctor understands the claimant's work duties and agrees that the disability prevents the claimant from performing them; uses the correct language to describe the disability to the insurance company; fills out forms on time; and is prepared to handle follow-up questions from the insurer. Ensuring such compliance can be difficult for a patient without the aid of a qualified attorney disability advisor.

Preface

A Disability Tsunami

In 2002, 1.3 million Social Security applications for disability benefits were filed, with an approval rate of 47 percent. Just 10 years later, the number of applicants had risen to 2.9 million, up *123 percent*, while the approval rate had diminished to 36 percent. Based on the 2010 average payment to those who qualified for benefits, this data represents more than $19.5 million of monthly benefits that will not be paid. When annualized, $23 trillion per year represents an overwhelming amount of disappointment—1.7 million Americans in a single year who will not collect benefits they thought they were entitled to.

Many initial disability claims are denied for simple mistakes and omissions that have absolutely nothing to do with the claimant's disability status. Think about what it might be like for a client to wait over a year to find out that his or her disability application was filed as "incomplete" for failing to answer just one question. After correcting this omission, the filer might have to wait another year or longer. *There must be a better way.* Those facing claim denials are filing an unprecedented number of appeals, further burdening the damaged system. As it is, appellants spend an average of nearly 17 months waiting for a judge to hear their appeal.

In addition, the Social Security Administration (SSA) system has been operating on overload for many years. Can overload lead to breakdown? Perhaps. Because elected officials prefer to align themselves with solvable problems, addressing Social Security is often swept under the rug. Currently, some 750,000 Americans are stuck in the Social Security disability backlog. The inability to pay bills causes Americans enormous mental anguish, which in turn stresses relationships, households, and mental health, potentially causing far-reaching repercussions such as burdening the nation's divorce courts and medical institutions.

According to data obtained through the Freedom of Information Act, more than 25 percent of veterans of the Iraq and Afghanistan wars seeking care at the Department of Veterans Affairs (VA) have posttraumatic stress disorder (PTSD). This statistic does not include vets who suffer mental illness but have not sought treatment due to the stigma associated with PTSD. Some PTSD claimants are diagnosed as having a preexisting "personality disorder" and therefore never receive benefits. As *USA Today* reported: "22,500 Veterans' PTSD Disability Claims Denied as Personality Disorder." How is it possible that a personality disorder, assuming it existed prior to military service, can be diagnosed when psychological evaluations are not done prior to military induction? In the meantime, for denied or undiagnosed suffering veterans and their families, life is hard—they may be forced to go on welfare and food stamps, their home may be foreclosed, drugs and alcohol frequently disrupt the home, and homelessness or even suicide may occur.

One often-insurmountable obstacle is the VA disability benefit application process. The VA has a long history of heavy bureaucracy. The VA disability claim form itself is more than 20 pages long, presenting a daunting task as the average citizen tries to complete it. The word *intimidation* comes to mind as a reason many veterans will never file a claim for benefits they are entitled to and may well be eligible for. In early 2018, outgoing VA secretary David Shulkin claimed to have improved the efficiency of disability claims and appeals processing, including a system that allows applicants to check their status online. Regrettably, long delays in disability claims processing still continue today, and promises for improvements in claims handling remain just that, with no relief in sight.

The U.S. Census Bureau recently projected a 75 percent increase in the age 65-plus population by the year 2030. This increase would bring the number of Americans 65 years of age and older to 69 million, or more than 20 percent of the entire population of the United States. An aging population carries with it an automatic growth in the number of disabled people.

In 2011, a massive earthquake in Japan created a 33-foot tsunami wave that caused over 1,000 deaths and billions of dollars in property damage. Our nightly news was filled with international panic, and vivid reporting continued for almost two years. The word *tsunami* automatically makes most of us think "disaster," and that is exactly what we face with increasing disability claims. When caused by Mother Nature, a tsunami is not preventable and comes with little warning. But we can see the "disability tsunami" on the horizon. With the Social Security disability trust fund scheduled to run dry in the not too distant future, this crisis is occurring at the worst imaginable time. Americans who experience disabilities need help collecting the benefits they are entitled to.

Attorneys, as this book argues, are critical allies in helping disabled claimants collect their rightful disability benefits. While we do not know exactly how many disabled claimants have filed claims directly with private insurers, the SSA, and the VA, we do know that if an attorney disability claim advisor had assisted in the process, many of these claimants would not have ended up having their claims denied.

☆ ☆ ☆

A Lawyer's Guide to Filing Long-Term Disability Claims and Appeals has been created for the legal advisors of individuals who are filing disability claims or appeals with their disability insurer, the SSA, or the VA. Different approaches to handling each disability claim are necessary because contractual provisions can vary dramatically, especially the definition of total or partial disability.

Your client may be filing a long-term disability (LTD) claim for the first time. Many others will be trying to understand why their claim was denied and how to appeal this denial. The primary objective in filing a disability claim is always to do it right the first time. You will encounter this reminder multiple times throughout this publication—especially in Chapter 4.

Filing a Social Security disability claim entails another claims-handling process. Many claimants file disability claims simultaneously with commercial disability insurers and the SSA. The definition of disability with private insurers is almost always more liberal than Social Security's stringent definition, which amounts to being totally disabled from doing all jobs. As such, many claimants will be eligible to collect from their disability insurers but at the same time are not eligible for Social Security disability benefits.

Filing a service-connected disability claim with the VA is a unique process. Benefits are based on the "degree of disability," starting at 0 percent, unlike traditional disability insurance. Moreover, qualifying for a VA disability may also provide access to free medical care, as well as a multitude of other beneficial services for the veteran and his or her family.

This publication is likewise a valuable resource for lawyers who are counseling clients considering the purchase of group or individual disability coverage, or both, as it discusses all the many definitions of disability. I explain the types of coverage and the related terminology, as well as how to achieve full protection. Furthermore, I have included a brief history of disability claims (Chapter 2), along with the perspectives of the many players in the claims process.

My primary objective is to use my decades of on-the-job experience to help attorneys understand the LTD claims process and guide their clients through it successfully.

This unique resource will help attorneys learn about four types of long-term disability insurance: individual, group, Social Security, and Veterans Affairs. They will obtain detailed information about the claims process, including common reasons claims are denied, frequent filing mistakes, and how to guide clients through effective communication with claims examiners and physicians.

Attorneys, in gaining this knowledge, will be able to successfully negotiate claims even when a client suffers depression in addition to a primary physical disability, a common occurrence. With the help of this book, lawyers can improve outcomes for harder-to-prove claims, such as claims from those clients suffering from chronic pain, fibromyalgia, and chronic fatigue. The facts are clear: claimants who have these types of "self-reported" disabilities and work with an experienced attorney have a measurably greater chance of having their claim approved than those without an attorney. The specially annotated claim form in Chapter 4 will serve as a particularly valuable tool. Chapter 11, which includes invaluable content on current law and regulations, will be updated as appropriate in future editions.

Finally, this publication will help attorneys give sound advice to their disabled clients about the possibility of returning to work, future insurance options, and employee rights. Should a disabled claimant recover to some extent and have the opportunity to work, they are eligible for returning to work under a transition program, having their work station adapted to their needs, and other rights granted to America's disabled population.

Chapter 1

Chance of Becoming Disabled

The acquisition of a disability comes with a host of side consequences. Indeed, outcomes are specific to each individual, but all are playing out against a rising swell of disability claims nationally that is swiftly becoming a crisis. Attorneys can be central players in helping clients navigate an increasingly unforgiving landscape—and be better able to claim the benefits they deserve.

Risks of Becoming Disabled

The likelihood of anyone becoming totally disabled varies depending on age, gender, and occupation. The statistics used in this book are for disabilities lasting 90 days or longer. If someone is disabled for 90 days, there is a high probability that his or her disability will last much longer, possibly for months or years, or even for the rest of his or her life. (Regrettably, insuring shorter-term disabilities such as sprained ankles, rotator cuff repair, or pneumonia would raise the cost of disability insurance by 20% to 30%.)

Some prevalent facts (and perceptions) on disability are as follows:[1]

- Over 36 million Americans today are classified as disabled, which represents 12 percent of the total population. Of those disabled, 50 percent are between the ages of 18 and 64.
- **Perception:** A total of 64 percent of workers say their chance of long-term disability during their career is only 1 or 2 percent.
- **Reality:** Just over one in four (25%) of today's 20-year-olds will become disabled before they retire.
- In total, 8.8 million workers, over 5 percent of the workforce, are receiving Social Security Disability Insurance (SSDI) today.

An article in the *American Journal of Medicine,* reporting on the results of a national study on medical bankruptcy in the United States, found the following:

- A total of 62 percent of personal bankruptcies in 2007 were related to medical conditions.
- Most of the sufferers were well-educated, middle-class homeowners.
- Their mean age was 45 years.
- Three quarters had medical insurance.
- Income loss was the major factor in their bankruptcy.
- Medical bankruptcy rates have risen substantially in recent years.

The Council for Disability Awareness (CDA) provides data from 19 of its member companies representing over

---

1 *See, e.g.*, the website for the National Fibromyalgia Association, http://www.fmaware.org.

75 percent of the commercial disability insurance marketplace. It reports that:

- Every seven seconds a working-age American will experience the beginnings of a long-term disability.
- Most people are not remotely prepared to experience the consequences of a long-term disability or the financial and psychological impact on their families.
- Eighty-four percent of corporate human resource professionals say the average employee can survive no more than six months without a paycheck, and 77 percent of financial advisors concur.
- The average LTD claim lasts over two-and-a-half years.

As these findings suggest, when people are young and distracted with family and ambition, they understandably give little thought to the likelihood of becoming disabled. However, reinforcing the data just presented, the Society of Actuaries tells us that the average 40-year-old faces a 20 percent chance of experiencing a long-term disability (i.e., a disability lasting at least 90 days) before reaching age 65, and one worker in seven will be disabled for five years or more sometime before normal retirement age.

Issues and Consequences

The average American, then, does not anticipate becoming disabled. One day your potential client is healthy, pleased to be working, with cares and concerns that center on everyday matters. Like tens of millions of other hardworking Americans, they allow themselves to remain willfully unaware of the risks and consequences of becoming disabled. And then "it" happens. The "it" might be headaches that won't go away, followed by an MRI, followed by a visit with a neurologist. Or the "it" might be awakening at 3 a.m. with stabbing chest pains, a spouse calling 911, and waking up a day later in intensive care. There are thousands of causes of long-term disability. Unfortunately, too many people discover the inadequacies of their disability insurance programs only after they are already facing a lifelong disability. Insurance clauses and policy terminology can make it difficult to truly understand the benefits. And then, once disabled, a potential client can struggle mightily to navigate the claims process and successfully collect benefits.

In many ways, the cause of the "it" doesn't matter—what matters are the issues someone faces when becoming totally disabled. The "it" has been best described as being like walking into a wall—and not at a normal walking speed but rather at 25 miles per hour. After that collision, this person's life as he or she knew it has effectively ended, so dramatic is the change.

One major consequence of disability can be home loss. For many people, jobs become an important part of identity formation. When health problems prevent potential clients from making a mortgage payment, perhaps the first they have ever missed, the impact can be devastating. The home carries with it enormous psychological value. It is the place where we shelter our families and seek refuge from the world, as well as a source of pride and satisfaction. It is not surprising that the leading cause of mortgage foreclosure in the United States today is a family member's health problem (as shown by the statistics on medical bankruptcy published in the *American Journal of Medicine*). We can infer that these statistics typically reflect disabilities experienced by household breadwinners.

As a window into the financial state of many American families, we can look at the mortgage foreclosure disaster that shook the country in 2008. Many households didn't have enough money to meet the downpayment on a home, so a second bank gave them a second mortgage. Or the original bank decided the downpayment wasn't necessary after all, given that houses were then appreciating at 5 percent per year or more. So many adages were proved wrong, notably: "Real estate doesn't ever go down in value" and "Our house will quickly be worth more than what we owe." Many homes were purchased with the income of both spouses working full-time jobs, which meant that when one member of the family lost income, many homeowners were unable to meet their mortgage payments. Many families lost their homes because of a disability.

Chapter 2

A Brief History of Disability Insurance

To serve their clients as effectively as possible, attorneys must understand disability insurance as it has been offered over the last five decades and its evolution to present-day policy forms. The disability insurance business has taken numerous twists and turns over this period, and the products offered by the major disability insurers have changed dramatically. This is largely because claims issues from past years have had an adverse impact on the attitudes of both policy and claims examiners. Someone filing a claim on a disability insurance policy purchased within the last decade will have very different contractual provisions than the person who purchased coverage 30 years ago. This brief history of disability insurance will give the professional legal advisor an understanding of how the current climate has been shaped by insurers' past adverse claims experiences.

End of an Era

Up until the mid-1980s, the industry standard was to offer disability products featuring two main areas of coverage: protection in one's own occupation for two, three, or five years, or until age 65, depending on the insured individual's occupation; and partial or residual disability protection without the requirement of a prior total disability. Typically, this coverage was limited by very few policy exclusions, primarily for disabilities acquired during war or an act of war, self-inflicted injuries, or commission of a felony; and no benefits would be paid during incarceration.

In 1976, a leading market-share disability insurer introduced a new benefit termed the "zero day residual." In disability contracts that paid benefits for either a long-term total or partial disability, zero day residual meant the insured did not have to go through a prior period of total disability before being eligible for residual benefits. At the end of the policy elimination period, benefits would be payable based on any combination of total or partial disability days. Insurers that previously had offered the best disability contracts only to professionals such as architects, attorneys, accountants, dentists, or physicians began to offer the same liberal policy forms to business executives and members of other select occupations. In the drive for market share, lifetime benefit periods and liberal definitions of total disability were on the rise. Proof of income was typically not necessary, and underwriting standards were liberal.

Financial Losses, Tougher Standards

During this period of low rates and liberalized underwriting, the incidence of disability began to increase markedly for unanticipated reasons. There was an almost overnight increase in claims. At the same time, the recessionary economy of the late 1980s, with poor investment returns, impacted insurers' claims reserves. The tide had turned.

Let's look at a theoretical scenario of what might have happened when a business executive who purchased a $6,000/month individual disability insurance policy to insure his $100,000 income developed a minor medical ailment. As no proof of income was necessary when he purchased his coverage, he realized that his $6,000/month disability insurance was better than his $4,000/month net income. The insurance was issued without restriction, although he had been treated for a bad back and he was seeing a psychotherapist because his business was failing and his wife was threatening to leave him. So he found a way to stretch a marginal, questionable disability into a long-term claim to benefit himself. It did not take very many fabricated claims to destroy the profitability of an insurer's entire book of business.

In addition, new causes of disability, including HIV/AIDS, chronic fatigue syndrome, carpal tunnel syndrome, and fibromyalgia, started to become prevalent. Modern social-influence claims (drugs and alcohol abuse, personality disorders, mental/nervous breakdowns) began appearing at an alarming rate, too. A study conducted by one major disability insurer discovered that 10 percent of new claims came from some form of psychiatric disorder. It was also found that a psychiatric disorder was a contributing cause of disability for nearly 30 to 40 percent of this insurer's long-term disability claims. Indeed, psychiatric disability is now one of the leading causes of Social Security disability claims.

The same study identified a dramatic increase in certain causes of disability over a recent four-year period:

- Psychiatric conditions—up 85 percent
- Severe back pain—up 120 percent
- HIV/AIDS—up 169 percent
- Carpal tunnel syndrome—up 520 percent
- Epstein–Barr virus—up 800 percent

The drive for market share with short-term insurer profitability in mind was yielding long-term claims—and losses. The financial statements of disability insurers reported rapidly deteriorating loss ratios. The insurers had learned that liberal definitions of total disability at high amounts of indemnity with lifetime benefit periods could not be offered profitably over extended periods of time. Rigid claims practices became the order of the day. Claims that would have been paid without question in previous years began to be denied outright, contested, or "negotiated."

The insurers' deteriorating loss ratios led to significant regret, driving drastic changes in the LTD claims approval process, such as the following:

- Liberalized underwriting standards disappeared.
- Long-term "own occupation" definitions of total disability began to disappear.
- Restrictions on mental and nervous conditions, and drug- and alcohol-related claims became more common.
- "Soft-tissue" restrictions began to appear for conditions such as chronic fatigue, carpal tunnel, and fibromyalgia.

The New Era: Today's Disability Claims Procedures

The simple fact is that 20 years ago, as many as two dozen quality individual disability insurers were in business, whereas today fewer than half that number remain. The shrinking field tells us a lot, however. The profit margins of insurers are so narrow that they struggle to generate any significant profit. Other businesses looking to increase profit either have to increase sales or cut their costs of doing business. Sometimes they borrow from their banks and expand into new areas. The startup costs hopefully get offset by new sales. With a disability insurer, one of two things usually happens. The first and most obvious adjustment is that they offer less liberal policy forms and/or more restrictive benefits to new insureds. But since the older policies are noncancellable, the newer policies with diminished benefits do not help profit margins on older policy forms. The only remedy for that is for insurers to toughen up on claims, something that is happening much more these days, as evidenced by the diminishing Social Security disability approval rate, which fell from 56 percent in 2000 to 33 percent in 2015.

We no longer see the "annuity" definitions of disability that insured occupations. A disability annuity definition insures an individual in his or her own occupation or specialty. Historically, if an insured became disabled from his specific occupation, he could collect full benefits for the duration of his benefit period. This benefit was possible regardless of whether he was still working or possibly even enjoying a higher income at another job.

With some insurers today, "guaranteed renewable" coverage has become their standard. The insurer cannot cancel the coverage, but he or she can increase the premium rate on a "class" basis. Blood testing and financial documentation are now the norm. And when an insured does become disabled, diligent claims management and aggressive rehabilitation programs are enforced.

The present norm in group LTD programs is to provide mental and nervous disorder protection for the first two years of benefits. After this period of time, the claimant must be institutionalized (confined to a hospital that specializes in the treatment of mental/nervous disorders) to continue to receive benefits. Some insurers now simply limit mental disorder claims to a two-year maximum without the additional wording about hospitalization. In fact, individual disability insurers have also begun to offer coverage with mental/nervous disorder restrictions, similar to group LTD.

Over the past two decades, improvements in medical technology have prolonged lives dramatically. Heart bypass surgery, angioplasty, transplant surgery, and many modern forms of cancer treatment did not exist just 20 years ago. While modern medical advancements are keeping individuals living longer lives, as they age these people are experiencing chronic or disabling conditions. A study spanning two decades revealed a 32 percent reduction in mortality from the four leading causes of death—heart disease, hypertension, cerebrovascular disease, and diabetes. The morbidity (disability) risk increased 55 percent over the very same timeframe.

Corporate Disability Insurance

The majority of corporate decisions relative to purchase of disability insurance are initiated by insurance brokers and employee benefit consultants. In the highly competitive corporate insurance world, the cost of medical insurance tends to dominate the attention of brokers and their clients. Whereas the medical insurance premium for a single employee might be $700 to $900/month, the cost of life and disability insurance for the same employee might be less than $50 a month. Regrettably, the diminished attention devoted to disability insurance may result in a lack of good advice provided by insurance advisors. This is particularly evident in the world of small businesses with fewer than 100 employees. Since more than 90 percent of businesses in the United States fall into this category, much of corporate America may not be getting sound disability insurance counseling.

Life insurance agents used to automatically recommend disability coverage to their life insurance clients; they were a predominant source of writing disability insurance, either with their primary company or one of the many disability insurers that accepted "brokerage" business. Today the number of life insurance companies that offer disability insurance has diminished markedly. A significant exodus of brokerage disability insurers has also taken place. With over two-thirds of the disability marketplace downsizing, one might assume that the insurers remaining would be doing much more business than previously. Unfortunately, this is not the case. The sad truth is that insurance agents and brokers are less inclined to offer disability insurance to their clientele today. The tougher underwriting standards, added to the educational requirements imposed by the various states, have put disability insurance on the back burner. Attorneys experienced in handling disability insurance claims can help by motivating their firm's individual and corporate clients to purchase disability insurance coverage. Aligning with a competent insurance advisor can be beneficial to a firm. It can actually become an added profit center, particularly for firms with small-business clients.

ERISA: Core Legislation for Disability Benefits

Central to understanding U.S. disability benefits is familiarity with the Employment Retirement Income Security Act of 1974 (ERISA), also known as the Pension Reform Act. Administered by the Employee Benefits Security Administration (EBSA), a division of the Department of Labor, along with the Department of the Treasury and the Pension Benefit Guaranty Corporation, an independent U.S. agency, ERISA established standards for group benefit packages, including those for disability insurance.

When ERISA was first unveiled 44 years ago, much of the publicity centered on its consumer protections for pension plans. But the provisions for disability insurance are strikingly important as well, and studying them is a requirement for any lawyer representing disability insurance claimants. (Visit the Labor Department's webpage for the basics: https://www.dol.gov/general/topic/health-plans/erisa.) Specifically, ERISA sets minimum standards for most voluntarily established pension and health plans in private industry that provide protection for those individuals covered. ERISA requires that plans provide participants with plan information, including plan features and funding; provides fiduciary responsibilities for those who manage and control plan assets; requires plans to establish a grievance and appeals process for participants to get benefits from their plans; and gives participants the right to sue for benefits and breaches of fiduciary duty.

The term "fiduciary responsibilities" is reminiscent of the period when corporate pension plans were first being scrutinized and 401(k)s were administered by banks, investment firms, insurance companies, and others. Many worried over the lack of protections for consumers, and ERISA made clear that an employer's responsibilities were being watched by federal regulators. In reviewing the Labor Department website, a lawyer can find the pertinent terms on disability insurance in the "Group Health and Disability Plans Benefit Claims Procedure Regulation" (see the Additional Resources section of this book), a booklet on the rules that apply to group health and disability benefit claims. Under "Compliance Assistance," the text states that ERISA covers retirement, health, and other welfare benefit plans (e.g., life, disability and apprenticeship plans), a touchstone for attorneys and their clients.

Chapter 3

The Disability Insurance Maze

This chapter covers, in some detail, four types of claims attorneys may face, depending on the claimant's line of work:

- **Individual disability insurance:** This insurance can be purchased, for example, by any employee whose employer does not provide group disability coverage.
- **Employer-provided group long-term disability (LTD) coverage:** This coverage is typical for many businesses.
- **Social Security Administration disability claims:** Those eligible include individuals who have worked at jobs that qualify for Social Security disability benefits.
- **VA disability claims:** These disability benefits are for members of the U.S. armed forces insured by the Department of Veterans Affairs.

Each of these types of disability insurance can have completely different contractual definitions of disability. Their claims systems and processes can also differ from one another. Adding complexity to this already complicated picture are the court system's different interpretations of policy terminology and varying outcomes of litigation on the same or similar issues. Furthermore, disability insurance claims can be mired in controversy when the claimant has both physical (medical) and mental health issues or when the cause of disability is chronic pain or another "self-reported" disability.

Some workers may have multiple forms of disability insurance. For example, a client of our firm is a skilled printing press operator. He originally purchased his own individual disability insurance through his employer's payroll deduction program. His union also automatically provided him with group LTD insurance. His group LTD benefits would be offset by Social Security disability benefits at the time of claim. The point here is that this individual has three completely different forms of disability insurance, each requiring a different approach and separate criteria for filing a claim. Another hypothetical example is that of a veteran who has a "10 percent" VA disability. Several years after acquiring a service-connected disability, he has recovered enough to return to work as a civilian. He might then be covered by a group LTD plan, working at a job where he is eligible for Social Security disability benefits. Again, the same individual ends up being insured by multiple disability programs, all with varying claims criteria.

Factual versus Legal Disabilities

The courts make a distinction between "factual disabilities" and "legal disabilities" (see, e.g., *Solomon v. Royal Maccabees Life Ins. Co.*, 243 Mich. App. 375, 382–83, 622 N.W.2d 101, 104 [2000]). A factual disability is a physical or mental condition that renders the insured unable to perform his occupation, whereas a legal disability, by contrast, is a condition imposed by law that forecloses the insured from performing his occupation (see *Massachusetts Mut. Life Ins. Co. v. Jefferson*, 104 S.W.3d 13, 26–27 [Tenn. Ct. App. 2002]).

Examples of legal disabilities include the inability to work due to incarceration, loss or suspension of a professional license, or restrictions imposed by a licensing board. For examples, see *Massachusetts Mut. Life Ins. Co. v. Ouellette,* 159 Vt. 187, 617 A.2d 132

(1992) (regarding an incarcerated optometrist not entitled to disability benefits); *Massachusetts Mut. Life Ins. Co. v. Millstein,* 129 F.3d 688, 691 (2d Cir. 1997) (regarding a lawyer prevented from practicing because of the loss of his license, not his alleged medical conditions); and *Zenk v. Paul Revere Life Ins. Co.*, 171 F.Supp.2d 929, 935 (D. Minn. 2000) (a case centering on ability to practice medicine, which ceased only when the plaintiff decided to voluntarily surrender his medical license).

Disability insurance comes into play when insured people seek benefits based on their medical conditions, claiming that but for their factual disabilities, they would still be working. As discussed below, courts evaluate the nature and timing of the disability, in keeping with the general principle that legal disabilities are not compensable.

The courts hold that, as a general rule, disability policies provide coverage for factual disabilities but not for legal disabilities (see *Allmerica Fin. Life Ins. & Annuity Co. v. Llewellyn,* 139 F.3d 664, 666 [9th Cir. 1997] citing *Brumer v. National Life of Vermont,* 874 F.Supp. 60, 64 [E.D.N.Y. 1995]).

The distinction between factual disabilities and legal disabilities is typically rather clear. Conflicts can arise, however, when an insured has, concurrently, both a legal disability and a factual disability.[1]

Group Long-Term Disability Coverage

Group LTD contracts usually have similar provisions across most insurers. The most common approach for total disabilities is to insure employees against the risk of disability in their "own occupation" for a set period of time, which is usually two, three, or five years, to age 65, or to Social Security normal retirement age (SSNRA). Then, after the "own occupation" period, the insured individual is almost always insured in an occupation for which he

1 *See* Keiko J. Kojima, "Blurred Lines: The Convergence of Mental/Physical Disability, Partial/Total Disability, and Legal/Factual Disability" (April 2017), iframe.dri.org/DRI/course-materials/2017-ERISA/pdfs/06_Kojima.pdf. *Heinonline is credited as the source of this content from the public domain.*

or she is suited by "education, training, or experience." The other common approach is to insure the individual in "any occupation" without regard to education, training, or experience.

Both consumers and their advisors frequently misunderstand the contractual differences between group and individual "noncancellable" disability insurance. Some noncancellable, or "noncan," policy forms offer "true" own occupation protection, that is, in one's principal occupation. If the claimants are unable to perform the material and substantial duties of their occupation, they are eligible for full total disability benefits, even if they are able to work at another job. "True" own occupation protection has become harder to find in policies issued after the early 1990s. The term "noncan" implies not only that the coverage cannot be canceled but also that there is a guaranteed level premium rate to at least age 65, or SSNRA.

Group LTD typically does not offer true own occupation benefits, and the term "long-term own occupation income protection" is commonly used. This implies that income from another occupation will be used to offset total disability benefits. Group LTD coverage can be canceled at renewal time, but group insurers are unlikely to cancel coverage because they can increase their premium rates at renewal time. Group LTD benefits are offset by Social Security, workers' compensation, state cash sickness, and other employer-sponsored benefits. Individual noncan policies are usually not offset by other benefits, although this offset has become a new trend in recent years.

Group LTD is an inexpensive way to insure a large group of people and focuses on the overall needs of an entire employee group. The guaranteed issue feature is clearly advantageous when compared to the medical underwriting requirements of noncancellable or guaranteed renewable individual coverage. "Noncan" coverage is designed to provide better protection for the needs of the individual.

It's unnecessary to favor one form of coverage over the other; each has its own distinctive benefits. Noncan coverage has the edge in contractual features, and yet it is much more expensive than group LTD. Group LTD has an edge in cost and ease of issuance. Regrettably, many people do not discover the inadequacies of their disability programs until after they either have become uninsurable or have already become disabled.

As stated in a representative disability policy, you have a disability when it is determined that:

- You are limited from performing the material and substantial duties of your regular occupation due to your sickness or injury, and you have a 15 to 20 percent or more loss in your indexed monthly earnings due to the same sickness or injury.
- After 24 months of payments, you are disabled when the insurer determines that because of the same sickness or injury, you are unable to perform the duties of any gainful occupation for which you are reasonably fitted by education, training, or experience.

Individual Disability Coverage

Over the past three decades, several different approaches have emerged for insuring individuals against the risk of long-term disability. We will analyze the most common forms of disability coverage that cover most contingencies and see how they compare. The coverage types can be roughly grouped into three categories: earnings only coverage, limited own occupation coverage, and own occupation coverage.

Earnings Only Coverage

An earnings only contract offers no special protection in one's own occupation. Total disability benefits are paid if the individual has experienced a loss of earnings. If the insured individual returns to work in his own or any other occupation, he collects a percentage of his monthly benefit based on the percentage of income he has lost.

Example: *A senior-level corporate executive working for a small construction company suffers a massive heart attack. Prior to becoming disabled, he was working 60-hour weeks and was earning*

$100,000 a year. He is insured to 60 percent of his income, which is $60,000, or $5,000 per month. After an initial period of total disability, he returns to his previous job, but his physician insists he only work half-days. Let's assume that through this reduction in hours the executive's income drops to $60,000, or 60 percent of what he was earning predisability. What will he collect?

First, we look at the income he has lost. This is his initial salary of $100,000 minus his current income of $60,000, which gives us an income loss of $40,000. We then divide this figure by his income before disability ($100,000) to give us his lost income as a percentage (40%). When we multiply this by his $5,000/month benefit ($5,000 × 0.40), we find he is still eligible for a $2,000/month benefit. Therefore, under an earnings only policy the executive could earn $60,000 from his job and receive another $24,000 ($2,000/month) from his disability insurer. This means that he could be collecting 84 percent of his predisability earnings ($84,000 divided by $100,000 × 100).

Own Occupation Coverage

The most liberal form of coverage is protection that provides coverage in the insured's regular occupation. With a true "own occupation" to age 65 (or SSNRA) definition of total disability, the insured can expect to receive own occupation income protection benefits, even when she is able to work part time at a reduced income.

Note the actual wording from an LTD contract:

***"Total Disability"** will be defined as follows:*

1. *During the Elimination Period and "Own Occupation" period, it means that due to an Injury or Sickness, the Insured Employee is unable to perform each of the main duties of his or her regular occupation.*
2. *After the "Own Occupation" Period, it means that due to an Injury or Sickness the Insured Employee is unable to perform each of the main duties of any gainful occupation which his or her training, education, or experience will reasonably allow.*

This approach offers full occupation protection combined with residual benefits. If the insured individual cannot perform the duties of her own occupation, she receives 100 percent full total disability benefits, even though she may be able to work in some other field. Residual (or partial disability) benefits are paid if the insured person returns to her own occupation while partially disabled and suffers a continuous loss of income.

Example: *Continuing with the example given in the Earnings Only Coverage section, let's assume the construction company executive returns to work earning $60,000 in each of two scenarios:*

1. *He returns to his former job working at reduced capacity, in which case he would be paid exactly as was described in the previous earnings only example.*
2. *He is unable to return to his former job because the physical and emotional demands are excessive. Instead, he begins to work on a part-time basis in a builders' supply house. His income falls dramatically, but the day-to-day pressures of managing his own business are gone.*

Under a true own occupation policy, the executive would be eligible to collect full benefits ($5,000/month), as well as receive the income from his new clerical job.

Limited Own Occupation Coverage

The "some occupation" form of coverage provides a limited own occupation definition lasting typically two, three, or five years. After the limited own occupation period, benefits are based on the percentage of lost income.

No industry study appears to be readily available indicating what percentage of America's workforce is covered by an own occupation definition to age 65. This full own occupation coverage would typically be for executives earning $50,000-plus annually. It is the norm to cover all other employees (e.g., blue-collar, lower-income, clerical) under a 24-month "own occupation" definition of total disability. Based on our own employee benefits practice, we would suggest that 80 to 90 percent or more of all businesses have 24-month limitations.

Disability Insurance Contractual Provisions

"Zero Day" Residual Disability

When residual/long-term partial disability benefits were first offered, insurers required a prior period of total disability before benefits would be paid. However, many claimants start out with a partial disability. Zero day residual benefits solve this problem by not requiring any prior days of total disability before partial benefits are payable. Today, most quality disability insurance carriers offer this critically important contractual feature.

Many insurers refer to zero day disability benefits. An insured can misunderstand zero day and assume that it means benefits are payable immediately (after zero days). However, as clarified here, the term "zero day" refers to the requirement that an insured does not have to have any days of prior total disability (zero days) to be eligible for benefits after the policy elimination period.

Waiver of Premium

Once an insured is considered totally disabled (typically, 90 days), the insurance company waives further premium payments for as long as the disability continues. This provision usually requires a disability that starts prior to a certain age. Should the disability occur after the age of 60, premiums will not be waived.

Trial Workday Provision

In many circumstances, an insured person will try to return to work to determine if she can handle the demands of her job while still in the stages of recovery. The trial workday provision allows the claimant a specific period of time back on the job, usually 15, 30, 60, or 90 days, depending on the policy elimination period. With an LTD program that has a long waiting period before benefits begin, say 180 days, this gives an insured person the opportunity to see if she can function at full capacity without starting the policy waiting period all over again should the insured person revert to being disabled.

Recurrent Disability Clause

Once an insured individual has been on claim for some time, the chance exists that her disability will recur as she recovers and returns to work. The recurrent disability clause typically provides a six-month period during which no break will occur in benefit payments if the insured person suffers a recurrent disability from the same or a related cause. The objective is to give the recovering employee the opportunity to get back to work without starting the waiting period all over again.

Presumptive Disability

If a disability prevents the insured from being able to use their hands or causes them to lose their eyesight, speech, or hearing, the insurance company automatically "presumes" they are disabled. It will pay full total disability benefits, even if they are able to work at their regular job in some capacity.

The "presumptive" clause can be very valuable. A cardiologist needs normal hearing to listen to heart sounds. A trial attorney needs unimpaired speech to deliver an effective summation in the courtroom. A neurosurgeon must have full use of his hands to function at his job. A self-employed CPA must have normal vision to be able to read tax forms.

Preexisting Condition Limitation (with Group LTD)

The most common preexisting condition clause insures an employee for a preexisting condition after he or she has been insured for 12 months. A preexisting condition is defined as a condition for which the employee has received medical treatment or advice during the three-month period prior to the effective date of coverage. For example, an insulin-dependent person with diabetes would have to be covered by an LTD program for one year before becoming eligible for benefits arising from a complication from diabetes. This is commonly referred to as a 3/12 preexisting condition clause.

There are other "pre-ex" clauses such as 3/6/12. This means the preexisting condition is defined the same way as in 3/12 (the employee has been treated for a condition within three months of the effective date of coverage), but employees can become insured sooner for the preexisting condition if they are treatment free for six months. The industry standard is 3/12 for larger groups, with more restrictive provisions for smaller groups (typically, fewer than 25 employees).

Protections under ERISA

As summarized at the close of Chapter 2, the Employee Retirement Income Security Act of 1974 (ERISA) protects most individuals covered by private LTD plans.

ERISA: Summary Plan Descriptions

Under ERISA, plan administrators must provide every insured person with a summary plan description (SPD) that identifies plan benefits and features and explains how to file a claim for benefits. If for some reason claim-filing details are not part of the SPD, a letter should be sent to the plan administrator, or human resources department, certified mail return receipt requested.

ERISA disability claims must be decided within a "reasonable period of time" but in no case later than 45 days after receipt of the claim. Should more time be needed beyond the plan's control, the plan must inform the claimant during the first 45-day period specifically why more time is needed and/or what any unresolved issues are and/or if additional information is required. Then the timeframe may be extended up to an additional 30 days. If a claim is denied, the plan administrator must provide written notice stating specifically why it was denied, with a clear description of the appeal process.

Appeal

The plan must provide copies of all documents, records, and any other information relative to the claim upon request and free of charge. As part of the appeal process, additional supporting documentation relevant to the claim must be submitted to the person specified in the denial notice within 180 days from notice of denial. The appeal must be evaluated by a new reviewer who looks at all submitted documentation and is not supposed to give any consideration to the prior claim denial. I personally believe that this is usually not practical or possible, so assume there must be new, compelling details to further document the validity of the claim.

Protecting a Disabled Claimant's Confidentiality under HIPAA

Attorneys need to exert great caution when dealing with a disabled claimant while obtaining the claimant's medical documentation to support his ERISA disability claim (see Appendix A for a case study on ERISA).

HIPAA: A Patient's Rights

Thanks to passage of the Health Insurance Portability and Accountability Act (HIPAA) in 1996, disabled claimants now have extensive rights as patients.

A Patient's Rights to Medical Records

HIPAA provides patients the right to obtain a copy of their own medical records from their medical provider, with a few exceptions. HIPAA allows health care providers to withhold some medical records, which include:

- Psychotherapy notes
- Information the provider is gathering for lawsuits
- Medical information that the provider believes could reasonably endanger one's life, physical safety, or the safety of another person

If the provider denies the request for medical records, it usually must provide a denial letter. The patient may be able to appeal the denial.

When Can You Get Your Requested Medical Records?

HIPAA requires that medical providers make copies of medical records available within 30 days of a patient's request. If it will take more than 30 days, the medical provider must provide a reason for not producing the requested medical records. Some states require that records be provided to the patient sooner than 30 days. For a list of state laws governing access to medical records, visit the Center of Medical Records Rights and Privacy at Georgetown University's Health Policy Institute online at http://hpi.georgetown.edu/privacy/records.html.

ERISA and the "Treating Physician" Rule in ERISA Plan Disability Determinations

A disability claimant's treating physician, the person who provides the hands-on medical care, has the best firsthand knowledge of the claimant and his or her medical condition. Therefore, you might assume that the treating physician should be in the best position to assist in determining the disability status.

The "treating physician rule" was originally developed as a means to control disability determinations by administrative law judges under the Social Security Act. ERISA regulates the manner in which plans process benefits claims. For example, plans must notify participants whose claims have been denied in writing, setting forth the specific reasons for the denial.

Prior to ERISA, the treating physician was the single most important ally for disabled claimants. However, a landmark 2003 U.S. Supreme Court case, *Black & Decker Disability Plan v. Nord,* determined that "ERISA does not require plan administrators to accord special deference to the opinions of treating physicians."

The net effect of this decision was to undo the protections provided by ERISA and to create an adverse consequence: without use of the "treating physician" rule, an LTD insurer can use its own medical consultants to evaluate a claimant's medical records and documentation. A huge obstacle is created when the LTD insurer denies or terminates an existing claim without the support of the treating physician.

From a disability insurance claim perspective, we have already stressed that the single most important factor impacting the likelihood of collecting disability benefits is the attending physician's report. That is the medical professional's statement that substantiates how the disabling medical condition is preventing the disabled claimant from performing the material and substantial duties of his or her occupation. The controversy begins when the insurer's claims examiner or the insurer's medical consultant questions the judgment or findings of the treating physician.

Unfortunately, many circuit courts did not apply the treating physician rule. The inconsistency was eventually clarified upon appeal to the U.S. Supreme Court. The Court ruled unanimously that ERISA 29 U.S.C. 1001 *et seq.* does not require plan administrators of employer-sponsored compensation plans to accord special deference to the opinions of treating physicians when deciding whether workers are eligible for disability benefits. (For an earlier study on the treating physician rule, see a paper by James Goodley in the *Journal of Contemporary Health Law and Policy*[2]; for updated material on this topic, based on changes to the law in 2017, see an article by the legal publisher Nolo.[3])

---

2 "The Effect of *Metropolitan Life v. Glenn* on ERISA Benefit Denials: Time for the 'Treating Physician Rule,'" vol. 26, no. 2 (2010): 403–40, https://scholarship.law.edu/cgi/viewcontent.cgi?article=1069&context=jchlp.

3 Aaron Hotfelder, "When Can Social Security Decide Not to Follow My Treating Doctor's Opinion?" Nolo, n.d., https://www.nolo.com/legal-encyclopedia/when-can-social-security-decide-not-follow-my-treating-doctors-opinion.html.

Chapter 4

The Claims Process

The actual process of completing a long-term disability claim form is beyond the capabilities of many. Answering a seemingly endless list of questions, with so much at risk, may become an insurmountable task for some. Claimants may have their disability insurance policy but not understand all the terminology. Or they are getting ready to file an LTD claim with an insurer, and they are not quite sure they have done it right. They may have heard or read that it can be hard to collect LTD benefits. They may have already filed an LTD claim that has been contested or denied. They are unsure about the next step to take. It is at this point that an attorney should become involved. We would not ordinarily think of filing an LTD claim as a presentation, but that is just what is needed—a carefully thought-out presentation to the insurer.

The evolution of long-term disability insurance in recent years necessitates a more intensive approach to filing LTD claims. Your involvement as a professional advisor in filing an LTD claim has become much more of a necessity. We know the Social Security disability denial rate has increased from 34 to 65 percent over a recent 10-year period. A struggling economy has produced a dramatic increase in the filing of disability claims by insureds covered by both individual disability policies and group LTD contracts. During times of economic downturns, many people tend to become more desperate, and so the number of questionable claims increases. This includes trying to "stretch" a marginal or partial disability into a total disability claim. Questionable disability claims will always be denied unless they are supported by skilled, reliable medical documentation attesting to the disability.

The key issue from your perspective as a professional advisor will come down to your ability to determine what claims are valid before investing your valuable time. It is imperative that you clearly understand the LTD claims process and how it fits with the current generation of LTD policy forms.

Professional advisors have the opportunity to provide "team support" and comfort, which claimants greatly appreciate when faced with the emotional upset and financial consequences of a long-term disability. You can outline the claims process itself to claimants so that they know exactly what to expect. Explain their rights to them. Then review all areas of the claimant's disability coverage so that all claim forms are submitted at the same time. In effect, you can act as the point person. With you "quarterbacking" the claims process, the claimant will not feel alone in dealing with strangers. You are his ally.

In this document, we encourage you to place yourself in the claimant's shoes, and we have described how a claimant may be feeling. Still, there is no way anyone can appreciate and understand what it is like to become disabled in the blink of an eye, unless they have experienced it. Disability affects not only the claimant but his family and friends as well. His life will never be the same. In addition to making sure the i's are all dotted, your assistance can give your client an enormous psychological boost. You are on the same team together.

Parts of an LTD Claim

A group LTD claim has three parts:

1. The employee portion, identifying the date and cause of disability.
2. The employer portion, confirming the date of disability, salary at the point of disability, and other work details.

3. The attending physician's report. The attending physician will need to clearly identify the date of the disability, its cause, and the prognosis. Know that LTD claims examiners are always prepared to check the credentials of the physician attesting to the disability. The claimant may want to ask the attending physician if he or she would recommend seeking the opinion of a specialist to reconfirm the disability.

After reviewing these basics, the next step is to refer to the definition of disability in the group LTD contract. It will read something like the following.

Disability or disabled means that:

- During the elimination period, you are prevented from performing the essential duties of your occupation.
- Following the elimination period, you are prevented from performing the essential duties of your occupation, and as a result your current monthly earnings are less than 80 percent of your indexed predisability earnings.

Before continuing, make sure you understand the preexisting condition limitation, which states something akin to the following.

No benefit will be payable under the plan for any disability that is due to, contributed to, by, or results from a preexisting condition, unless such disability begins:

- After the last day of 90 consecutive days while insured, during which you receive no medical care for the preexisting condition; or
- After the last day of 365 consecutive days, during which you have been continuously insured under this plan.

Preexisting condition defined

1. Any accidental bodily injury, sickness, mental illness, pregnancy, or episode of substance abuse; or
2. Any manifestations, symptoms, findings, or aggravation related to or resulting from such accidental bodily injury,

sickness, mental illness, pregnancy, or substance abuse for which you received medical care during the 90-day period that ends the day before your effective date of coverage.

Medical care is received when:

1. A physician is consulted or medical advice is given; or
2. Treatment is recommended, prescribed by, or received from a physician.

Treatment includes but is not limited to:

1. Medical examinations, tests, attendance, or observation; and
2. Use of drugs, medicines, medical services, supplies, or equipment.

The key point here is that if policyholders were being treated for a medical condition in the 90 days prior to the effective date of coverage, they will not be covered for that condition until they have been insured for 12 months. (They are covered for other conditions.)

Filing an effective claim also requires an understanding of the mental/nervous disorders limitation. In group LTD programs, the norm is to terminate mental and nervous disorder protection after two years of disability or to provide it only if the insured person is institutionalized (confined to a hospital that specializes in the treatment of mental or nervous disorders). It is to the insurer's benefit if the claimant can be classified as mentally ill, limiting benefits to two years. When a medical disability is compounded by psychological issues, make sure it is noted that the psychological disability is the result of the primary (medical) disability rather than a preexisting battle with depression or a similar mental health challenge. For example, if the claimant is now severely depressed in part because of a disabling heart condition, then it must be specified that the disabling condition is the heart condition.

Supplementing the LTD Claim

Presentations of long-term disability claims can be enhanced immensely by supplementing your LTD claim with research. Do an Internet search for articles relevant to the disability in medical and psychiatric journals. Consider having the claimant's supervisor or a co-worker issue a written statement describing changes she has observed since she first became disabled. Some examples include the following: "He was unable to stay focused on his job." "She called in late frequently and could not do her job for sustained periods of time." "She began to react emotionally to the pain she was experiencing." "He would forget simple tasks he had done before." "I noticed he was unable to sit or stand for long periods of time." "She's not as reliable anymore." If you ask for such testimony, be sure to emphasize that the co-worker should only record actual observations. He or she should never feel compelled to invent supporting material.

Have the signature on the statement notarized. When this supplemental evidence, which can be highly influential, is presented, the notary's signature and stamp will fend off any doubt about the document's validity. The supplemental statement should also contain the co-worker or supervisor's observations about the claimant's work capabilities before becoming disabled. The person supplying supplemental evidence should identify his or her relationship to the claimant, the length of time he or she has known them, and the frequency of their contact with each other before the claimant became disabled.

Doing It Right the First Time

When the LTD claim form is submitted with information that results in the claim being denied, the claimant is already at a significant disadvantage. Let's assume that a disabled claimant ends up filing a disability appeal correctly after the initial claim was presented with incomplete or incorrect information. The likelihood of the denial being overturned is substantially lower than the chance the original claim had of being approved. *It is critical to do it right the first time.*

The claims examiner's job is to evaluate LTD claims thoroughly and to pay valid claims while denying those that are incomplete, inaccurate, or potentially fraudulent. Typically, LTD claims, regardless of whether they are approved, are reviewed by the claims department manager. Frequently, staff or outside medical consultants are also involved in the process. An on-staff attorney may be consulted as insurers are well aware that claim denials lead to litigation. Thus, an LTD claim denial ultimately involves three or four separate insurance company professionals, representing at least three different departments or divisions of the insurer. Because multiple LTD insurance company departments are involved in a denied claim and they have all reached an agreement, the task of getting them all to change their minds is challenging and time consuming.

Common Reasons Disability Claims Are Denied

It is absolutely imperative that disability income claims be submitted correctly the first time around. If there is incomplete information that requires further clarification, claimants run the risk of their claim being contested. Attorneys need to pay special attention to the following pitfalls:

- Lack of clarity about the occupational duties of the insured individual's job.
- Claims information that does not clearly support the inability to perform the occupation being performed at the point of disability.
- An attending physician's statement that does not clearly validate the disability being reported.
- The appearance that the claimant is choosing not to return to work when the cause of disability and the doctor's report indicate that recovery could, and should, be possible.
- What appears to be a marginal or partial disability that is being stretched into a total disability.

Empirical knowledge of the most common reasons claims are denied is impossible to obtain, for it is confidential and proprietary information. Disability claims examiners have no reason to volunteer this information or to make it available to the general public. Based on my three decades of dealing almost exclusively with disability insurers, the following are my own observations of the frequent reasons disability claims are denied.

First, the majority of the working population is unaccustomed to completing long, detailed applications. One representative major disability insurer's long-term disability application contains dozens of questions, which can lead to confusion, inattention to detail, and mistakes. Fortunately, a national disability claims association has outlined the acceptable criteria for the application process, so at least there is some consistency among claims questions across the leading disability insurers.

Second, each claim is filed individually by individuals. There is no centralized place, either physically or virtually, where disability applicants can communicate or consult with each other. The loneliness of each individual fending for him- or herself is a major disadvantage for claimants, especially if they have not sought the services of an attorney specializing in disability claims. As of the publishing of this text, we are not aware of any nationally recognized, reputable source that outlines how to correctly file long-term disability claims.

The claimant's attending physician is the cause of numerous issues affecting claim denial. While in reality a high percentage of claims are denied, most applicants tend to assume their benefits will be paid just because their attending physician has deemed them disabled. Since a claimant's physician will be attesting to his or her patient's disability, it is necessary that the physician and his or her staff be familiar with the insurer's format. The office staff is likely to be very busy and to be processing many claims at a time, and so will probably need regular follow-up. The insurer's disability claims examiner will be communicating directly with the physician who is attesting to a total disability for additional details. New information thus obtained may lead to questioning the possibility of recovery to a nondisabled status. There may well be a partial and not a total disability, or the disability may not be related to the claimant's ability to perform the essential duties of his or her occupation or profession. At the same time, our society accords a lot of respect to doctors. There is a form of politeness in the claimant's relationship with his or her physician that is not typically extended to other skilled professionals. This can make it difficult for patients to assert their needs and rights during the disability claim process. However, our doctors are charged with taking care of our health and welfare, which includes helping to satisfy a disability insurer's criteria.

With regard to the medical professional who is attesting to a disability, there are many potential issues. Is he or she willing to cooperate with the claimant throughout the claims process? Is he or she a recognized specialist in the treatment of the particular medical condition that is disabling the claimant? For example, a primary care physician with a specialty in internal medicine should not be attesting to a psychiatric disability. This is not an unlikely scenario, as more than half the antidepressant medications prescribed nationally are reportedly prescribed by personal physicians. Another example would be a disabling back condition that has been treated by a chiropractor with spinal adjustments on a weekly basis. Has an MRI revealed a herniated disk or a bone spur on the claimant's spinal column? Might surgical intervention improve the condition enough to allow the claimant to return to work with a bad back? Details of weekly chiropractic adjustments usually are not enough to qualify the patient for disability benefits. The critically important point is that a disability must be certified by a physician skilled in the treatment of the claimant's specific cause of disability.

Another potential source of claims denial is either the claimant's or the doctor's lack of understanding of what is being insured. It is imperative to recognize the importance of being insured against the inability to perform one's specific occupation at the point of disability. This does not necessarily mean the exact occupation being performed when disabled. The policy wording may refer to a similar occupation in today's work world. The following wording was taken from a modern-day group long-term disability policy:

> Your occupation means Your Occupation as it is recognized in the general workplace. Your occupation does not mean the specific job you are performing for a specific employer or at a specific location.

There are literally hundreds of major causes of disability, and there are numerous occupations in the work world with a wide variance in occupational duties. It needs to be substantiated that the cause of disability leaves the insured unable to perform the essential duties of their occupation—the occupation they were performing when they became disabled.

At the same time, a particular medical condition that totally disables one individual may have no bearing on someone else's disability. For example, severe arthritis in a heart surgeon's hands creates a total disability, whereas the trial attorney can continue to function with arthritic hands. Loss of hearing or inability to speak renders the trial attorney incapable of continuing at his or her job but may not greatly affect a dentist. The professional with a bad back, whether a manual laborer or a dentist, becomes completely incapacitated, whereas the psychotherapist sitting in a chair may function well even with a bad back.

The Role of Claims Examiners

In assisting disabled claimants, it is helpful to understand the perspective of a disability insurer's claims examiner, whose job necessitates the evaluation of every detail of each claim he is assigned. Each insured has a unique job description and a particular disability caused by a specific medical impairment, which is sometimes complicated by a wide assortment of medical maladies. The claims examiner must carefully assess all of these inputs. The goal of each claims examiner is to pay legitimate, fully documented disability claims and deny all others.

For claim examiners, many claims they process end up being paid without any hassle. They receive properly completed claim forms substantiating the claimants' inability to perform work, for which there is adequate documentation. Let's call this the "black and white" side. These claims are filed completely, and there is no reason for the claims examiner to request additional information. The claims examiner begins to develop an attitude about a particular claimant—clearly, she is severely disabled, with all the supporting documentation to approve her claim. Using the recent Social Security disability approval rate of 35 percent, this represents about one-third of all claimants. If we consider the 65 percent Social Security denial rate, why is it so high?

First, there is the "gray" side. The claims examiner may receive incomplete forms. He or she cannot determine if the claimant was disabled "badly enough" based on the doctor's report. It is not clear how long the claimant has actually been disabled, either totally or partially, or whether there is a clear, definable disability. Or perhaps the job description makes it difficult to identify which occupational duties the claimant cannot perform. When there is not enough information, telephone calls and written letters are needed to communicate with the attending physician, the employer, and/or the claimant. As a result, a significant amount of time is needed to gain the clarity needed to make a long-term disability claim determination.

Then we have the "dark" side: this is when the claimant's "disability" hasn't interrupted his golf game. When the examiner calls seeking additional information, the claimant might be on vacation in Aspen (during ski season of course). When he returns the phone call, he is angry that he has not received his check yet and says he plans to file a complaint with the president of the insurance company, his agent, or his attorney. He may be highly indignant and may threaten a lawsuit. In these cases, a "true" disability has not been established. As another example, a claimant may be stating that his bad back is preventing him from returning to his job. However, the real problem is that his former job was already filled and his boss is delighted with his new employee. Our claimant simply cannot find a new job and is starting to think he is better off taking early retirement now by collecting disability benefits.

We could continue on with an endless list of situations where a claimant is trying to stretch a marginal disability into a total disability and may well be indignantly thinking, "I've paid premiums all these years and the insurer owes it to me."

After the claims examiners make a decision of denial, they report to a supervisor or manager with a recommendation to deny this claim. The claim file will have already been reviewed by a medical consultant with a specialized background in this particular cause of disability. Each variable (occupation, occupational duties, age, likelihood of recovery, amount of monthly benefit, total expected payout, etc.) may dictate the need (and likelihood) of video surveillance. From the claims examiner's perspective, it is easy to dispute a disability claim after showing video footage of a claimant's round of golf when the claimant supposedly has a debilitating back condition that is preventing him from working. Today, video surveillance is accepted as a primary method of disputing a claim.

Dealing with this range of claim experiences on a daily basis causes examiners to exercise caution and be suspicious about validating a claim. Think about how you would feel if many of the people you deal with every single day, week in and week out, were not being straight with you. It can become hard to trust claim applicants in this position. Understanding this up front will be helpful in your dealings with your clientele and claims examiners. So what is the best way to work with the claims examiner?

Communicating with the Claims Examiner

Disabled claimants need to be extremely cautious in speaking directly with their claims examiner for several reasons. First and foremost, we can assume that the claims examiner will appear to be pleasant, cooperative, and maybe even personable. This can be disarming to the claimant. The examiner may speak in a positive way about the possibility of claim payment. It may seem that he or she is on the claimant's side. However, in reality, claims examiners are focused solely on evaluating the claim; their allegiance is to their employer, the insurance company.

Disability insurer claims examiners are trained to carefully ask questions that elicit certain information. The interview will be recorded. The American public is now accustomed to statements about the need to record the conversation for "quality control," for "training purposes," or for "quality assurance," and may not pay much attention when these statements are made. However, these conversations will be on the record and cannot be undone.

At the same time, it is not helpful if a disabled claimant is non-communicative or uncooperative with his or her disability insurer. We need to arrive at a state of give and take between the claimant and the insurer. Keep in mind that claims examiners are looking for additional details so that they can verify the claim. The vast majority of disability insurers, especially those with solid, long-standing reputations and excellent financial ratings, will always pay clearly documented disability claims.

Remind the claimants that they are not to get angry or upset. They are used to going to work and being healthy. If they do get upset, it is completely understandable. If they are uncomfortable with the questions they are being asked, or if they are unsure about an answer and are worried they might say the wrong thing, tell them to pause the conversation. Tell your clients to ask the claims examiner for an 800 number and say that they will call back within a day or two. Or, better still, have them ask the claims examiner to put the questions in writing. Calling this time-out will allow you to regroup and refocus. The claimants need to make sure they answer every question correctly. They need an opportunity to think through their answers and discuss them with you. Following is a positive example of what a claimant might say to an examiner when queried via telephone.

> My understanding is that there is a federal law, HIPAA, which protects the privacy of people like me, especially when it involves my medical information. So I need to be cautious about talking to anyone about my private affairs, especially someone I don't know. You can understand how upsetting it is to me to have a medical impairment that will affect me the rest of my life. But, at the same time, I certainly don't want to delay you in obtaining the added medical information you are seeking, as my

benefits should be starting soon. I'm assuming you received the letter from the attorney who is representing me. Is that correct? I think the best option would be for you to contact my attorney directly. Otherwise, if you must hear something from me, I need to be absolutely sure we're both on the same page. I don't want to share very personal information over the telephone. If you could please send me a letter stating what information you need, I assure you I will respond in writing within two weeks.

Video Surveillance

Video surveillance is a valued tool when substantiating a disability claim. Is it legal? Absolutely. Concealed high-resolution digital cameras make irrefutable evidence when presented in front of a jury. Since disabled claimants frequently are not aware of the surveillance, their lives while disabled become an open book. The videotape tells a very powerful story, and that is also why today's jurors are predisposed to be comfortable with viewing an insurer's video surveillance documenting that a claimant is not as disabled as he or she claims. However, while video surveillance has become an effective defense of a disability claim for insurers, at the same time the court system continues to address multiple legal issues. The question of invasion of privacy and trespass looms large. The all-important issue of balancing the claimant's right to privacy with the defendant's right to investigate sits at the top of the controversy.

Independent Medical Exams and Functional Capacity Evaluations

An independent medical exam (IME) is performed by a physician who is not the claimant's treating physician. The claimant can use the results of the exam to support a claim for disability. Meanwhile, the disability insurer may use the IME to dispute or deny a claim for benefits. IMEs are also utilized when there is disagreement over the claimant's medical (or psychiatric) condition, diagnosis, or prognosis. An IME should be an unbiased exam and diagnosis of the claimant's condition. The following wording was taken from an actual disability policy:

> *After three months of continuous sick leave, you will be contacted by a claims examiner to initiate a claim. Your claim will be coordinated between human resources and the XYZ insurance company. You will be required to provide proof:*
>
> - *that you are under the regular care of a physician;*
> - *of the date your disability began;*
> - *of the cause of your disability; and*
> - *of the extent of your disability, that is, the restrictions and limitations preventing you from performing your regular occupation.*

XYZ insurance company may request that you undergo an independent medical evaluation to qualify for LTD benefits or to maintain them.

A functional capacity evaluation (FCE), also known as a functional capacity exam, consists of an extensive battery of tests to determine a claimant's physical capabilities regarding his or her ability to return to work. It can determine the ability to perform certain job functions that may not have been part of the claimant's daily work routine. The results of an FCE are typically compared with the Department of Labor's occupational standards of sedentary, light, medium, or heavy work. On the one hand, FCEs may yield positive evidence substantiating and confirming a valid disability. On the other hand, since the exam can be interpreted in different ways, the result can negatively impact a claim for disability benefits.

It is important for the attorney advisor to caution his clients that an IME means that the disability insurer wants documentation of the cause of disability, stating a specific medical diagnosis by a reputable, unbiased physician who has the recognized, creditable expertise to make an objective evaluation. Claimants' medical records must clearly substantiate their inability to perform the duties of their regular occupation, supported by medical and/or psychiatric records submitted by skilled professionals, as well as medical documentation that supports the disability claim in question. It is important to remember, however, that the medical professionals conducting IMEs and FCEs are representing the claimant's disability insurer and not the claimant. It is imperative that the claimant conduct him- or herself professionally. Refusing to cooperate is within their rights, but it raises a red flag to the insurer.

When claimants are asked to undergo an IME, they need to discuss how to handle it, or not, with their attorney disability claims advisor. If claimants and their physician feel the IME physician is representing the claimants' condition in an unfair manner or is ignoring the opinions and statements made by the claimant physician, we suggest you ask for the credentials of the physician performing the IME. Is the extent of the physician's medical practice limited to IMEs, thereby making claimants financially reliant on one or more insurance companies? If so, question whether there might be bias. If you judge that bias exists, then claimants are within their rights to insist upon an evaluation by a medical examiner who is truly independent.

Remind your clients that confidentiality is an absolute must. We live in an age of electronic media where many people stay in touch via Facebook, LinkedIn, Twitter, and the like. Today's claims professionals check social networking sites, chat rooms, public posts, and any other online source of information where claimants might share their daily activities. If claimants are seen to be engaging in activities that do not corroborate their disability claim, the insurer will use this as evidence for a claim denial.

The Claimant–Physician Relationship

Doctors undergo exhaustive education, training, and evaluation to achieve professional success. However, today's MD needs to be much more than a medical specialist. The day-to-day business end of practicing medicine also necessitates business management skills and compliance with many regulations. Health Maintenance Organization (HMO) criteria, hospital bureaucracy, and HIPAA policies all must be adhered to, and at the same time, in today's litigious society, there is always the risk of a lawsuit. Primary care physicians see patients an average of 28 hours a week and spend much of the rest of their time handling correspondence and follow-up, seeing patients in the hospital, and initiating managed care referrals. Keeping patients healthy and caring for them through a wide assortment of medical ills creates the utmost ongoing challenge.

Let's address the day-to-day office routine in today's medical environment. A disability claim form may arrive along with the rest of the MD's office mail. The office staff usually puts the envelope aside and deals with all such matters on a monthly basis. In one such case, the administrative assistant might pull out all the claimant patient's office notes and records covering an ongoing, two-decades-long, doctor–patient relationship. Years of office notes are left attached to the Attending Physician Statement for certification of the patient's long-term disability. What happens, however, if several more disability claim forms arrive on the doctor's desk during the month and the doctor has been working 12-hour days for two months now and cannot stand even the thought of more paperwork? Most MDs want to practice medicine and treat patients, not fill out more forms.

What is the MD's diagnosis, and, more importantly, what is the claimant's prognosis? Is the claimant totally disabled from his or her regular job? Is the claimant unable to perform the material and substantial duties of his or her regular job? Can the claimant be expected to recover? Can he or she return to the work world at another job? Can the claimant's workday or workplace accommodate his or her disability as required under the Americans with Disabilities Act? Will the claimant be capable and/or willing to make those changes?

How many MDs are aware of disabled patients' work duties? Probably not many. Has this MD ever had to certify a patient's disability previously? Has the physician ever had to leave his or her daily practice to testify on behalf of a disabled patient, especially a patient whose disability claim has been denied?

Trusting one's physician with our health and our lives is not an automatic occurrence. It can take years to build a relationship with our primary care physician. When people are disabled, they are trusting that their doctor will certify their disability and that he or she is knowledgeable about the claims process. However, this trust can be detrimental to achieving a successful claim.

In this way, claimants are hindered by their relationships with their physicians.

Dealing with a Noncooperative Doctor

It can be distressing for patients to discover that their physician, whom they may have known for decades, is not cooperative in helping them file a long-term disability claim and attesting to their disability. A number of reasons may account for the physician's reticence.

First, it may be the process itself. The practice of medicine involves a hectic routine. LTD claims generally require additional work that can disrupt an office routine, necessitating forms to complete and telephone calls to make and receive. The physician may have previously been asked to testify on behalf of a patient, perhaps after a lengthy delay or postponement, and may not want to do so again. Involvement with attorneys can also be unsettling for physicians.

Another reason a doctor may not be assisting is her disbelief that true disability exists. It always helps to take a step back and to perform an objective evaluation of the disability claim. Review carefully what the doctor is saying and ask yourself the following questions: Is the claimant trying to stretch a partial or marginal disability into a total disability? Is the doctor simply trying to say that she cannot ethically support the disability claimant's statements and that the claimant is unwilling to listen?

Some treating physicians may have difficulty making a hard-and-fast statement that there is total disability or permanent disability or permanent partial disability. With constant improvements in modern medicine, there is always the possibility that a new medical treatment or surgical procedure will be developed that could help in recovery. Yet, even with this understanding, how do you get the claimant classified as disabled now?

One tempting solution in any of these scenarios is to seek the assistance of another physician who might be less busy and more willing to help in the process. However, starting with a new doctor may do more harm than good. Note that in ERISA, as noted in Chapter 3, the "treating physician" who provides "hands-on" medical care has the best firsthand knowledge of the claimant's medical condition. Therefore, this physician is best positioned to assist in determining the disability status. This means the current doctor can be a valuable asset. (For a general introduction to ERISA, see Chapter 2.)

The attending physician's help with a long-term disability claim can be obtained if the physician recognizes that we are talking about being disabled today, not forever. The claimant cannot sustain full-time work *today*. If there is a Social Security disability that is expected to last 12 months or longer, the claimant needs to be eligible for benefits at the end of the 12th month. If the group LTD has a six-month waiting period, the claimant needs to be declared eligible for benefits at the end of the sixth month.

Professional advisors need to be aware of the attending physician's perspective; likewise, the doctor must understand the claimant's point of view. The claimant should start by having a personal conversation with his doctor. Physicians need to look beyond the additional demands that an LTD or Social Security claim may impose on their schedule. It is important, and sometimes necessary, for them to be reminded that the claimant's future financial survival depends on their cooperation. The bottom line is that the attending physician's cooperation is absolutely critical.

Major Mistakes to Avoid

To initiate a long-term disability claim, the claimant can obtain an LTD claim form from the human resources (HR) department at their place of employment. HR should then tell the claimant to have her doctor complete the attending physician portion. Then HR will complete the employer statement and be ready to submit it to the insurer. These three components are described next.

Employer's Statement

Key information includes date of hire, occupation, income at the point of disability, and the date the claimant stopped working due to her disability. It is imperative to include a job description with all work duties submitted with the employer's statement.

Employee's Statement

The claimant's portion of the claim form gives her the opportunity to state why she stopped working at her job. This is her documentation of the cause and date of the disability, as well as expectations regarding recovery and return to work.

Attending Physician's Statement

This statement is the attending physician's chance to support the LTD claim with the medical specifics. The wording used is very important. There may be an inclination to leave the form with the physician, or more likely an office staff person, to complete and return, but this should not be done.

Mistake 1

Leaving the attending physician's form with anyone but the attending physician is a major mistake. Do not trust the doctor will complete the form in a timely manner and send it to the insurer. Follow-up is extremely important. A physician responding to an insurance company's inquiry in one month would be very impressive—but highly unlikely; two to three months is more the norm. In filing a claim after 90 days of disability, if the LTD plan has a 90-day waiting period before benefits begin, there will be at least a four- to five-month time lag between the date of disability and the claims examiner's receipt of the attending physician's forms. How many people can go five months without a paycheck?

Mistake 2

Do not expect the doctor to understand the type of work the claimant does or why the claimant cannot do his job. When the claimant speaks with his doctor, it is very important to have clarity on this point. To determine what a good claimant response might look like, let's imagine I have just become disabled.

I start by calling my physician's office to request an appointment to discuss my medical condition and how it is preventing me from returning to work. When I meet with my doctor, I ask for a clear explanation of my diagnosis, if I haven't already been given an explanation of the medical condition that has disabled me. I also must hear my doctor's specific medical prognosis and how I can expect my disability to affect my life from this point on. Most important of all, I need to hear my doctor's perception of my disability and how it will impact my ability to return to my current job or to perform any future job for which I am suited. I need to hear from my physician that he clearly understands the duties of my job and how the medical condition he is attesting to will continue to prevent me from returning to work. I bring a job description to leave with my doctor so that there will be no misunderstanding about my work duties. I also ask when I can expect the attending physician's statement to be sent. Does my doctor have any doubts about my impairments? I want to make absolutely sure there is a clear agreement with my doctor that I will be unable to return to work.

The lack of claimant–physician communication will certainly create an obstacle to payment of benefits. If each party is telling a different story, the claim is likely to be denied.

Mistake 3

Sometimes the physician's statement is not worded strongly enough or does not clearly identify the extent of the claimant's disability. Note the following examples of the necessary stronger wording.

Weak: Unable to do his job
Strong: Cannot sustain full-time work at his job

Weak: Unable to work due to his disability
Strong: Completely unable to perform all the important duties of his job

Weak: Could work for several hours daily, several days per week
Strong: Unable to sustain level of activity sufficient to perform his job on a daily basis

Weak: Cannot maintain clear thinking for long periods
Strong: Unable to concentrate, complete tasks, stay organized and focused, or relate to others and has memory impairment

Mistake 4

It is important that the right person is certifying the disability. In this day and age of HMOs, health care is directed by one's primary care physician (PCP). When the PCP is an internist and a heart attack necessitates treatment by a cardiologist, the cardiologist should be the medical professional who confirms the disability (the heart condition). The cardiologist will supply the PCP with the claimant's medical records referencing the cardiac condition, diagnosis, prognosis, and indicated course of treatment; the PCP will then have a clear picture of the claimant's cardiac condition.

Mistake 5

When the physician's form is returned, the norm is for the claimant to immediately send it along to the insurer's claims department. Do not do this. The claim will probably be turned down if you do not insist upon seeing the medical records that the attending physician submits to the insurance company. The medical records belong to the claimants; they have every right to have them.

When you review the sample LTD claim form included with this publication, you will note how the attending physician identifies the cause of disability, dates of medical treatment, prognosis, and so on. However, in simply stating the cause of the disability, the doctor gives the insurer only a small portion of the information the claims examiner needs to approve or deny the claim. As soon as an LTD claim form arrives on the claims examiner's desk, the examiner requests medical records from all treating physicians. The medical records themselves tell the most important parts of the story. Identifying the medical treatment (exams, tests, medications, etc.), the dates of disability (possibly beginning with a partial disability eventually leading to a total disability), and attempts at rehabilitation, such as physical therapy, paints the clearest possible picture.

Mistake 6

Allowing the claimant to speak freely with the claims examiner is a major mistake. The claims examiner may well try to elicit information that will weaken the claim.

Successfully Filing a Claim

When filing an LTD claim, prepare, prepare, and prepare some more. As the claimant fills out the long-term disability claim form, be sure to keep in mind these key factors:

- Successfully collecting benefits will depend not only on the attending physician attesting to the claimant's medical condition, but also on how that medical condition prevents the claimant from performing the duties of his occupation. His occupation refers to the job he was performing on the day he became disabled.
- Make absolutely sure the physician is verifying how the claimant's medical condition affects the ability to do the duties of her job/profession before the claim is submitted and that everyone agrees with the doctor's statements.
- The attending physician should report any psychological (secondary) problems that the claimant is experiencing due to the medical (primary) disability.
- Make sure the physical aspects of the claimant's job are clearly defined—the physician will indicate that the claimant is unable to perform the most important duties of her job as well as the percentage of time that she performs those duties.
- Make sure the employer reports the claimant's last day of work consistent with the date the attending physician says the claimant was disabled.
- Make sure all doctors include office notes, test results, hospital discharge summaries, and consulting physician reports, and submit all medical documentation to the insurer at the same time.
- If the claimant has been paying premiums "post-tax" to be eligible for tax-free benefits, the claimant's employer should have been reporting post-tax premiums to allow for tax-free benefits.
- If the claimant is totally disabled, make sure he asks his insurer about applying for a disability waiver of premium

on his group life insurance so that his group life insurance continues.

- If the claimant is totally disabled, she may well be uninsurable and not be able to qualify medically for new life or disability insurance. Do not neglect the guaranteed group life and LTD conversion options.
- The claimant will have a conversion privilege to make a decision on converting coverages before the conversion period (usually 30 days) expires upon termination of employment.

Sample LTD Claim Form

<table>
<tr><td colspan="4">EMPLOYEE'S STATEMENT (PLEASE PRINT) (Answer all questions to avoid delay.)</td></tr>
<tr><td colspan="4">Type of Coverage (CHECK ALL THAT APPLY)
☐ Short-Term Disability ☐ Long-Term Disability ☐ Individual Disability</td></tr>
<tr><td colspan="2">Policy Numbers:</td><td colspan="2">The State in which You Work:</td></tr>
<tr><td colspan="4">1. Claimant's Name</td></tr>
<tr><td colspan="4">Home Address (Street, City, State, Zip)</td></tr>
<tr><td>Home Phone Number
( )</td><td>Date of Birth</td><td>Social Security Number</td><td>☐ Male
☐ Female</td></tr>
<tr><td colspan="2">2. Is this condition due to ☐ Accident ☐ Sickness?</td><td colspan="2">Is this disability related to your employment? ☐ Yes ☐ No</td></tr>
<tr><td colspan="4">Describe the injury incurred (what, how, where, when) or the nature and details of the sickness and when it began:</td></tr>
<tr><td colspan="4">You have been unable to work because of this condition as of what date?</td></tr>
<tr><td colspan="4">3. Employer's Name and Address</td></tr>
<tr><td colspan="4">Claimant's Work Phone Number ( )</td></tr>
<tr><td>Occupational Title</td><td>List the duties of your occupation at the time of your disability.
Duty</td><td colspan="2"># of weekly hours spent at each duty
Hours</td></tr>
</table>

Make sure the date of disability on the doctor's report coincides with the employee and employer statement.

Have you returned to work? If yes, When? Part Time: Full Time:		
Hours per week:		
If you have not returned to work, when do you expect to return? Part Time: Full Time:		

> Here's where the claimants need to specify how their medical disability prevents them from performing the duties of their job/profession.

> Make sure all doctors include office notes, test results, hospital discharge summaries, and consulting physician reports. All should be submitted to the claims examiner at the same time.

How does your injury or sickness impede your ability to do your occupational duties?
4. Information about physicians and hospitals **NOTE: TO AVOID DELAY IN EVALUATING YOUR CLAIM, ADVISE YOUR DOCTOR(S) TO ATTACH COPIES OF ALL MEDICAL RECORDS.**
First medical attention for the current disability was given by (complete below):

Doctor's Name	Doctor's Specialty
Address (Street, City, State, Zip)	Phone Number ( )
Hospital Name	Hospital Phone Number ( )
Address (Street, City, State, Zip)	
Dates of Confinement: From: To:	From: To:

(Continued)

<table>
<tr><td colspan="6">If other doctors or hospitals were consulted for the disabling condition, please note below.</td></tr>
<tr><td colspan="6">5. Information about Care and Treatment (if additional space is needed, please provide details on a separate page).</td></tr>
<tr><td colspan="2">Doctor who first provided medical attention to you for your current disability.</td><td colspan="2">Doctor's Specialty</td><td colspan="2">Telephone ( )
Fax ( )</td></tr>
<tr><td colspan="3">Doctor's Address</td><td colspan="3">Date(s) you were seen by this doctor
From________ To_______</td></tr>
<tr><td colspan="6">List all other physicians and/or hospitals you have seen for this condition below:</td></tr>
<tr><td colspan="2">Doctor's Name</td><td colspan="2">Doctor's Specialty</td><td colspan="2">Telephone ( )
Fax ( )</td></tr>
<tr><td colspan="3">Doctor's Address</td><td colspan="3">Date(s) you were seen by this doctor
From________ To_______</td></tr>
<tr><td colspan="2">Doctor's Name</td><td colspan="2">Doctor's Specialty</td><td colspan="2">Telephone ( )
Fax ( )</td></tr>
<tr><td colspan="2"></td><td colspan="2"></td><td colspan="2"></td></tr>
<tr><td colspan="3">Doctor's Address</td><td colspan="3">Date(s) you were seen by this doctor
From________ To_______</td></tr>
<tr><td colspan="2">Name of Hospital</td><td colspan="2">Department of Treatment</td><td colspan="2">Telephone ( )
Fax ( )</td></tr>
<tr><td colspan="3">Hospital's Address</td><td colspan="3">Date(s) you were treated at the hospital
From________ To_______</td></tr>
<tr><td colspan="6">Have you ever had the same or a similar condition in the past? ___Yes ___No
If Yes, provide the following information concerning past treatments.</td></tr>
</table>

Doctor's Name	Doctor's Specialty	Telephone ( ) Fax ( )

Doctor's Address	Date(s) you were seen by this doctor From________ To_______

Name of Hospital	Department of Treatment	Telephone ( ) Fax ( )

Hospital's Address	Date(s) you were treated at the hospital From________ To_______

Signature (required for all claims)

Any person who knowingly and with intent to injure, defraud, or deceive any insurer files a statement of claim or an application containing any false, incomplete, or misleading information is guilty of a felony of the third degree.

The above statements are true and complete to the best of my knowledge and belief.

X ____________________________________ ______________________________

Signature of Employee Date

<table>
<tr><td colspan="6">EMPLOYER'S STATEMENT (PLEASE PRINT)</td></tr>
<tr><td colspan="6">Type of Coverage (CHECK ALL THAT APPLY)</td></tr>
<tr><td colspan="6">☐ Short-Term Disability ☐ Long-Term Disability ☐ Individual Disability</td></tr>
<tr><td colspan="3">1. Employer Name</td><td colspan="3">Employer's Phone Number ( )</td></tr>
<tr><td colspan="6">Employer Address (Street, City, State, Zip)</td></tr>
<tr><td colspan="3">Policy Numbers</td><td colspan="3">Division/Class Description</td></tr>
<tr><td colspan="6">2. Claimant's Name</td></tr>
<tr><td>Claimant's Home Phone</td><td>Date of Birth</td><td>Social Security Number</td><td>Date of Hire</td><td>Effective Date of Insurance</td><td>Date Last Worked</td></tr>
<tr><td colspan="6">Claimant's Work Status: ☐ Full Time ☐ Part time ☐ Exempt ☐ Nonexempt</td></tr>
<tr><td colspan="6">General Information about the Claimant's Job</td></tr>
<tr><td colspan="3">3. Job Title</td><td colspan="3">Minimum education or training required</td></tr>
<tr><td colspan="3">Does the claimant perform supervisory function? ☐ Yes ☐ No</td><td colspan="3">If yes, how many people are supervised?</td></tr>
<tr><td colspan="6">4. Describe job duties:</td></tr>
<tr><td colspan="3">Duty</td><td colspan="3"># of Weekly Hours Spent at Duty</td></tr>
<tr><td colspan="3">Duty</td><td colspan="3"># of Weekly Hours Spent at Duty</td></tr>
<tr><td colspan="3">Duty</td><td colspan="3"># of Weekly Hours Spent at Duty</td></tr>
</table>

Name of Direct Supervisor	Telephone Number of Direct Supervisor ( )

> If the claimant has been paying premiums "post-tax," he or she should be eligible for tax-free benefits. Here is where the employer reports this.

> If the claimant is totally disabled, make sure he or she asks the insurer about waiver of premium on their group life insurance coverage.

Please attach a copy of the claimant's job description.

5. How was claimant paid? (please check one)

☐ Hourly ☐ Commissions ☐ Salaried ☐ Salary and Bonus ☐ Commissions Only ☐ Salary and Commissions

What is the earnings figure you use to compute premium payments for this claimant? $

Salary/Wage prior to date last worked **(Refer to earnings definition in your contract).**

☐ Weekly ☐ Bi-Weekly ☐ Semi-Monthly ☐ Monthly $___	Bonuses (per mo.) $___	Overtime (prior year) $___	Commissions (per mo.) $___	W-2 Earnings $___

6. Information needed for withholding and reporting taxes

Does employee contribute post-tax dollars toward the premium? ☐ Yes ☐ No
If yes, what percent is paid by the employee?

___% Pre-tax ___Post-tax ___ ? If you leave this section blank, we will assume it is 100% employer contribution or any portion paid by the employee is paid with pre-tax dollars and calculate FICA taxes accordingly.

PHYSICIAN'S STATEMENT (Answer all questions to avoid delay.)

A. General Information

Patient's Name:	Employer's Name:	Policy Number:

Patient Social Security Number:	Height:	Weight:	Blood Pressure:	Date of Birth:

(Continued)

B. Complete the following for normal pregnancy; then go to Section E.

Date of patient's last menstrual period?	Expected date of delivery?

Expected length of postpartum recovery?	First date of treatment?	Last date of treatment?

> This is where the physician should report psychological problems the claimant may be experiencing due to the medical disability.

C. Complete the following for all conditions except normal pregnancy.

Primary diagnosis (including ICD-9 or DSM code)	Symptoms
What diagnostic testing has been done?	Objective Findings

Are there secondary conditions contributing to the patient's disability?
___ Yes ___ No

If Yes, what are they? (include ICD-9 or DSM)

If this is a cardiac condition, what is the functional capacity (as referenced by the American Heart Association)? ___ Ejection Fraction ___ Class 1–No Limitation
___ Class 2–Slight Limitation ___ Class 3–Marked Limitation
___ Complete Limitation

If this is a psychiatric condition, what is the current GAF (Global Assessment of Functioning) score?	In the past year, what was the patient's highest GAF score?

When did symptoms first appear?	Date of patient's first visit?	Date patient was first unable to work?

Date of patient's last visit?	How often do you see this patient?
Is the patient's condition work related? ___ Yes ___ No If **Yes**, please explain.	
Has patient undergone surgery, or is he or she expected to have surgery in the future? ___ Yes ___ No If **Yes**, answer the following: Date of Surgery: Surgical Procedure? Result:	
What medication is the patient currently taking or has been prescribed?	
Please indicate other types and frequencies of treatment.	
Has the patient been referred to a medical rehabilitation or therapy program? ___ Yes ___ No If **Yes**, give details.	
Have you referred the patient for other types of consultations? ___ Yes ___ No If **Yes**, give details.	
Has the patient been hospital confined? ___ Yes ___ No If **Yes**, please complete the following. Name of Hospital Address of Hospital Date of Confinement From _____ To _____	
D. Information about the patient's inability to work	
Briefly describe the patient's restrictions. (SHOULD NOT DO)	
Briefly describe the patient's limitations. (CANNOT DO)	
What is the prognosis for recovery?	

(Continued)

Has the patient achieved maximum medical improvement? ___ Yes ___ No If **No**, please complete the following.
How soon do you expect fundamental changes in the patient's medical condition? __ 1–2 months   __5–6 months   __1 year or more __ 3–4 months   __6 months to a year   __Never
Give details concerning expected improvement or deterioration.
What is your treatment plan for the patient's return to work or return to prior level of function?
In an eight-hour workday, the patient can: **(Circle full hourly capacity for <u>each</u> activity)** Sit 1 2 3 4 5 6 7 8 Stand 1 2 3 4 5 6 7 8 Walk 1 2 3 4 5 6 7 8

Are there restrictions in:	Yes	No	If **Yes**, please fully explain below.
Driving/Operating motorized equipment	___	___	________
Lifting/Carrying	___	___	________
Use of hands in repetitive actions	___	___	________
Use of feet in repetitive movements	___	___	________
Bending	___	___	________
Squatting	___	___	________
Crawling	___	___	________
Climbing	___	___	________
Reaching above shoulder level	___	___	________
Other	___	___	________

If necessary, make sure the physician understands that he or she only needs to certify that the claimant is disabled at the end of the elimination period (when benefits start) and not for the rest of their life.

When do you expect the patient to return to prior level of functioning?	Would you recommend vocational rehabilitation for this patient? ___Yes ___No
E. Required Attachments and Signature	
After you have fully completed this form, please attach copies of the following materials. • Office notes for the period of treatment received • Hospital discharge summaries • Test results showing objective findings • Consulting physician reports	
Your Name	Degree
Specialty	Telephone No. ( ) Fax No. ( )
Address	
Any person who knowingly and with intent to injure, defraud, or deceive any insurer files a statement of claim or an application containing any false, incomplete, or misleading information is guilty of a felony of the third degree. **X**____________________________ ____________________ Signature of Attending Physician (no stamp) Date	

The Definition of Disability Revisited

The distinction between a total disability and a partial disability claim often falls into a gray area. The line between the two becomes particularly blurred when claimants continue to work in their occupation while claiming to be totally disabled. Typical cases include doctors or dentists who continue to own and manage their practices and physicians who claim to be restricted from performing certain procedures, such as surgery, which they characterize as the defining features of their occupation. Claimants in these situations maintain that their disabilities are total disabilities, not partial disabilities, because they are unable to perform a core aspect of their occupation, even if they are still able to perform other essential duties that allow them to keep practicing.

This debate is an open question in most jurisdictions. Courts that have confronted the issue have taken one of two approaches. In the first approach, courts hold that in order to recover total disability benefits, an insured must show that his disability prevented him from performing all of those duties, not just some of them. *See, e.g., Conway v. Paul Revere Life Ins. Co.*, No: 5:99CV150–T, 2002 WL 31770489, *9 (W.D.N.C. 2002), *aff'd*, 70 F.App'x. 117, 2003 WL 21730096 (4th Cir. 2003); *Yahiro v. Nw. Mut. Life Ins. Co.*, 168 F.Supp.2d 511 (D.Md. 2001); *Dym v. Provident Life & Accident Ins. Co.*, 19 F.Supp.2d 1147 (S.D.Cal. 1998). In the second approach, the courts have concluded that the definitions of total disability and residual disability are ambiguous, and they have held that an insured can be totally disabled despite being able to perform one or more substantial and material duties. *See, e.g., Giddens v. The Equitable Life Assurance Soc'y of the United States*, 445 F.3d 1286 (11th Cir. 2006) (rejecting "all" substantial and material duties interpretation); *Dowdle v. Nat. Life Ins. Co.*, 407 F.3d 967 (8th Cir. 2005) (discussing the two lines of cases and holding that where the insured's disability prevented him from performing the most important part of his occupation as an orthopedic surgeon, he was entitled to total disability benefits under Minnesota law).

Under the second approach, courts find that an insured does not have to establish an inability to perform "all material duties" in order to be totally disabled under the policy. *See, e.g., Dowdle v.*

Nat. Life Ins. Co., 407 F.3d 967 (8th Cir. 2005) (insured was totally disabled by reason of his inability to perform orthopedic surgery, notwithstanding his continuing ability to manage nonsurgical patients); *Stoneman v. Paul Revere Life Ins. Co.*, No. 12-15334, 2013 WL 6768616 (E.D. Mich. Dec. 20, 2013). The courts may emphasize the inequities that could result if the test were taken to the extreme—a claimant who could not perform most of her material duties would not be entitled to benefits simply because she could perform one material duty. *See Gross v. UnumProvident Life Ins. Co.*, 319 F.Supp.2d 1129, 1141 (C.D. Cal. 2004). ("[A] literal interpretation of the total disability clause would defeat the very purpose of insurance against total disability because it rarely happens that an insured is so completely disabled that he can transact no business duty whatsoever.") From a practical standpoint, this scenario does not play out because the battles over total disability occur when insureds demonstrate far greater work capacity; nonetheless, insureds still rely on this hypothetical. Courts rejecting the "all material duties" approach attempt to find a middle ground, recognizing that a claimant still has to prove he is unable to perform the vast majority or most of his material duties. This still leaves room for insurers to maintain that the claimant is unable to satisfy the definition of total disability even under the standard of the second approach.

The context of *Giddens* is important. *Giddens* is not a case where the insured continued to work or was only slightly limited in his job duties. Rather, Dr. Allen Giddens was unable to perform the "vast majority" of the substantial duties of his occupation. Courts have distinguished *Giddens* on this ground. *See, e.g. Berenguer v. Lincoln Nat. Life Ins. Co.*, No. 2:06CV190, 2006 WL 3327643, at *17 (E.D. Va. Nov. 15, 2006) (even under the standard in *Giddens*, the plaintiff would still not be totally disabled because he was capable of engaging in the duties of an office-based gynecological practitioner); *Repass v. Nw. Mut. Life Ins. Co.*, 684 F.Supp.2d 779, 783 (S.D.W. Va. 2009) (the court was not required to choose among the different approaches because even under the more favorable *Giddens* standard, the plaintiff still could not show he was totally disabled under the terms of the policy at the critical time). The facts that compelled the court's discussion of total disability in

Giddens are instructive. The insured in *Giddens* submitted evidence during the claim that his real estate development activities were only a passive investment carried on by his wife, but he later characterized his occupation as involving entrepreneurial, financial, planning, coordinating, and administrative duties. This explains how the "all" material duties question became one of the main issues in the case, whereas it may not have been an issue in other similar cases where the insured was not working in any capacity.[1]

Lump-Sum Settlements

Lump-sum settlements have become a noteworthy method of claims management in recent years. Disability insurers have markedly increased the number of lump-sum offers, and it is important to understand the insurer's objectives. Lump-sum settlements can be a "win–win" situation for both the insurer and the claimant.

As the number of claimants has risen, with increasing amounts of monthly indemnity, insurers must substantially increase their cash reserves. Sufficient reserves represent the capital that must be set aside to honor all expected future claim payments at a given point in time. Although a predictable percentage of claimants will either die earlier than the normal life expectancy of a nondisabled person or recover from their disability, the insurer must still maintain sufficient reserves. Lump-sum settlements can free up substantial amounts of capital to be diverted in a more productive direction.

After many months, even years, of fatigue, pain, and frustration dealing with medical issues and insurance paperwork, a lump-sum offer can be difficult to turn down. The desire to just put it behind the claimant may be very powerful. Yet there are too many instances in which claimants have unnecessarily sacrificed tens and hundreds of thousands of dollars in future benefits. In this instance, the attorney claim advisor can be enormously helpful in evaluating the pros and cons of a lump-sum settlement.

---

1 This section is sourced from Keiko J. Kojima, "Blurred Lines," iframe.dri.org/DRI/course-materials/2017-ERISA/pdfs/06_Kojima.pdf. *Heinonline is credited as the source of this content from the public domain.*

The claimant should ask why he is now being offered a cash settlement, after years of struggle and doubt. The answer is that it is all about the money or, better put, about the time value of money. The insurer realizes the claimant may eventually become eligible for monthly benefits. The claimant would rather pay, say, $200,000 today versus $350,000 over the next 20 years. Or the insurer realizes that defending the case in court, even if the insurer wins, could cost much more than a lump-sum settlement—and if the insurer loses, even worse. In addition, if the claimant is in a state where she is eligible to collect for damages in addition to monthly benefits, the ultimate settlement can be "off the charts."

Lump sums may be offered in exchange for "return of the policy" in instances in which there is a disputed claim. Return of the policy means that the insured person surrenders his or her policy to the insurer, giving up the opportunity to file any future claims, in exchange for a lump-sum settlement. This can occur when the claimant has a questionable degree of impairment and may be in conflict with the insurer's contractual definitions. The claimant is offered lump-sum compensation for a "perceived" disability, and the insurer is relieved of all future liability.

Many factors influence an insurer's decision to offer a lump-sum settlement. The expected duration of the payout period is usually at the top of the list. Someone who is terminally ill is unlikely to receive a lump-sum settlement. Other key factors include the amount of cash the insurer would have to place in a reserve fund and current interest and bond rates. In many instances, the cost of defending marginal claims may exceed the settlement offered. Lump-sum settlement awards or "commutations" may be offered when the claimant is permanently and totally disabled and there is no significant increase in mortality (chance of early death). In exchange for surrender of the policy, the insurer offers a single sum settlement or a "restructured" guaranteed periodic schedule of payments. Not all permanent disability claims are candidates for the commutation of benefits, as the claimant's psychological well-being and financial situation influence the decision.

When the claim meets the necessary criteria, the insurer may offer a lump-sum payment as an alternative to continuing to receive regular contractual benefits. If the claimant is not interested in pursuing a lump-sum settlement, the contractual benefits continue. However, should the claimant's medical condition improve, he or she then runs the risk of having future benefits contested. Should the claimant ever recover from his disability and return to work, is there a likelihood that the disability will recur? Should recovery occur, the claimant will then no longer be insured for other causes of disability. In such instances, insurers have been known to make a lump-sum offer verbally and/or insist that a decision be made immediately. In this event, the claimant should ask for the offer in writing and insist upon sufficient time to make a decision. The claimant will need adequate time to seek financial and legal expertise. Again, be mindful of the claimant's present psychological and emotional state. Is it possible that depression or anxiety might be impairing his ability to make a clear-headed decision? A trusted professional advisor is of great value in these situations.

The amount of the lump sum will predictably be less than collecting a regular long-term disability check, payable monthly, until normal retirement time. For example, imagine the claimant is presently age 50 and eligible for $5,000 per month until age 65. The expected payout will total $900,000 by age 65 ($5,000/month × 12 months × 15 years). Would a $600,000 lump-sum payment be acceptable today? Most astute investors with disabilities would love to have $600,000 in hand today to invest over the next 15 years. What if the disability limits the expected lifespan so that the claimants would likely never collect the full $900,000? In such a case, the decision to accept a lump-sum award may not be easy. You can be sure the disability insurer has already explored the various alternatives.

Claimants who are interested in a lump sum or a guaranteed restructured schedule of payments are always urged to consult with their professional financial advisors. Decision making should include the following questions: Is the claimant an astute investor? Is the claimant financially comfortable today? What is the likelihood that the disability will result in an early death (prior to age 65)? This issue should be discussed with his physician. If the claimant has a terminal illness, a lump-sum settlement may be advantageous. However, in dealing with the receipt of a large sum, it is important to remember that a lump-sum settlement offer does not have to be accepted. Whatever happens, the claimant should not make any quick decision. Claimants are best advised to discuss the "bird-in-hand" approach with their financial planning and other trusted investment advisors. They will need a clear understanding of the lump-sum award system. It can definitely be a "win–win" for insurer and claimant alike. The primary objective is for the claimant to understand all the various ramifications.

Structured Settlements

As an alternative to a lump-sum settlement, another method of settling disability claims is through a "structured settlement." The insurer might pay an immediate lump sum, for example, one-third or one-half of the total amount, followed by periodic payments. The insurer also purchases for the claimant an annuity or other financial product to guarantee a lifetime income.

One advantage of a structured settlement is that an annuity or U.S. Treasury security can be tax-free on the federal and state levels. When compared to a lump sum, which also can be tax-free, the proceeds are taxable when invested and interest or dividends are received. A structured settlement is not without risk. The entity making the regular payments may go bankrupt, even though insurers do careful due diligence. Utilizing a custodial account would be a viable option. Make sure to ask the insurer offering the structured settlement how it can guarantee all the proceeds being offered to the claimant.

When is a structured settlement better than a lump-sum settlement or regular monthly installments? It is not feasible to recommend one settlement vehicle over another. Time and circumstances create ever-changing conditions, and there is no one-size-fits-all solution. Our objective is simply to make attorney advisors aware of the various options offered by disability insurers in lieu of regular monthly payments. As always, claimants are urged to consult trusted financial advisors for the best option suitable to their particular needs.

Chapter 5

Disability Claimants and Mental Health

Medical researchers have conducted numerous studies on the recovery rate of the U.S. disabled population. It has been well documented that those who become disabled from a medical or psychological condition where recovery is possible or probable recover faster when they can maintain a positive outlook. Having effective disability insurance increases the likelihood of such a positive outlook. [*Note:* When examining the psychological effects of disability, we distinguish here between someone who is born with a life-altering disability (e.g., blindness, loss of a limb, paralysis, a congenital heart defect) and a fully able individual who suddenly experiences disability leading to career loss, given that the mindset is likely to be very different.]

For attorneys assisting in the disability claims process, it is particularly important that they understand how depression can impact their disabled client. Consider that over a 20-year timeframe the use of antidepressants has skyrocketed. Reportedly, one in ten Americans is now taking antidepressant medication. Yet, only one-third to half of those suffering from major depression have their condition diagnosed by medical professionals. Over their lifetime, more than 10 percent of men and 20 percent of women will suffer an episode of major depression.

According to the Diagnostic and Statistical Manual of Mental Disorder (DSM-5), a diagnosis of a major depressive episode is appropriate when the patient has been in a depressed mood or has felt no interest in daily activities for at least two weeks, and also has a least five symptoms that impair functioning almost daily. These symptoms may include unintentional weight gain or loss, difficulty sleeping, agitation, or slowed reaction as noticed by others, fatigue, low energy, feelings of excessive guilt or worthlessness, difficulty concentrating, as well as recurrent thoughts of death.

Although some claimants do attempt to file a disability claim with depression as the primary disability, far more will experience depression as a secondary disability resulting from their primary physical disability, particularly those facing chronic illness. We define chronic illness as an illness that will continue for a very long period of time and almost always cannot be cured completely. It is not surprising that depression occurs more frequently in people who have serious medical conditions than in the nondisabled population.

As many as one-third of chronically ill patients report mild to moderate symptoms of depression. Consider the statistical likelihood of depression among patients suffering from the following medical conditions:

- Heart attack: 40–65 percent
- Coronary artery disease (without heart attack): 18–20 percent
- Parkinson's disease: 40 percent
- Multiple sclerosis: 40 percent
- Stroke: 10–27 percent
- Cancer: 25 percent
- Diabetes: 25 percent

Individuals who become disabled, frequently with no advanced warning, are immediately impacted by stress and often have difficulty coping with the changes to their physical and emotional well-being. Major treatments required for primary disabilities are often unpleasant and can produce a long list of side effects. For example, cancer patients who opt for chemotherapy commonly experience nausea, stomach upset, and sleep disturbances, as well as weight loss, which adds to their weakened state. Anxiety and feelings of helplessness are common among them. In addition, many drug treatments for physical illnesses are known to have depressive side effects, which can add to the difficulties of a patient who is already experiencing some degree of depression.

Pain, fatigue, and a loss of energy complicate a patient's life. And depression certainly intensifies existing pain. An impaired capacity to work as well as increased difficulty in maintaining social relationships impact one's sense of identity and self-esteem. The condition may well affect mobility, independence, and lifestyle.

The difficulties associated with the first diagnosis of physical illness can precipitate a depressed state, which can be exacerbated as the disease progresses. If a claimant diagnosed with a serious physical illness has a past history of depression, recurrence of the condition is more likely than it is for someone who previously was never depressed. Sometimes a lower or impaired mood state is connected with substance abuse.

The "fallout" after becoming disabled is likened to the stages of mourning experienced by those who are advised of their impending death—shock, denial, anger, depression, and eventually, hopefully, adjustment and acceptance. Psychological counseling can be of enormous help to the person progressing through the stages of adjustment and possible recovery. Cognitive-behavioral therapy (CBT) is known to be helpful with issues involving changes in appearance and bodily functions.

In certain situations, the depression caused by chronic illness tends to aggravate the primary cause of disability. Depression and chronic illness can create a vicious circle that works to intensify the pain and fatigue caused by the primary illness. Depression is more likely to occur for the following conditions:

- *Vascular diseases* such as:
    - *Heart disease,* especially after a heart attack. Depression can impair recovery and increases the risk of another heart attack.

  - *Stroke,* as well as "ministrokes" (transient ischemic attacks [TIAs]), with depression a factor in prolonging illness.
  - *Hypertension diseases* of the nervous system.
- *Parkinson's disease,* with an estimated rate of depression exceeding 40 percent. Adding uncertainty, some of the symptoms of Parkinson's are also similar to the symptoms of depression.
- *Dementia*
- *Multiple sclerosis,* for which depression is frequently a complicating factor. Here, it is difficult to separate the effects of multiple sclerosis on the brain from the effects of underlying depression.
- *Cancer*
- *Diabetes*
- *PTSD,* for which a study by the National Institute of Mental Health identified more than 40 percent comorbidity with depression.

Attorneys handling LTD claims for clients should have a clear understanding of the complications created when depression is secondary to a medical disability. You can expect depression to be an issue as much as half the time when a medical condition is the primary cause of disability. The following are the key points to remember:

- It is important to determine whether clients have had previous episodes of depression prior to their debilitating illness and whether they have taken an antidepressant without a specific diagnosis of depression.
- The focus on establishing a total disability in the claims process should be the primary disabling medical condition and not depression.
- Depression is secondary to the cause of disability and is one more factor influencing the unlikelihood of recovery and return to work.

- When the insurance coverage is group LTD, you can automatically assume there will be a mental/nervous (M/N) disorder restriction after two years of disability. Keep in mind that in recent years some of the individual disability insurers have also started to include a M/N disorder restriction.
- If the primary cause of disability is found to be a mental or nervous disorder, the claimant will need to be institutionalized after two years in order to continue receiving benefits.
- The disability claims examiner will be looking to determine if he can establish that this is a M/N disorder claim and that if the insured was not depressed the claimant could return to work.

24-Month Mental/Nervous Disorder Limitation

The standard for group LTD is to provide mental and nervous disorder protection for the first 24 months of benefits. Then, to continue to receive benefits, the claimant must be institutionalized (confined to a hospital that specializes in the treatment of M/N disorders). Both depression and anxiety are included under the 24-month M/N restriction. Increasingly, the M/N disorder restriction is being extended to include disabilities from alcoholism and drug addiction.

Let's now consider disabilities caused by a heart attack or cancer, two leading causes of long-term disability. Frequently, depression will occur as a secondary disability. The claimant may recover from the heart attack or cancer but not from the subsequent depression. The heart attack disables these claimants, and then the depression keeps them disabled or complicates their recovery. If the insurer defines the disability as depression, benefits will be capped at two years. It is imperative that professional advisors stress and validate that the heart condition is the primary cause of disability, with depression as a secondary disability. This observation is especially important for disabilities such as chronic pain or chronic fatigue syndrome (usually referred to as "self-reported" disabilities) that are accompanied by high rates of depression or anxiety and are often classified in the M/N category. Attorney advisors should be sure to provide medical evidence that supports the primary cause of disability so that the claimant's depression does not become the primary claim under group LTD contracts.

Mental Health Parity in Disability Insurance

Medical (health care) insurance has historically been the most popular employer-sponsored benefit when compared with dental, life, disability, and long-term care coverage. Surveys repeatedly and consistently show that when employees are asked about their most valued employee benefits, their medical insurance comes out on top and by a large margin.

The recurrent issue of employers providing equal coverage for both mental and physical health care for employees was finally resolved with passage of the Mental Health Parity Act. The Patient Protection and Affordable Care Act of 2008 (ACA) gave every American ready access to health care coverage, including mental health and substance abuse disorder services in parity with medical/surgical benefits. Note that the ACA is a federal law covering all Americans for their health insurance coverage but not for disability benefits. The Mental Health Parity and Addiction Equity Act of 2008 (MHPAEA) was intended to improve access to affordable mental health care. MHPAEA requires that most private group health insurance plans offer parity with medical and surgical benefits, but not within employer-sponsored disability programs. This is particularly relevant when considering the likelihood of working Americans needing restriction-free disability coverage, that is, with no M/N disorder restrictions.

Several issues keep surfacing in the court system relative to parity in benefit levels for mental health and physical disabilities. Prior to the arrival of health care reform (the ACA), there were inconsistencies from state to state in several notable areas. Depending on the state in question, medical underwriting was allowed by state insurance department regulators. There were exclusionary provisions as well as waiting periods for certain benefits. And, most important of all, benefit maximums may have differed depending on whether the benefit being paid was for physical or mental illness. The ACA successfully forced medical insurers to provide restriction-free coverage without preexisting condition restrictions from thc inception date of coverage.

Mental Health Parity in Long-Term Disability Benefits

To date, no elected official has carried the banner of parity in both medical/surgical and mental health benefits in all employer-sponsored benefit programs. Disability insurance is designed to replace a portion of a claimant's earnings on a restriction-free basis except in an employer-sponsored group disability program. The industry standard is to pay benefits for a 24-month maximum in cases of mental disability. Note that ERISA preempts state regulation of employee benefits.

The Americans with Disabilities Act of 1990 (ADA) made it unlawful for employers to discriminate against a qualified individual with a disability. The Supreme Court ruled that determining whether a person has an ADA disability hinges on consideration of whether that person is substantially limited in performing a "major life activity" as determined "when using a mitigating measure." If that person has little or no difficulty performing any major life activity because he uses a "mitigating measure," then that individual will not meet the ADA's definition of disability.

Passage of the Affordable Care Act gave every citizen in the United States equal access to medical coverage universally with the removal of waiting periods, preexisting-condition restrictions, guaranteed issue coverage (with no medical underwriting required), and, lastly, same (equal) coverage for both physical (medical) and mental health benefits. But in the United States employers are not required by law to provide short- or long-term disability coverage. Employers are required to provide worker's compensation insurance for individuals injured on the job. In addition, six states and territories (California, Hawaii, New Jersey, New York, Rhode Island, and Puerto Rico) have "state cash sickness laws." These are essentially short-term disability coverage, with benefits differing from state to state.

Because U.S. employers are not required by law to offer short- or long-term disability benefits, the policy provisions in employer-sponsored disability programs are selected at the discretion of each individual employer. Consider the following:

- The industry standard for physical disabilities is to provide benefits to age 65 or Social Security normal retirement age (SSNRA), whichever is later.
- We refer to LTD as usually paying benefits to people age 65 or SSNRA (whichever is later), but LTD disability plans can be limited to a one-, two-, three-, five-, or even ten-year duration. (See the section on cost-containment LTD restrictions in Chapter 6.) LTD plans commonly insure executives and professionals in their own occupation for the duration of benefits, whereas blue-collar, gray-collar, lower-paid, or unskilled workers can be restricted to "own occupation" coverage for one or two years.
- LTD coverage almost always covers the insured in their own occupation. However, they can also be covered by a definition of disability that makes no reference to the insured's occupation (otherwise known as an "any occupation" disability contract).
- A 60 percent LTD benefit can be capped at \$3,000/month, \$5,000/month, and so on.
- An insured may be covered for total disability but not partial or residual benefits.
- Sometimes LTD benefits are only offered after an employee has gone through a probationary period, for example, a period of one, two, or three months.
- U.S. employers can continue to lawfully include 24-month M/N limitations, as every employee has the exact same coverage. If a federal law were ever passed to force employers to remove the 24-month limitation, every U.S. employer could then be required to pay an extra premium of 25 to 30 percent. This could lead to a rush of employers trying to terminate their disability programs or find alternative solutions such as offering employees the option of paying the extra premium

or giving every employee the option of electing to have voluntary individual LTD and having them pay the premiums themselves. Voluntary LTD coverage would have severe limitations, creating yet more controversy. (See Appendix B for a discussion of thc courts' treatment of parity in LTD benefits.)

Further Analysis

To explore the dilemma of the 24-month mental/nervous restriction, I offer my experience during my several-decades-long career in the employee benefit business. Let's examine the situation if an employer client of ours were to insist that we offer their employees restriction-free disability benefits, that is, with no M/N restrictions.

First, we are faced with the task of finding a group LTD insurer that is willing to remove the M/N restriction for an additional 15 to 20 percent premium or more. In a recent query, none of our "go-to" companies were willing to remove the M/N restriction at any added cost. The actuaries tell us that, since physical disability claims issues are compounded when a psychiatric disorder is also involved, it is not possible to develop an acceptable and reasonable premium increase that employers would be willing to pay.

Another option would be to offer two LTD plans to the same employer, one with the M/N restriction and the other without. Our firm has explored this situation, and it has never been a viable option. Moreover, the actuaries remind us of what we refer to as "adverse selection" against a disability insurer. This is similar to the addition of a limiting preexisting condition clause when insuring a large group of employees without medical evidence of insurability. The point here is that, based on experience, employees who already struggle with mental health challenges will be those most interested in group long-term disability without the M/N disorder restriction. Yet another option might be to combine restriction-free individual disability coverage with traditional group LTD coverage, but as noted earlier, this has not been practical or achievable in today's employee benefits arena.

In conclusion, if a new law or regulation were ever enacted to force U.S. employers to offer restriction-free disability coverage, the future security of millions of American workers would be subjected to corporate CFOs revisiting the cost and quality of their company-sponsored LTD programs. Restriction-free group LTD (i.e., coverage with no drug, alcohol, mental, or nervous restrictions) would increase costs substantially. The alternative would result in employers offering voluntary employee-paid LTD with higher rates than corporate-paid group LTD. This would put those American workers at risk of having no protection whatsoever for a long-term disability.

State Law Approaches to Parity[1]

In recent years, ERISA cases have been leading the way in developing the law on mental/physical disability claim issues. The majority of reported decisions on the subject are ERISA cases rather than individual disability claims. This may be because mental illness limitations may be more prevalent in group ERISA-governed policies, given that the decisions of state lower courts adjudicating non-ERISA cases are not reported, or because ERISA cases are more likely to proceed to the motion briefing stage where these issues are addressed.

Nonetheless, non-ERISA cases often draw on the holdings and concepts in ERISA cases and vice versa. For example, in *Bosetti v. U.S. Life Ins. Co. in City of N.Y.*, 175 Cal.App.4th 1208, 96 Cal.Rptr. 3d 744, 762 (2009), a non-ERISA action, the California Court of Appeal discussed Ninth Circuit ERISA cases, such as *Patterson v. Hughes Aircraft Co.*, 11 F.3d 948 (9th Cir. 1993) and *Lang v. Long-Term Disability Plan of Sponsor Applied Remote Tech., Inc.*, 125 F.3d 794 (9th Cir. 1997), without making a distinction between ERISA and non-ERISA cases. In turn, ERISA cases, such as *Johnson v. Gen. Am. Life Ins. Co.*, 178 F.Supp.2d 644 (W.D.Va. 2001), acknowledge the parties' citation to non-ERISA authorities, including *Elam v. First Unum Life Ins. Co.*, 72 Ark.App. 54, 32 S.W.3d 486, 490 (2000) (reversed by *Elam v. First Unum Life Ins. Co.*, 346 Ark. 291, 298, 57

1 Attorneys are encouraged to carefully review the page on ERISA on the Department of Labor website: https://www.dol.gov/general/topic/retirement/erisa.

S.W.3d 165, 170 [2001]) and *Akins v. Washington Metro. Area Transit Authority*, 729 F.Supp. 903, 906 (D.D.C. 1990). Note that plaintiffs may point out that ERISA cases adjudicated under the *de novo* standard of review, rather than those adjudicated under the abuse of discretion standard, are more appropriate for comparison because *de novo* cases do not give deference to the insurer's claim decision. Also, the doctrine of *contra proferentum* (ambiguities are construed against the drafter) may not apply in abuse of discretion cases. See, for example, *Johnson v. Am. United Life Ins. Co.*, 716 F.3d 813, 820 (4th Cir. 2013). (If plain language remains ambiguous after application of the primary principles of contract construction, then the courts are "compelled to apply the rule of *contra proferentum* and construe the terms strictly in favor of the insured.")

Many policies now identify specific mental disorders, which provide examples of the types of mental illnesses subject to the limitation. See, for example, *Simonia v. Glendale Nissan/Infiniti Disability Plan*, 378 F.App'x 725 (9th Cir. 2010) (unpublished) (limitation applied where the plan defined mental disorder as a disorder found in the Diagnostic Standards Manual, and depressive disorders were found in that manual); *Randles v. Galichia Med. Grp., P.A.*, No. 05-1374 WEB, 2006 WL 3760251, at *2 (D.Kan. Dec. 18, 2006). (Evidence showed that disability was caused or exacerbated by a mental disorder, which was defined as follows: "Mental Disorder includes, but is not limited to, bipolar affective disorder, organic brain syndrome, schizophrenia, psychotic illness, manic depressive illness, depression and depressive disorder, anxiety and anxiety disorders.") Even if the subject policy does not identify the specific mental disorder at issue, insurers can use these examples to serve as guideposts.

Since policies in recent years are more likely to cite specific examples of mental illnesses, such as depression or anxiety disorders, or to reference DSM-5 in their definition of mental illnesses, insurers can benefit from distinguishing the insured's cited cases based on the policy language and/or factual situation.[2]

---

2 The source of this section is Keiko J. Kojima, "Blurred Lines," iframe.dri.org/DRI/course-materials/2017-ERISA/pdfs/06_Kojima.pdf. *HeinOnline is credited as the source of this content from the public domain.*

Chapter 6

Self-Reported Disabilities

Becoming afflicted with chronic fatigue syndrome (CFS), carpal tunnel syndrome (CTS), fibromyalgia (FM), or multiple chemical sensitivity (MCS) can be confusing for early sufferers. We say confusing because, unlike the case for cancer patients or stroke victims, attaining a specific diagnosis can be frustrating and complicated. These illnesses can be grouped as "self-reported" disabilities. When a patient is recovering from a major heart attack, the attending physician hears the difference in heart sounds. An EKG shows a cardiologist the extent of the damage, and the reported diminished capacity is identified on a stress test. An MRI shows the orthopedic surgeon the location of a ligament tear. Self-reported or "subjective" disabilities, however, cannot be easily diagnosed with traditional medical exams and testing.

The Social Security Administration's publication "A Guide for Health Professionals" refers to chronic fatigue syndrome as follows: "Statements merely recounting the symptoms of the applicant or providing only a diagnosis will not establish a medical impairment for purposes of Social Security benefits." In other words, if you cannot provide the SSA with specific medical documentation, the agency will not rely on your reporting of symptoms for the purposes of establishing that you are disabled. Therefore, if there is no specific medical test documenting such disabilities, where does the chronic pain or chronic fatigue claimant turn? In the next section, we suggest ways to improve the chances of helping your client collect from a disability insurer for a self-reported disability, focusing on specific ailments. A review of court cases addressing subjective disabilities can be found in Appendix C.

Chronic Pain

Chronic pain, also referred to as fibromyalgia, affects up to 10 million people in the United States, the majority of whom are women. It is characterized by widespread pain, often accompanied with sleep and/or thinking difficulties, and sometimes depression. Definitive causes are unknown, and treatment is palliative. This can make the condition difficult to diagnose, especially for physicians who may not be familiar with it. A growing body of research has established this condition as a recognized disease and has removed early assumptions that it was mentally-based. The courts' treatment of chronic pain continues to evolve as the body of data grows and the number of diagnostic techniques and specialists increases. A further description of chronic pain can be found in Appendix D.

Pain as a disability in the Social Security determination process is both a controversial and an important issue in claims evaluations. At its heart is the issue of what sort of proof is required to demonstrate that pain resulting from the medically determined impairment prevents the claimant from engaging in substantial gainful activity. One of the leading court of appeals decisions on the issue explains the proper approach as follows: "while the claimant has the burden of proving that the disability results from a medically determinable physical or mental impairment, direct medical evidence of the cause and effect relationship between the impairment and the degree of the claimant's subjective complaints need not be produced." A further discussion of how the SSA and the courts have dealt with pain is found in Appendices E and F.

Chronic Fatigue Syndrome

CFS, also referred to as immune dysfunction syndrome, begins for many after a bout with a cold, bronchitis, an intestinal bug, hepatitis, or mononucleosis. For some it begins during a period of high stress, and for others it develops more gradually with no other illness or event precipitating it. Unlike the flu, which will go away in a few days or weeks, CFS symptoms can last more than six months, frequently resulting in a lifelong disability. Symptoms include fatigue, weakness, muscle and joint aches, difficulty concentrating, headaches, and tender lymph nodes. CFS sufferers report weakness and debilitating fatigue that is unrelieved by rest, resulting in substantially lowered activity levels. In addition, people with CFS report four or more of the following additional symptoms: sore throat, multi-joint pain (without accompanying swelling or redness), headaches, impaired memory, tender lymph nodes, and sleep that fails to refresh. When symptoms persist for at least six months, CFS can be properly diagnosed. Since these symptoms are similar to those for many other diseases, physicians who have had little experience in this area often find it difficult to specifically diagnose CFS.

In the early 1980s, the media began reporting on a "new" illness that they called "yuppie flu." The condition got this tagline because most people seeking treatment were well-educated women in their 30s and 40s. (CFS is diagnosed almost four times more frequently in women than in men.) Over time, people belonging to all socioeconomic groups have been diagnosed with the condition, dimming the inappropriate association with "yuppies."

Chronic fatigue, carpal tunnel, and fibromyalgia tend to include depression as a symptom. In the early years of awareness of these illnesses, patients were frequently diagnosed with "depression" when treatment for the depression did not alleviate their other symptoms. To this day, some members of the medical community have insufficient knowledge of or doubt the validity of CFS.

There is no recognized specific treatment for CFS. Studies show that cognitive-behavioral therapy and exercise programs have helped many sufferers. Antidepressant medication has also been helpful to some. (Certain antidepressants, however, increase fatigue, a symptom from which the patient is seeking relief. The attending physician can increase the dosage slowly or prescribe a more active antidepressant to alleviate the fatigue factor.) And, of special value given the uncertainties of CFS, emotional support and counseling can help in coping with the ups and downs of the illness.

One major disability insurer reported CFS to be the fastest-growing disability in recent years. The Centers for Disease Control and Prevention estimate that CFS affects about one million Americans, and many others have similar conditions that do not meet the criteria for CFS.

Cost-Containment Provisions

In recent years, an increasing number of LTD insurers have been utilizing "cost-containment" restrictions. Such cost-containment limitations restrict claim payments when the disabling condition is chronic fatigue syndrome, carpal tunnel, fibromyalgia, and chemical sensitivities, all of which are commonly referred to as self-reported disabilities.

As described earlier, the controversy surrounds the lack of objective proof of disability, forcing the insurer to rely on statements made by the disabled claimant. Note that many disability policies require the claimant to provide objective medical proof of disability [*Ecklund v. Continental Casualty Co.*, 415F. Supp.2d1353 (N.D. Ala. 2005)].

In filing a claim for any self-reported disability, it first must be established whether there is medical proof of disability wording. Considering the vast number of disability policies insuring working Americans today, the majority of such policies do not appear to include objective medical proof of disability wording.

Most group LTD insurers do not automatically include cost-containment restrictions, yet many group LTD insurers automatically will provide quotes to benefit advisors that have cost-containment wording. If there is little difference in premium rates (usually less than 5%) for removing cost-containment wording, why offer more restrictive LTD insurance? Simply put, the answer is profitability. Insurers want to pay fewer claims, not more. This is why consumers need to exercise caveat emptor—buyer beware. Employee benefit advisors must help employers and employees become educated consumers. As an employee benefit advisor, my suggestion is to avoid cost-containment/self-reported disability restrictions at all costs. There are already too many adverse scenarios possible for claimants throughout the disability insurer's handling of long-term disability claims.

LTD Claims for Self-Reported Disabilities

The following fictitious case studies give a sense of the obstacles faced by individuals pursuing long-term disability claims based on chronic fatigue syndrome.

Case #1

Kathy was a certified public accountant working for a large accounting firm in downtown Boston. She began to feel an increasing level of fatigue, which she attributed to trying to balance a full-time job with being a mom to two young, very active children. Resting more on weekends and having an au pair move in to help carry the load didn't seem to help. Her fatigue, along with new symptoms, prompted a visit to her physician, who referred Kathy to a specialist. Two months later a diagnosis of chronic fatigue syndrome surprised her, but at least she now knew what she was dealing with. After another six months, Kathy finally began to feel she was regaining some control over her life. Her new employment arrangement allowed her to work part-time from home, and she could rest when necessary. In cutting back on her hours, she came to understand that her firm's LTD program included partial disability benefits that would cover most of the difference in lost wages. However, she didn't realize that her LTD coverage didn't cover "self-reported" disabilities.

Case #2

Brenda's chronic fatigue had been making it increasingly difficult to keep up with the demands of her job. Assuming that her individual disability policy covered all different contingencies, she asked her physician to complete his portion of the LTD claim form. Brenda was surprised and angry when she learned that her doctor only considered her partially disabled. Her anger turned to fear when she learned that her individual disability policy only covered her for total disability.

In one unofficial survey conducted among individuals experiencing CFS claims difficulties with their insurers, certain disturbing commonalities surfaced:

- More than 25 percent of respondents were reportedly told there was no medical evidence of their disability and were denied benefits outright.
- More than 50 percent were told that they were suffering from a psychological (mental/nervous) disorder and that their group disability benefits were limited to 24 months based on the standard 24-month limitation on M/N disorders.
- Of the remaining 25 percent, many were offered small lump-sum payments in exchange for withdrawing their claims. Unfortunately, a single-sum check can become very attractive after a long battle with an insurer, especially when the claimants suspect they may ultimately collect no benefits at all.
- A small percentage of other respondents were reportedly declared eligible for benefits based on recognition of a physical illness.

All these claimants filed their claims in good faith with what they felt was sufficient medical documentation of their disability. Most experienced a very long, harrowing battle lasting from several months to as long as several years. Many were asked to be examined by a consulting physician, who may or may not have been adequately familiar with CFS. Keep in mind that the SSA specifically states that self-reported symptoms "will not establish a medical impairment for purposes of Social Security benefits." So where do we go from here?

As noted previously, insufficient preparation and inadequate presentation of a long-term disability claim form substantially increase the likelihood that the application will be denied. This is especially true when the claim stems from chronic fatigue or another self-reported disability.

For the professional legal claims advisor meeting with a new disability claimant and reviewing his or her disability insurance contracts, step one should be to evaluate the definition of total and partial (or residual) disability. Does it state the claimant's inability to perform one or more of the material daily duties of their occupation, and/or is there reference to performing the duties of the claimant's occupation in a reduced capacity or in a reduced amount of time?

Step two is to evaluate any policy restrictions and exclusions, keeping in mind that you can expect a 24-month M/N disorder limitation on group LTD contracts. Make sure there are no cost-containment restrictions for self-reported disabilities. Remember that another factor complicating self-reported disabilities is depression, which is included in the M/N restriction. If the condition includes depression, and especially if there have been prior episodes of depression, it is highly probable that the claims examiner will want to pay the claim under the M/N disorder limitation, thereby restricting benefits to two years. It is obviously to the claimant's benefit when the claim is due to a medical disability that is not a mental disorder. If depression and/or anxiety are included in the diagnosis, make sure the physician stresses that they are secondary to the medical illness.

Complete documentation of the chronic fatigue syndrome (or other self-reported disability), supported by irrefutable evidence from the treating physician(s), is absolutely essential in the initial filing of the claim. Is the treating physician a specialist in the treatment of CFS? Very few doctors are. If he or she is not a specialist, take heed. Because of the specialized nature of the CFS diagnosis, the insurer will expect the physician to have expertise, which adds credibility, in the treatment of the condition. A disability insurer looks for expertise in the treatment of any illness but especially in diagnosing CFS. This, however, does not mean a change in doctors. The claimant's primary care physician may already have referred him to a CFS specialist for diagnosis and initial treatment. In such a case, the PCP would probably follow the course of treatment, with an occasional update from the specialist.

What type of testing has been utilized to confirm a CFS diagnosis? When CFS was first being recognized as a unique and difficult-to-diagnose illness, considerable controversy surrounded the various methods of diagnosis. Leading CFS researchers and clinicians, the Centers for Disease Control and Prevention, and the National Center for Infectious Diseases developed various guidelines for evaluating the condition.

Remember that you absolutely must have the complete cooperation of the attending physician as well as his or her agreement with the claimant as to the extent of their disability. What has been the doctor's experience in helping other patients with CFS obtain disability benefits? Has he or she had significant success or great difficulty?

File the CFS claim as early as possible. Since we know in advance that significant documentation will be needed, probably including an independent medical exam by a physician representing the insurer, the claims process must begin early. If the insurer needs to write to several doctors, their responses can take four to six weeks or more to obtain. Be prepared for an insurance company representative to call the claimant directly to verify the details of the claim. Along with requesting an exam by an independent medical examiner, the representative may want to visit the claimant at home. Despite claimants' arguments to the contrary, a review of medical information on paper can reasonably be assisted by a personal visit. If the claimant is to be examined by an independent medical examiner, ask him about his background and experience with diagnosing CFS patients. Ask if he has any bias against chronic fatigue claims. Expect to be treated fairly and respectfully. If the claimant feels a claims examiner is being abusive, do not hesitate to file a complaint with the consumer division of your state's department of insurance.

Subjective Pain: A Valid Claim under ERISA

A ruling by the Seventh Circuit Court of Appeals acknowledges that "subjective pain" must be considered by an insurer under ERISA. A former TV station manager had received disability benefits from her insurer for several years. The insurer then terminated her benefits (for osteoarthritis), stating that the station manager had recovered "enough" to return to work at a desk job. The claimant filed suit against the insurer alleging that her subjective pain was enough to make her eligible for continuity of benefits.

In this situation, the plan ignored the evidence provided in the FCE (functional capacity evaluation) and affirmed that the complaints of pain were reliable. Because the vast majority of long-term disability claims are supported by medical tests and exams, the Seventh Circuit Court of Appeals opens the door to claimants who become disabled but cannot substantiate their disability with objective medical evidence.

The court ruled as follows:

> Even if the source of pain cannot be located, it nonetheless can be real. Furthermore, here the plan ignored the evidence in the [functional capacity evaluation (FCE)] that [the plaintiff's] complaints of pain were reliable. Under these circumstances, we believe it was incumbent on the plan (or the plan's consultant) to do more than just dismiss the complaints out of hand. Instead, the plan must explain why, despite evidence to the contrary in the FCE, it nevertheless finds [the plaintiff's] complaints of pain unreliable and why, if the complaints in fact are reliable, the pain [the plaintiff] is experiencing is not completely debilitating.

The holding of this case is important to anyone who is disabled since, while most disability claims are supported by objective medical testing, some are not. This case opens the door for those who have been denied disability payments simply because current medical technology could not validate their pain by objective means.

Establishing a CFS Claim with the SSA

On April 3, 2014, SSR14-1p: Titles II and XVI replaced the SSA's long-standing SSR99-2p. With the evolution of SSR14-1p: Titles II and XVI, Social Security clarified its policy on (1) how it develops evidence establishing that a disabled individual has a medically determinable impairment (MDI) of CFS and (2) their evaluation of CFS relative to disability claims and continuing disability reviews (under Titles II and XVI) of the Social Security Act.

If a patient's licensed physician diagnoses CFS, but that diagnosis is not consistent with other evidence in the person's case record, evidence of another MDI will cause the review to be evaluated under the rules that apply for that impairment and not under SSR14-1p: Titles II and XVI. When a licensed physician (a medical or osteopathic doctor) has diagnosed an MDI of CFS, the treatment notes will be reviewed for consistency and a determination will be made relative to whether the symptoms have remained stable, or may possibly have improved or worsened. In addition, the disabled person's physical strength and functional abilities will need to be diagnosed. This is why the credentials of the diagnosing physician are critically important in the handling of a CFS claim with the SSA.

SSR14-1p may be the best primer for understanding Social Security's determination of total disability. Disabled individuals tend to believe and expect their disability claims will be approved if their attending physician reports they are medically disabled. However, as previously emphasized, disability claim payments are not about the claimant's medical condition by itself; they are based on how the medical condition impacts the disabled individual's ability to work. The claim outcome will be determined by how the claimant's specific medical condition(s) causes specific and significant work limitations.

- Social Security considers an individual disabled when the person is unable to engage in any substantial gainful activity by reason of any medically determinable physical or mental impairments which can be expected to result in death or can be expected to last for a continuous period of not less than 12 months. Social Security requires that the impairment be established by medical evidence consisting of signs, symptoms, and laboratory findings. A claimant may not be found disabled based on a statement of symptoms alone. However, a CFS (or fibromyalgia) disability claim can include self-reported symptoms among the determining factors in establishing total disability. The benchmark for CFS is the presence of clinically evaluated, persistent, or relapsing chronic fatigue that:

  - is of new or definite onset;
  - can't be explained by any other physical or mental disorder;
  - is not the result of ongoing exertion;
  - is not substantially alleviated by rest; or
- Results in substantial reduction in prior levels of occupational/educational and social/or personal activities.

Diagnostic symptoms—four or more specific symptoms that persist or recur during six months or more of consecutive illness (and did not predate the fatigue) that are:

- Post-exertional malaise lasting more than 24 hours;
- Self-reported impairments in short-term memory or concentration severe enough;
- Sore throat;
- Tender cervical or axillary lymph nodes, muscle pain;
- Multi-joint pains without joint swelling; redness;
- Headaches of a new type or severity; and
- Waking unrefreshed.

Other symptoms a person with CFS may exhibit:

- Muscle weakness;
- Disturbed sleep patterns;
- Visual difficulties;
- Orthostatic intolerance (lightheadedness, fainting, dizzy, added fatigue with prolonged standing);
- Respiratory difficulties;
- Cardiovascular abnormalities;
- Gastrointestinal discomfort; and
- Urinary or bladder problems

Chapter 7

Social Security Disability Claims

Recent published data relative to the approval and denial rates of Social Security disability claims reveals that, in 2010, there were 2.7 million individuals who filed a formal disability claim with the SSA. Keep in mind the Social Security definition of disability: The law defines disability as the inability to engage in any substantial gainful activity (SGA) by reason of any medically determinable physical or mental impairment(s) that can be expected to result in death or that has lasted or can be expected to last for a continuous period of not less than 12 months. I am personally unaware of any other tougher, more stringent wording of the definition of disability in any disability programs available in the United States today. Essentially this means "totally disabled from any occupation" and is as tough as it gets.

Many political leaders have pointed out weaknesses in our current Social Security system. Regardless of how much tweaking the present system requires, most claimants have devoted their hard-earned dollars to SSA disability protection. As long as the SSA exists, nothing should dissuade working citizens from filing a claim. It is their right under federal law. This does not mean they will become entitled to benefits for which they are not eligible, nor should it imply that valid claims will be turned down. It does mean that (1) the claimant must be legitimately totally disabled under the current Social Security definition and (2) it is their job, or the job of their professional advisors, to prove that the claimant is totally disabled.

Some applicants mistakenly believe their claim is an entitlement. Actually, a disability claim is an application for benefits; but many claimants think they are automatically entitled to disability benefits simply because they've had SSA deductions withheld from their paycheck during their working career. The U.S. court system assumes that everyone is innocent until proven guilty beyond a reasonable doubt, whereas filing a Social Security disability claim works almost in the reverse—claimants and their attending physicians, using appropriate medical records, must prove the claimants are legitimately totally disabled.

Social Security benefits are based on total disability, which is defined earlier in this chapter as a disability that is expected to last 12 months or longer and end in death. Personal disability insurance usually provides partial or "residual" disability benefits for which benefits can be paid based on a percentage of lost income; total disability is frequently not necessary. However, LTD benefits are offset by Social Security benefits. It is to the insurer's advantage to help claimants qualify for Social Security benefits, as it is money the insurer will not have to pay. Disability insurers almost always have a skilled team to assist claimants in filing for and qualifying for Social Security disability payments.

Filing a Social Security Disability Claim

The SSA's updated disability determination system was introduced in the New England region in August 2006. The objective of this new process was to shorten the decision time of claims, paying benefits to people "who are obviously disabled" much sooner than was being done under the prior system.

Key features of the updated approach include the following:

- Favorable decisions can be expected within 20 days after the state agency receives the claim.

- A new Medical-Vocational Expert System composed of a national network of medical, psychological, and vocational experts provides the expertise to make accurate and timely decisions.
- Upon request by the claimant, a federal reviewing official will review state disability determinations, eliminating the current "reconsideration" process.

When to Apply

1. Application can be made when claimants and their physician agree that the claimants are unable to work, when the claimants can satisfy Social Security's definition of disability, and when they are approaching the end of the waiting period.
2. The impairment is expected to last at least 12 months.
3. Claimants must be unable to perform other types of work.
4. Claimants are presently not earning more than $1,000 a month.

Where and How to Apply

1. At their local Social Security office.
2. By calling the local Social Security office to set up an appointment.
3. By filing the application online at www.ssa.gov.
4. Through an in-person or telephone interview (which can be arranged through the local Social Security office).

After the application for benefits is completed at the local Social Security office, it is forwarded to Disability Determination Services (DDS). The DDS examiner then requests the claimant's medical records. The decision to pay benefits to the claimant will be determined by the medical records.

What medical records are used in the case evaluation? The DDS examiner will request all medical records that are relevant in making a disability determination. The primary care physician's records will usually be the most important source of information, as he or she knows the claimant best. This, however, may not be the case if the PCP has referred the claimant to a medical specialist who is treating the claimant's specific disabling condition. For example, suppose the cause for a claim is a permanent back disorder that confines the claimant to a wheelchair, requiring treatment by a neurosurgeon. The medical records will show (from the PCP and neurosurgeon) that the claimant has lost the ability to stand, bend, or walk, and suffers from extreme loss of range of motion. This claim will be supported by the specific diagnosis and prognosis resulting in these limitations and inability to work.

It is unlikely that anyone can become eligible for benefits without a personal interview. Based on claimants' ability (or lack thereof) to travel, walk, or move about in any way, they are certainly within their rights to ask the Social Security representative to come to their home. This is a reasonable request and can actually be helpful.

The Three C's: Continued, Consistent, Competent

The chances of collecting Social Security disability benefits are significantly bolstered if the claimant can demonstrate the three C's: continued, consistent, and competent medical care.

- *Continued:* If the claimant is experiencing debilitating pain, it is assumed that he will seek appropriate medical care. Someone with a bad back who rarely sees his doctors, except for chiropractic adjustments, will of course provoke numerous questions as to the legitimacy of his disability.
- *Consistent:* Medical attention should be consistently given and should be consistent with the type of disability. Let's say the cause of a claim is an automobile accident that left the claimant permanently paralyzed. It is understood that he will probably need to see his doctors less often than someone whose heart attack led to bypass surgery and now has the possibility of recovery.
- *Competent:* Administrative law judges (ALJs) tend to question claimants with disabilities whom they feel are not

receiving professional care based on prevailing standards of medical care. Practitioners of acupuncture, chiropractic care, massage therapies, and other holistic treatments can help provide relief from pain. Any method of treatment that can improve one's health and better manage pain is welcomed in demonstrating disability. However, ALJs tend to rule most favorably when they are provided with evidence of care by a skilled physician rather than a practitioner of an alternative therapy.

Residual Functional Capacity Assessments

During the claims process, the DDS examiner reviews the work done prior to disability and prepares a residual functional capacity (RFC) assessment that identifies the claimant's ability to perform sedentary, light, or medium work. Based on those limitations, a decision is made relative to the claimant's perceived ability to return to his or her former line of work. For example, if a claimant's old job required a "medium" level of exertion, and the RFC indicates the claimant's capability is now "sedentary" work, it would be unreasonable to expect the claimant to return to his or her prior "medium" level of exertion. The SSA residual functional capacity assessment as described in the Code of Federal Regulations can be found in Appendix G.

The Social Security Administration places substantial value on an RFC completed by the claimant's attending physician, assuming the claimant's doctor is a recognized medical expert in the claimant's area of disability. When a mental condition exists compounding the effects of a physical disability, a mental RFC should also be submitted. When the form is completed by a mental health professional, it can dovetail with handling the physical disability, boosting the claimant's overall prospects. Naturally, issues associated with concentration, attention, social interaction with other employees, memory, or clear thinking can impact recovery and return to work.

For a Social Security Disability Insurance (SSDI) or Supplemental Security Income (SSI) case, it is extremely important that the treating doctors give an opinion on the claimant's residual functional capacity—in other words, show how much the claimant can lift, how long he can stand, and how far he can walk. If nonexertional limitations such as memory difficulties or difficulties concentrating are a factor, the doctor should note these problems as well because they can further limit the jobs the SSA will be able to find the claimant can do. If the claimant is suffering from a psychiatric condition such as depression, the treating psychiatrist should point out any limitations created by the condition. The RFC can be reported on residual functional capacity forms or forms covering ability to do work-related activities. Do not rely on the SSA to perform this evaluation. In the absence of this evaluation, the SSA decision will be based solely on what their doctors say about the claimant's limitations.

"Other Work"

Once it is determined that the claimant is unable to return to past work, a decision is made relative to the likelihood that the claimant will be able to do "other work" based on his or her training or experience. This determination is based on the claimant's exertional limits as decided by the RFC.

The Listing of Impairments

The impairment listing manual "contains medical criteria that apply to the evaluation of impairments." Technically called *Disability Evaluation under Social Security* and informally known as the "Blue Book," this publication includes the Listing of Impairments. Each particular medical condition has less to do with the disability determination than with the claimant's ability to do work. Although the listing includes numerous medical conditions, it may not be helpful in every situation. This is because the claimant's particular condition may not be listed, or its severity may make it impossible to perform a normal disability evaluation. Someone else with the very same cause of disability may be better able to return to work due to a more successful physical therapy regimen. Or the claimant may have an additional medical condition (e.g., arthritis) that further diminishes his or her ability to return to the work world.

A False Assumption

Many disability benefit applicants assume that they will be eligible for Social Security benefits if their personal disability insurance or their employer-sponsored LTD insurers are paying them benefits. This is an erroneous assumption. First, the SSA has the strictest definition of disability. Social Security definitions are considered "severe," whereas personal or group disability insurance provisions are almost always more liberal. Second, Social Security places a huge emphasis on one's residual functional capacity. Personal individual disability or group LTD insurance almost always focuses on the inability to do one's job at the point of disability. Many individuals who file disability claims formerly held executive positions in which thinking and verbal skills were paramount. The RFC focuses more on occupational duties that are outside of white-collar jobs and that have lower physical demands.

Social Security Pre-Hearing Documentation (Sample Hearing Brief)

As stated previously, inasmuch as over 60 percent of Social Security disability claims are denied, it is imperative that claims be filed correctly the first time. We are unable to determine the number of Social Security disability claims filed directly by claimants versus those that are filed with the help of attorney advisors. However, we assume that law firms specializing in representing Social Security disability claimants will do more thorough preparation than a claimant filing a claim on his or her own. Plus, they will have a greater understanding of Social Security's rigorous claims process. Upon reviewing the numerous websites of law firms specializing in filing Social Security disability claims, one point clearly stands out: their percentage of successful claim approvals exceeds the approval rates published by the SSA.

Gordon P. Gates, a Maine attorney who specializes in filing Social Security disability claims, offers a sample hearing brief that exemplifies the benefits of an attorney-assisted claim.[1] Gates has presented a classic primer useful in preparing an initial Social Security claim or appeal. His sample hearing brief from a recent case led to a fully favorable on-the-record decision. Changes were made to protect the privacy of the claimant. Of note are the many methods used to clearly document the extent of the claimant Jane Smith's physical and mental disabilities. These methods included a neuropsychological evaluation, a neurological consult by a board-certified neurologist, treatment records of the primary care physician, a consultative exam report, a DDS review, and documentation of a finding of *disabled* under the medical vocational "grid rule" guidelines (201-14).

Using Social Security's "Grid Rules"

Attorneys who assist clients applying for Social Security disability benefits need to understand Social Security's grid rules, or medical vocational guidelines. The grid rules come into play when an individual has a severe medically determinable physical or mental impairment and is not working at a substantial gainful activity (SGA) level,[2] and when the impairment prevents an individual from performing past relevant work.

The "grids" are set up as a series of charts. Social Security will determine what level of exertion each claimant can perform in a work environment through an RFC assessment. The categories range from the least level of exertion to the most, sedentary, light, medium, heavy, and very heavy. Individuals who can perform at a heavy or very heavy level and do not have severe nonexertional limitations are generally not found to be disabled and therefore

1 Available at http://www.socialsecuritydisabilitylawyer.us/blog/sample-hearing-brief.html. Used with permission from the author.

2 Measured roughly by monthly earnings; see https://www.ssa.gov/oact/cola/sga.html.

do not have a grid chart. Based on Social Security's determination of exertional level, the claims examiner will then look at the corresponding grid chart and match age, education, and past work experience to come to a conclusion of disabled or not disabled. Since employers are less likely to offer entry-level positions to older disabled workers, the SSA grid rules authorize administrative law judges to classify the applicant as disabled after reaching a certain age, commonly at least age 50 or older, even though they might still be able to perform some level of work. Fortunately, the SSA recognizes that as we get older. it becomes more difficult to find a new job or learn new skills.

If claimants have both exertional (strength) and nonexertional limitations, the SSA will first determine if they can be found to be disabled based on exertional limitations alone. Exertional limitations are physical limitations such as impaired ability to lift, stand, or walk. Examples of nonexertional limitations include difficulty with memory or concentration, possibly stemming from a condition such as depression. If the "grids" direct a finding of "not disabled," the SSA will then consider any nonexertional limitations and how much those additional limitations would erode the ability to perform a job at that exertional level. For the Third Circuit's ruling on grid rules and nonexertional limitations, we refer you to *Sykes v. Apfel*, 228 F.3d 259 (3d Cir. 2000), which can be found in Appendix H.

As the "grids" show, disability and how it limits a claimant is not the only factor that decides whether they will be approved for SSDI benefits. In general, the older a claimant is, the better the chance of getting disability. The SSA believes that the older one is, the harder it is to adjust to new work. If you are 18 to 49 years of age, you are considered to be a "younger individual." However, the SSA separates this age group into 18–44 and 45–49, with 45- to 49-year olds considered less able to make an adjustment to other work. If you are 50 to 54 years of age, you are considered "closely approaching advanced age," and if you are 55 or older you are considered to be in "advanced age." The specific age category a claimant falls into is very important, especially if the claimant has purely exertional limitations from his or her disability; the older one is, the easier it is to get SSDI benefits for physical conditions.

Education is yet another important factor in the SSA's decision as to whether a claimant has a disability. The SSA believes that the higher a claimant's education, the easier it will be for the claimant to find other work. Educational level is broken down into several categories—from least educated to most. Little or no high school, for example, does not provide for direct entry into skilled work; being a high school graduate or more does provide for direct entry; and so on.

So how do you read the chart? You can begin by looking at what the SSA's RFC assessment says about the claimant and then find the corresponding chart. For example, if the SSA finds that a claimant is limited to sedentary work, look at the chart called "Grids for Sedentary Work." Let's say our claimant is 50 years old, has 12 years of education (is a high school graduate), and has past relevant work (has performed work in the past 15 years at the SGA level) as an unskilled heavy laborer. First look under the Age column; if a claimant is 50 years old, he or she is considered "closely approaching advanced age." Next look at the column for Education; this claimant is a "high school graduate or more (that does not provide for direct entry into skilled work)." Now look at the column for Previous Work Experience. The claimant's past relevant work was as an unskilled heavy laborer; therefore, Previous Work Experience is considered "unskilled or none." Now follow this row across to the Decision column to see if the finding is "disabled" or "not disabled." In this case, you should be in row Rule 201.12, and the finding is "disabled." Note that a "younger individual age 18–44" with the same education and previous work experience would not be considered disabled (Sedentary Work, Rule #201.27). Also, if the SSA had instead determined that our claimant had the RFC to perform "light" work, the claimant would be found to be not disabled, as per the "Grids for Light Work" (Rule #202.13).

Chart: Grids for Sedentary Work

Rule	Age	Education	Previous Work Experience	Decision
201.01	Advanced Age	Limited or less	Unskilled or none	Disabled
201.02	Advanced Age	Limited or less	Skilled or semiskilled—skills not transferable	Disabled
201.03	Advanced Age	Limited or less	Skilled or semiskilled—skills transferable	Not disabled
201.04	Advanced Age	High school graduate or more—does not provide for direct entry into skilled work	Unskilled or none	Disabled
201.05	Advanced Age	High school graduate or more—provides for direct entry into skilled work	Unskilled or none	Not disabled
201.06	Advanced Age	High school graduate or more—does not provide for direct entry into skilled work	Skilled or semiskilled—skills not transferable	Disabled

(Continued)

Chart: Grids for Sedentary Work

Rule	Age	Education	Previous Work Experience	Decision
201.07	Advanced Age	High school graduate or more—does not provide for direct entry into skilled work	Skilled or semiskilled—skills transferable	Not disabled
201.08	Advanced Age	High school graduate or more—provides for direct entry into skilled work	Skilled or semiskilled—skills not transferable	Not disabled
201.09	Closely approaching advanced age	Limited or less	Unskilled or none	Disabled
201.10	Closely approaching advanced age	Limited or less	Skilled or semiskilled—skills not transferable	Disabled
201.11	Closely approaching advanced age	Limited or less	Skilled or semiskilled—skills transferable	Not disabled
201.12	Closely approaching advanced age	High school graduate or more—does not provide for direct entry into skilled work	Unskilled or none	Disabled

Chart: Grids for Sedentary Work

Rule	Age	Education	Previous Work Experience	Decision
201.13	Closely approaching advanced age	High school graduate or more—provides for direct entry into skilled work	Unskilled or none	Not disabled
201.14	Closely approaching advanced age	High school graduate or more—does not provide for direct entry into skilled work	Skilled or semiskilled—skills not transferable	Disabled
201.15	Closely approaching advanced age	High school graduate or more—does not provide for direct entry into skilled work	Skilled or semiskilled—skills transferable	Not disabled
201.16	Closely approaching advanced age	High school graduate or more—provides for direct entry into skilled work	Skilled or semiskilled—skills not transferable	Not disabled
201.17	Younger individual age 45–49	Illiterate or unable to communicate in English	Unskilled or none	Disabled

(*Continued*)

Chart: Grids for Sedentary Work

Rule	Age	Education	Previous Work Experience	Decision
201.18	Younger individual age 45–49	Limited or less—at least literate and able to communicate in English	Unskilled or none	Not disabled
201.19	Younger individual age 45–49	Limited or less	Skilled or semiskilled—skills not transferable	Not disabled
201.20	Younger individual age 45–49	Limited or less	Skilled or semiskilled—skills transferable	Not disabled
201.21	Younger individual age 45–49	High school graduate or more	Skilled or semiskilled—skills not transferable	Not disabled
201.22	Younger individual age 45–49	High school graduate or more	Skilled or semiskilled—skills transferable	Not disabled
201.23	Younger individual age 18–44	Illiterate or unable to communicate in English	Unskilled or none	Not disabled
201.24	Younger individual age 18–44	Limited or less—at least literate and able to communicate in English	Unskilled or none	Not disabled
201.25	Younger individual age 18–44	Limited or less	Skilled or semiskilled—skills not transferable	Not disabled

Chart: Grids for Sedentary Work

Rule	Age	Education	Previous Work Experience	Decision
201.26	Younger individual age 18–44	Limited or less	Skilled or semiskilled—skills transferable	Not disabled
201.27	Younger individual age 18–44	High school graduate or more	Unskilled or none	Not disabled
201.28	Younger individual age 18–44	High school graduate or more	Skilled or semiskilled—skills not transferable	Not disabled
201.29	Younger individual age 18–44	High school graduate or more	Skilled or semiskilled—skills transferable	Not disabled

Source: "Ultimate Disability Guide," Kazmierczak & Kazmierczak, online version available at http://www.ultimatedisabilityguide.com/index.html.

Chart: Grids for Light Work

Rule	Age	Education	Previous Work Experience	Decision
202.01	Advanced Age	Limited or less	Unskilled or none	Disabled
202.02	Advanced Age	Limited or less	Skilled or semiskilled—skills not transferable	Disabled
202.03	Advanced Age	Limited or less	Skilled or semiskilled—skills transferable	Not disabled

(Continued)

Chart: Grids for Light Work

Rule	Age	Education	Previous Work Experience	Decision
202.04	Advanced Age	High school graduate or more-does not provide for direct entry into skilled work	Unskilled or none	Disabled
202.05	Advanced Age	High school graduate or more—provides for direct entry into skilled work	Unskilled or none	Not disabled
202.06	Advanced Age	High school graduate or more-does not provide for direct entry into skilled work	Skilled or semiskilled—skills not transferable	Disabled
202.07	Advanced Age	High school graduate or more—does not provide for direct entry into skilled work	Skilled or semiskilled—skills transferable	Not disabled
202.08	Advanced Age	High school graduate or more—provides for direct entry into skilled work	Skilled or semiskilled—skills not transferable	Not disabled

Chart: Grids for Light Work

Rule	Age	Education	Previous Work Experience	Decision
202.09	Closely approaching advanced age	Illiterate or unable to communicate in English	Unskilled or none	Disabled
202.10	Closely approaching advanced age	Limited or less—at least literate and able to communicate in English	Unskilled or none	Not disabled
202.11	Closely approaching advanced age	Limited or less	Skilled or semiskilled—skills not transferable	Not disabled
202.12	Closely approaching advanced age	Limited or less	Skilled or semiskilled—skills transferable	Not disabled
202.13	Closely approaching advanced age	High school graduate or more	Unskilled or none	Not disabled
202.14	Closely approaching advanced age	High school graduate or more	Skilled or semiskilled—skills not transferable	Not disabled
202.15	Closely approaching advanced age	High school graduate or more	Skilled or semiskilled—skills transferable	Not disabled

(*Continued*)

Chart: Grids for Light Work

Rule	Age	Education	Previous Work Experience	Decision
202.16	Younger individual	Illiterate or unable to communicate in English	Unskilled or none	Not disabled
202.17	Younger individual	Limited or less—at least literate and able to communicate in English	Unskilled or none	Not disabled
202.18	Younger individual	Limited or less	Skilled or semiskilled—skills not transferable	Not disabled
202.19	Younger individual	Limited or less	Skilled or semiskilled—skills transferable	Not disabled
202.20	Younger individual	High school graduate or more	Unskilled or none	Not disabled
202.21	Younger individual	High school graduate or more	Skilled or semiskilled—skills not transferable	Not disabled
202.22	Younger individual	High school graduate or more	Skilled or semiskilled—skills transferable	Not disabled

Source: "Ultimate Disability Guide," Kazmierczak & Kazmierczak, online version available at http://www.ultimatedisabilityguide.com/index.html.

Chart: Grids for Medium Work

Rule	Age	Education	Previous Work Experience	Decision
203.01	Closely approaching retirement age	Marginal or none	Unskilled or none	Disabled
203.02	Closely approaching retirement age	Limited or less	None	Disabled
203.03	Closely approaching retirement age	Limited	Unskilled	Not disabled
203.04	Closely approaching retirement age	Limited or less	Skilled or semiskilled—skills not transferable	Not disabled
203.05	Closely approaching retirement age	Limited or less	Skilled or semiskilled—skills transferable	Not disabled
203.06	Closely approaching retirement age	High school graduate or more	Unskilled or none	Not disabled
203.07	Closely approaching retirement age	High school graduate or more—does not provide for direct entry into skilled work	Skilled or semiskilled—skills not transferable	Not disabled
203.08	Closely approaching retirement age	High school graduate or more—does not provide for direct entry into skilled work	Skilled or semiskilled—skills transferable	Not disabled

(*Continued*)

Chart: Grids for Medium Work

Rule	Age	Education	Previous Work Experience	Decision
203.09	Closely approaching retirement age	High school graduate or more—provides for direct entry into skilled work	Skilled or semiskilled—skills not transferable	Not disabled
203.10	Advanced Age	Limited or less	None	Disabled
203.11	Advanced Age	Limited or less	Unskilled	Not disabled
203.12	Advanced Age	Limited or less	Skilled or semiskilled—skills not transferable	Not disabled
203.13	Advanced Age	Limited or less	Skilled or semiskilled—skills transferable	Not disabled
203.14	Advanced Age	High school graduate or more	Unskilled or none	Not disabled
203.15	Advanced Age	High school graduate or more—does not provide for direct entry into skilled work	Skilled or semiskilled—skills not transferable	Not disabled
203.16	Advanced Age	High school graduate or more—does not provide for direct entry into skilled work	Skilled or semiskilled—skills transferable	Not disabled

Chart: Grids for Medium Work

Rule	Age	Education	Previous Work Experience	Decision
203.17	Advanced Age	High school graduate or more—provides for direct entry into skilled work	Skilled or semiskilled—skills not transferable	Not disabled
203.18	Closely approaching advanced age	Limited or less	Unskilled or none	Not disabled
203.19	Closely approaching advanced age	Limited or less	Skilled or semiskilled—skills not transferable	Not disabled
203.20	Closely approaching advanced age	Limited or less	Skilled or semiskilled—skills transferable	Not disabled
203.21	Closely approaching advanced age	High school graduate or more	Unskilled or none	Not disabled
203.22	Closely approaching advanced age	High school graduate or more—does not provide for direct entry into skilled work	Skilled or semiskilled—skills not transferable	Not disabled
203.23	Closely approaching advanced age	High school graduate or more—does not provide for direct entry into skilled work	Skilled or semiskilled—skills transferable	Not disabled

(Continued)

Chart: Grids for Medium Work

Rule	Age	Education	Previous Work Experience	Decision
203.24	Closely approaching advanced age	High school graduate or more—provides for direct entry into skilled work	Skilled or semiskilled—skills not transferable	Not disabled
203.25	Younger individual	Limited or less	Unskilled or none	Not disabled
203.26	Younger individual	Limited or less	Skilled or semiskilled—skills not transferable	Not disabled
203.27	Younger individual	Limited or less	Skilled or semiskilled—skills transferable	Not disabled
203.28	Younger individual	High school graduate or more	Unskilled or none	Not disabled
203.29	Younger individual	High school graduate or more—does not provide for direct entry into skilled work	Skilled or semiskilled—skills not transferable	Not disabled
203.30	Younger individual	High school graduate or more-does not provide for direct entry into skilled work	Skilled or semiskilled—skills transferable	Not disabled

Chart: Grids for Medium Work

Rule	Age	Education	Previous Work Experience	Decision
203.31	Younger individual	High school graduate or more—provides for direct entry into skilled work	Skilled or semiskilled—skills not transferable	Not disabled

Source: "Ultimate Disability Guide," Kazmierczak & Kazmierczak, online version available at http://www.ultimatedisabilityguide.com/index.html.

The Interaction of Social Security Claims and Group LTD Claims

Group long-term disability insurers have the right to reduce LTD benefits by the amount the claimant is eligible to collect from Social Security. For example, if there is an LTD policy benefit of $3,000 per month and there is an expected $800 per month in Social Security disability benefits, the LTD policy "offsets" the $3,000/month and pays $2,200 per month.

Here is a sample of the wording from an actual LTD contract.

> **Reduction of Benefits:** *Your LTD benefits are reduced by other sources of income that are payable to you because of your disability. Income that will reduce your LTD benefits includes:*
>
> - *workers' compensation benefits or benefits provided under a similar law, state disability benefits, and other statutory benefits for disability, retirement, or unemployment;*
> - *benefits provided through company benefit plans, including the pension and business travel accident insurance plans; and*
> - *any Social Security benefits for which you are eligible.*

If any of these benefits are payable as a lump sum, the LTD benefit will be calculated as if the lump-sum benefit was to be paid monthly. The insurance company has the right to recover advanced Social Security benefits by direct payment or by offset against future LTD payments.

Insurers require that the claimant apply for Social Security disability benefits to continue to receive LTD benefits. If claimants are denied Social Security disability benefits, they will be required to request reconsideration, and they will need to provide the insurer with evidence of the appeal and of denial or award letters.

The LTD insurer will offer the services of its attorney to help with a Social Security appeal. Claimants do not have to use the insurer's attorney and are free to select their own attorney. However, keep in mind that the disability insurers use attorneys who specialize in handling Social Security disability claims; they understand the system. It is to the insurer's advantage to help the claimant have a successful Social Security claim. The claimant may already have a great relationship with a local attorney who has written up the claimant's will or settled his parents' estate, but unless the attorney understands the extensive intricacies of the Social Security system, he or she cannot be expected to be very effective.

Flow of Cases through the SSA Disability Process

The objective in analyzing these data is to impress upon our readers the magnitude of claims problems experienced by 2.7 million disabled individuals, as well as the importance of persistence and knowledge in the process. They need the help of attorney disability claims advisors in filing their disability claims.

In evaluating the chart "Progression of Cases through the Disability Process," certain important information becomes apparent.[3] Out of each 100 *Initial Claims* filed, 38 percent are allowed and 62 percent are denied. This is the high denial rate we have

3 See, e.g., https://books.google.com/books?id=kY-4CwAAQBAJ&pg=PA224&lpg=PA224&dq="Progression+of+Cases+Through+the+Disability+Process,"&source=bl&ots=QLPooOWK5R&sig=oTgzBD8n18hGKDg5xH_cwSoZA8E&hl=en&sa=X&ved=0ahUKEwiTpMjd-YzaAhVSS6wKHbK6A-cQ6AEILjAB.

repeatedly referenced in this work. Of those 62 claimants who were initially denied, just over a third (21) filed an appeal; however, only three were allowed at the first level of appeal, *Reconsideration*. Almost all those claimants denied at *Reconsideration* appealed again, and 12 were allowed at the *Hearing* appeal stage; seven were denied. Five of these seven cases appealed once more and went to the *Appeals Council Review*. One case was allowed at Appeals Council Review, while four were rejected.

The flowchart reveals that out of the 62 original claims denied, only 21 claimants followed through asking for reconsideration—66 percent gave up, not taking advantage of their right to appeal. Using the 2.7 million claimants reported in 2010, this represents over 1.1 million people who did not exercise their right to appeal and will not be receiving disability payments. At the second level of appeal, *Hearings*, 12 out of 18 were approved, or a 67 percent success rate. The vitally important lesson here is to appeal and remain determined. Those folks who "hang in there" and persist face a high probability of success—of the 21 claimants who appealed their initial denial, 76 percent were approved through the appeals process.

There are many reasons why claimants give up after their first claim attempt is denied. It may be that they have been advised that their claim is not strong enough to appeal. Or it may simply be that they are too discouraged or overwhelmed by the process or by their disability. Depression may also be a factor. Claimants may not be aware of their right to appeal or may not know what steps to take next. And as there is little to no support network for claimants, they are likely to feel isolated throughout the process.

Social Security Fee Agreements

Attorney disability claim advisors need to understand and follow the SSA's procedures for:

- The fee agreement process
- Conditions for approval of a fee agreement
- Exceptions to the fee agreement process

- Provisions that will not prevent SSA's approval of a fee agreement
- Provisions that will cause SSA to disapprove a fee agreement

The SSA has written fee agreement model language that complies with the statutory conditions for approval of a fee agreement. However, because a fee agreement is a contract between a representative and his or her client, each fee agreement is unique, may appear in any form, and may include provisions in addition to the fee. For example, a fee agreement may contain additional provisions for payment of out-of-pocket expenses for medical reports, for interest on an unpaid balance of an authorized fee, or for establishing a trust or escrow account. This information can be found in Appendix I, as well as on the Social Security Administration's website.

Chapter 8

Disability Claims with the Department of Veterans Affairs

Sadly, veterans today face a multitude of obstacles in filing disability claims. When our service members return from war, we have a huge moral obligation to care for them and help them function in, and enjoy, civilian life. Some will return with physical disabilities, such as the loss of a limb caused by a roadside mine. Others return with recurrent nightmares, flashbacks, and panic attacks that continue long after the daily horror of war has ended. Our nation provides these returnees, most of them young, with the extensive professional training and state-of-the-art weaponry needed for war; they also need the best medical care and rehabilitation programs when they come home, for injuries both physical and mental. We need to help our veterans take advantage of the extensive resources the system does offer, so that they can claim the assistance they require and deserve. U.S. Senator Kirsten Gillibrand (D-NY) has said that "one of the most troubling issues facing our veterans is the delay in processing benefit claims." She has also reported that "many veterans are unaware of the resources available to them, the benefits they are entitled to, or what state and local organizations are in place to support their transition out of the military and back to a civilian life."[1]

PTSD and Traumatic Brain Injury

A study by the RAND Corporation, the first of its kind produced by a nongovernmental group, offers an all-encompassing assessment of the psychological and cognitive needs of military service members. Contributors to the report determined that about 300,000 U.S. veterans of the Iraq and Afghanistan wars are suffering from posttraumatic stress disorder (PTSD) or major depression. The findings show that another 320,000 veterans suffer from traumatic brain injury (TBI); many of these veterans have never been evaluated by a physician for a brain injury.

PTSD is an anxiety disorder that occurs after a traumatic event. Sufferers may think their life or the lives of others are in danger, and feel they have no control over what is happening. For U.S. service members, roadside bombs are the cause of most TBI cases. Service members may experience ringing in their ears, memory lapses, headaches, and dizziness among other symptoms. People sometimes shake off these effects and return to combat, but many months later more serious symptoms can begin to develop. To this day, diagnosis and treatment are not state of the art. Relapse of PTSD symptoms often occurs stateside and is linked to unhealthy behaviors, including smoking, overeating, drug and alcohol use, and unsafe sex. All of these practices, coupled with increased irritability and depression, can lead to higher rates of physical health problems, suicides, and diminished lifespan. Other consequences of PTSD and TBI include disruption of marriage and the attendant psychological effects on children, as well as lost productivity in the workplace, which results in additional family financial burdens. Police, firefighters, and service members all have likely potential to experience nightmares, panic attacks, and flashbacks related to their work experiences.

---

1 Op-ed piece by Kirsten Gillibrand, *The Daily Gazette* (Schenectady, NY), May 25, 2008.

PTSD and other cognitive conditions become more intense when soldiers prepare to return to combat. A reported 15 to 20 percent of all soldiers fighting in Afghanistan show signs of PTSD or depression. That rate increases to 30 percent for soldiers on their third or fourth combat deployment. With a rising figure of 300,000-plus veterans suffering from PTSD, recent studies show that the VA continues to struggle to offer adequate mental health treatment. A *USA Today* story reported on the record level of health problems incurred by soldiers in the Afghanistan and Iraq wars. A study conducted by mental health teams from the Army Surgeon General's Office revealed that three in ten service members on their third tour admitted to emotional illnesses. In addition, military leaders tell us that the year-long break soldiers receive between successive 12- to 15-month combat deployments is not long enough.

Regrettably, in the early days of PTSD treatment, the psychological stigma faced by many soldiers discouraged them from filing disability claims. This continues to be a problem today. The VA's National Center for PTSD reports that one in five PTSD sufferers is afraid to get help. And one in three does not want anyone to know he or she is in therapy getting help. Regrettably, some of these PTSD sufferers become overly concerned about what their former fellow soldiers or other active military personnel will think about them. Sufferers worry that others "won't understand" or that they will be judged harshly for not being "strong enough" to cope on their own. The attorney claim advisor can be enormously helpful not only in assisting in the VA disability claim process but also in understanding the wealth of resources that are readily available.

Struggles Faced by Veterans

Soldiers returning from our foreign wars need a clear understanding of how and where to obtain assistance when they are experiencing the aftershock of battle. They may need help filing a disability claim for PTSD, seeking counseling, or just blending back into civilian society. Disengagement from military life is a traumatic process.

Even as an attorney who has never been in military combat, try to put yourself in the shoes of a returning veteran who is suffering from PTSD.

When a veteran returns home safely to his family after a successful tour of duty, the 24-hour days and months of endless fear and danger have finally ended. No more need to fear your demise will be around the corner. You are back to safety. No more enemies. No more sleepless nights. You are back home beside your loving family. And yet now is when the trouble begins. A silent battle. The war within. A battle away from the field of battle. The ever-dangerous war within your mind. You discover how easy it was to face your enemy. You knew who he was. He was on the other side right in front of you. You were trained well in how to confront danger. Today, long after wartime battles have ended, your angry outbursts are puzzling to you and troubling to your family. You may be feeling fear and isolation—wanting to hide, but no place feels safe. You do not realize it yet, but you are suffering from post-traumatic stress disorder. Here is where the mental toughness that is so necessary on the field of battle can resurface in a counterproductive way. You may tell yourself to just "stick it out," "be strong," "it'll all go away." But it doesn't.

Service members returning home face "minefields" in returning to civilian life and filing a disability claim. These can include the following:

- A lack of quality, helpful, user-friendly information compiled in one place.
- Anger, frustration, and fear. Many returning service members simply do not know where to turn to start rebuilding their lives.
- Dismay when faced with a mountain of disability claim forms. It may be unclear where to address the many questions and concerns that arise.
- Hearing about the denial of PTSD claims based on the judgment that it was a personality disorder. Claimants may be unaware of who can help them respond effectively to such a ruling.

- Lack of access to veterans' advocates generally. What range of advocates exists? Where can they be contacted?
- Lack of knowledge about eligibility for other benefits like education and home loans.
- Downgrading of a disability rating by the VA. What steps can be taken to advocate for one's cause?

Filing a VA Disability Claim

VA disability claims present a unique assortment of issues and problems. First and foremost, we are generally dealing with younger men and women who have chosen to put their health and very lives at risk to protect the United States. Unlike most of America's workforce, veterans have their entire lives ahead of them. The loss of an arm or a leg may not prevent a veteran from living a long, fulfilling life when a tour of duty has ended, but pursuing everyday activities is no longer simple.

Whereas America's civilian workforce has employer-provided medical and disability insurance through multiple commercial insurers, service members and veterans are covered under the federal VA health care system. Unlike civilian coverage, which insures a percentage of earned income (usually 60% or 70%), VA disability coverage is based on the assignment of a disability "award" or classification. The award is a percentage of disability, or a disability rating, beginning with 0 percent and rising to 100 percent. A veteran's extent of disability dictates whether he or she is eligible, along with family members, for free medical care and other VA-sponsored benefits such as rehabilitation assistance, educational and training services, home loan services, and life insurance. No benefits are paid for less than a 10 percent disability, and the percentage is based on a variety of factors, including the significant impact on a veteran's lifestyle—not just income and earning potential—caused by a combat-related disability.

Despite bipartisan efforts to fix the Department of Veterans Affairs, it continues to be plagued by many issues. Without going into the long history of these problems and how devastating they can be for veterans, what follows is a description of three setbacks facing disability claimants.

- **Processing time.** When a veteran submits a new claim for VA benefits, he or she must wait an average of 177 days, or almost six months, before getting the first decision. This six-month processing time is devoted primarily to the VA's gathering of evidence. If the claim is denied and the claimant decides to appeal, he or she must submit a notice of disagreement. On average, the time from receipt of the notice of disagreement to the issuance of a Board of Veterans' Appeals (BVA) decision is 971 days. Ultimately, a veteran may wait more than three years (177 days for the initial processing of a new client plus 971 days for the appeal to be eventually adjudicated) to finally get a favorable decision from the BVA granting him or her VA benefits and compensation.
- **Insufficient staffing.** Former VA Secretary Jim Nicholson once reported that 1,100 new staff had been hired in an effort to reduce the 177 days it takes the VA to issue the first decision on a new claim. Even with these new hires, the staffing at local VA regional offices remains woefully inadequate, as the numbers make clear—some 13,784 BVA employees are being tasked with processing and deciding more than 1.4 million new and backlogged claims.
- **Insufficient training.** The VA's Office of Inspector General conducted a survey of veterans service representatives ("raters") and decision review officers (DROs). The results of the survey revealed that within the previous year these professionals had received 10 hours or less of formal classroom instruction on rating policies and procedures.

Nevertheless, despite personnel upheavals in the VA, the ability of service members to track their claims online represents something of an advance. Attorneys can guide their clients by exploring these resources.[2]

---

2 See the VA's eBenefits page: https://www.ebenefits.va.gov/ebenefits/about/feature?feature=compensation-claim-appeal-status.

VA Right to Represent

Disabled veterans have the right to appoint an advisor to represent them (38 U.S.C.5902, 5903 and 5904), either a veterans service organization (VSO), an attorney, or a claims agent. We mention the VSO first because, unlike disability claims with disability insurers or the Social Security Administration, the Department of Veterans Affairs provides a preapproved list of VSOs nationally that do not charge for their services.

By law, organizations and individuals must have VA permission, which is referred to in the law as "recognition" or "accreditation," to represent veterans before the Department in their claims for VA benefits. This requirement ensures that veterans have qualified and competent representation. Only those organizations and individuals authorized by the VA to provide representation for veterans are included in the eBenefits "Representative Search" results. A VA-accredited attorney has applied to VA for accreditation, is licensed to practice law in at least one state, and is in good standing in the states, courts, and agencies in which in which the attorney is authorized to practice or appear for clients. A VA-accredited claims agent has applied to the VA for accreditation, has satisfied minimum character and fitness requirements, and has passed a written examination about VA benefits laws and procedures. The VA requires accredited attorneys and claims agents to complete continuing legal education courses to maintain their accreditation.

If you are recommending that claimants seek representation from a VSO, direct them to download a blank copy of the 21-22 form. This form can be printed and mailed or hand-delivered to the VSO of their choice. If the VSO agrees to assist in their claim, that organization will then submit it to the VA regional office on their behalf. VSOs are not part of the VA; they are recognized national and state organizations that help veterans and their dependents and survivors with their claims. These services are provided without charge.

If you are an accredited attorney or claims agent, a claimant may bring you a copy of the 21-22a form. If you agree to assist in the claim, you will then submit it to the VA regional office on your client's behalf. The fees charged by VA-accredited attorneys and agents may be based on a fixed fee, an hourly rate, a percentage of past-due benefits recovered, or any combination of these options. Veterans may choose to enter into a fee agreement providing that fees for representation will be paid by the VA directly out of any past-due benefits awarded to the veteran. Such a fee is limited to 20 percent of the total amount of past-due benefits awarded on the claim. A fee not exceeding 20 percent of past-due benefits awarded is presumed by the VA to be reasonable; a fee exceeding 33⅓ percent of past-due benefits awarded is presumed by the VA to be unreasonable.

PTSD versus Personality Disorder

Before you file a service-connected disability with the VA, you should have a clear understanding of potentially troublesome areas. An amputee has little difficulty in establishing the extent of his disability. There are no gray areas subject to individual interpretation or requiring second and third opinions. This is not the case for the PTSD and TBI disabilities that so many combat veterans face when they return to the homeland. A veteran's disability must be "service connected" or come from a prior condition that worsens due to the military service.

News Nation and the *Denver Post* reported that the U.S. military was illegally discharging veterans with "personality disorders." These conclusions were based on data collected from the Department of Defense resulting from Freedom of Information suits filed by the Veterans Services Clinic at Yale Law School on behalf of its clients, Vietnam Veterans of America. The Mayo Clinic defines a personality disorder as a mental disorder that usually develops in the teen or early adult years and is characteristic of a rigid and unhealthy pattern of behaving, thinking, and functioning.

In a recent six-year timeframe, the military discharged 22,500 service members who had filed PTSD claims that were denied due to "personality disorders." Unfortunately, once veterans have been diagnosed with a personality disorder, they can experience much more difficulty receiving benefits and treatment from the VA. Regrettably, when this diagnosis is made, these veterans are denied certain medical benefits not only for themselves but for their family members as well. In cases like these, the military automatically assumes a personality disorder existed prior to military service. This assumption puts the onus on the service member to prove that his or her "preexisting condition" was aggravated by military service—a difficult case to make.

Joshua Kors, a journalist who has reported on personality disorders for the *Nation,* writes that a personality disorder discharge is a contradiction in terms. Recruits who truly have a severe preexisting condition such as a personality disorder do not pass the rigorous prescreening process and are not accepted into the army. But the Department of Veterans Affairs is not required to provide medical care to soldiers dismissed with personality disorders due to the preexisting condition clause; the VA is only required to treat wounds sustained during service. Moreover, service members discharged under Chapter 5-13 of the Army's separation manual, "Separation Because of Personality Disorder," cannot collect disability benefits. To receive disability benefits, a soldier must be evaluated by a medical board, which must confirm that he or she is wounded and that the wounds stem from combat. This process usually takes several months, whereas a 5-13 discharge can be completed in a matter of days. When soldiers dismissed under 5-13 have not completed their military contract, they have to return a portion of their enlistment bonus. There are situations in which soldiers expect their final pay on discharge day and instead receive a bill from the Army for thousands of dollars.

The pre-induction physical for young men and women prior to acceptance into the U.S. armed forces does not include questions and/or evaluations relative to a personality disorder. Thus, upon discharge from military service, a VA disability claim based on a personality disorder will be denied because there is no identifiably clear evidence (proof) of personality disorder prior to the veteran's induction into military service. Not only are such veterans unable to receive VA disability benefits upon discharge, but they also lose other important benefits such as VA health care for themselves and their spouses and children. They further lose the benefit of any veteran hiring priorities. Unfortunately, there is a financial motivation for keeping the current personality disorder policy in place. Harvard professor Linda Bilmes's extensive study of the Iraq and Afghanistan wars shows that, by sticking to its policies on personality disorder discharges, the military potentially saves $8 billion in disability pay and $4.5 billion in medical care over the course of veterans' lifetimes.

A very real tragedy exists, exemplified by the feelings of betrayal experienced by returning soldiers who are denied benefits. We are reminded of the VA's own motto, drawn from Abraham Lincoln's second inaugural address: "To care for him who shall have borne the battle and for his widow and orphan." The bottom line is that discharged, emotionally troubled soldiers face a "double whammy." On one hand, it is apparent they will need skillful advice in appealing their VA disability claim; on the other hand, they will need help in returning to the workforce if their discharge paperwork reads "discharge for personality disorder."

Chapter 9

Group LTD Conversion Rights

Attorneys advising clients filing disability claims under employer-sponsored coverage need to understand the employee rights of disabled terminating employees. Totally disabled employees are particularly vulnerable and for several reasons. We can assume they were previously healthy and insurable before their disability. Upon termination of employment, they have a limited timeframe, usually 30 days, to invoke their conversion rights—that is, to sign up for conversion (sometimes referred to as portable) coverage that they can take with them without penalty. The attorney advisor is in an ideal position to make sure their disabled clients exercise their conversion rights. Unfortunately, the mindset of newly disabled individuals is such that they will need and appreciate a reminder about these rights.

Today the "industry standard" is to ensure that group life, short-term, and long-term disability contracts almost always include a waiver of premium provision. Premiums can be waived upon proof of disability per the policy contractual definition. Group short-term and long-term disability policy forms allow for employees to be out of work, disabled, with premiums waived by the insurer. This provision allows for benefits to continue without the employer or employee required to make premium payment. Moreover, it enables employees to become fully insured again upon recovering from their disability and returning to full-time employment.

Group life insurance operates in a very different manner. The group life waiver of premium typically requires a six- to nine-month continuation of total disability, and disability almost always must occur prior to age 60. The good news here is that an employee can become disabled at, say, age 55, file for waiver of premium, and collect benefits for another 15 years. Thus, death benefits are ultimately paid without the employer or former employee having had to pay a premium since the ninth month of the employee's disability.

After Employment Ends

Employee benefits (medical, dental, life, disability, long-term insurance coverage) are almost always tied to full-time employment, that is, working at least 24 to 30 hours per week. Because of the variance in benefit provisions with different insurers, it is not possible to cover all scenarios, but key issues deserve particular attention. As soon as claimants become disabled, they will need proper guidance from their benefit advisors, and before returning to work with a partial disability, they will need to discuss the loss of benefits with their benefits advisor. The claimant's attorney may well be called upon to make recommendations. That does not mean the attorney advisor should be expected to be an expert in the areas of life, disability, and other employee benefits coverage. Yet the attorney advisor is in the best position to identify these issues and to direct the claimant to professional insurance advisors.

If claimants have group long-term disability at their place of business and they become totally disabled, they may be losing all their employee benefits, possibly without even being aware it is happening. They may lose their employee benefits after only 30 days of being disabled, with literally no time to make benefit decisions that will impact them for the rest of their lives. Should they only be partially disabled, a whole new set of considerations are set in motion. Is continuation of their group life insurance possible if it is connected to full-time employment? Is there a waiver of premium (WP) provision that allows for continuation of group life insurance when disabled? (There almost always is.) Does it necessitate that the insured be totally disabled, or is a partial disability sufficient? (A partial disability is almost never sufficient.) Does the disability have to occur before age 65? (It almost always does.) If the insured was disabled while employed and is only partially disabled, when they are no longer considered an employee, how do they continue their group life insurance? (This is a great question for human resources personnel.) Are short-term disability benefits available, and does the definition of disability under the long-term disability plan differ from the short-term disability plan? (It almost always does.) What about the company-sponsored health care plan being continued under the Consolidated Omnibus Budget Reconciliation Act (COBRA)? What about the company-sponsored dental plan being continued under COBRA? Will the insured be eligible for Medicare after being disabled for two years if she is only partially disabled?

Communicating with HR

We are assuming that the claimant's new disability does not (and should not) lead to termination of employment. The attorney advisor should send notice to the head of human resources at the claimant's place of employment, or to whoever is in charge of employee benefit administration, and should request details on the claimant's conversion rights on their behalf (after the claimant has authorized the attorney to represent them).

Following is a sample attorney insurer communiqué:

```
To: Manager & Director of Human Resources
--------- Corporation

Boston, MA

Date:

Our client John Brown is now disabled and is
insured under the --------- Corporation Employee
Benefit Program and needs the forms to exercise
his/her rights under the following:

  BCBS MA Medical Insurance Plans insuring the
  Brown family

  Dental Insurance Plan insuring the Brown
  family

  Group Life Insurance

  Group Voluntary Life Insurance

  Long Term Disability

  Long Term Care Insurance

Mr./Mrs. does not have ready access to PDF's of
his/her employee benefit coverages. When
Mr. Brown decides which of his employee benefits
he wants to continue, our firm, --------- Law,
will advance all premiums due within 31 days of
Mr. Brown's termination of employment.
```

Group Life Insurance

When claimants become disabled so that they cannot perform their job and can start collecting group long-term disability benefits, they will eventually be terminated from their employer's employee benefit program. The key issue will be to maintain their group life insurance, which is possible, especially if there is a waiver of premium provision (assuming the disabled employee qualifies for waiver of premium), which exempts the insured from paying future premiums. Keep in mind that terminating employees have just one month to convert their group life insurance. Consider that insured employees who have become disabled are probably uninsurable for individual life insurance purposes, so they must be reminded to consider converting their group life insurance coverage before the month has expired. Group life insurance almost always includes a waiver of premium benefit if the insured is totally disabled and is under the age of 60. Some insurers extend the waiver of premium benefit for a disability occurring before age 65.

For decades, group life insurers have offered conversion rights to terminating employees. Conversion to whole life is an industry norm. Some insurers offer conversion to a one-year term, which then converts to whole life. With the increasing popularity of voluntary term life coverage, insurers began to allow for "porting," or continuing the coverage as term insurance. Since the employee has already been paying his or her voluntary life premium via automatic payroll deductions, upon termination of employment or loss of eligibility, it is advantageous to be allowed to continue life coverage as term insurance.

Note the following wording taken from a group life insurance contract:

> If you become totally disabled before age 60, your employee life insurance will be continued without further payment of premium, after nine months of total disability. However, you must continue to pay premiums until we approve your total disability. To be considered totally disabled, you must, because of injury or illness, be unable to do any work for which you are reasonably qualified by education, training, or experience.

Now let's look at a common definition of disability under a typical group LTD contract:

- **Total Disability:** After the initial own occupation definition, you will be totally disabled if you are unable to work in any occupation for which you are or may become suited by education, training, or experience. If you are employed and still earning wages or a salary, you will be considered "residually disabled."

- **Residual Disability:** You are residually disabled if due to sickness or injury you are unable to perform all the material duties of your own occupation on a full-time basis, but you are able to perform one or more of the material duties of your own occupation or any other occupation on a full-time or part-time basis; and you have a loss of earnings.

You will note that premiums can be waived under the group life insurance waiver of premium benefit after nine months of total disability. You also must remain totally disabled for nine consecutive months.

A group LTD contract can allow for benefit payments beginning sooner than 90 days, but most LTD plans have a waiting period of 90 days or longer. Hence, long-term disability benefits can begin sooner than they do under a waiver of premium provision. Benefits can also begin after a combination of total and/or partial disability days (versus total disability only under a group life insurance waiver of premium provision). We are explaining these differences to show that it is possible for claimants to collect group LTD benefits while partially disabled, and not be disabled "enough," and be eligible to have premiums waived on their group life insurance.

If the employee has become partially disabled, disability benefits are calculated based on income, either at their income prior to becoming disabled or at their lower income now that they have become partially disabled. Will their group life insurance benefit, typically based on a formula of one, two, or three times earnings, be based on one times earnings at the point of disability or one times their (lower) partial disability earnings?

Unfortunately for those insured under group LTD plans, when a partial disability claim is approved, insured individuals do not realize that their employer-sponsored benefits can be affected substantially, especially if their partial disability status continues for an extended period of time. How will the premium be paid when they are partially disabled? (Keep in mind that waiver of premium is applicable only for total disability, not partial.) Who pays the premium for the LTD if the claimant remains partially disabled for an extended period of time? Will the claimant remain eligible for group life insurance if he or she works less than 30 hours per week when eligibility requires 30 hours per week of employment?

The Lifespan of Benefits

Six years ago, David became totally disabled, preventing him from being able to do his job at the museum. When he passed away many years later, the group life insurance benefit was payable to his beneficiary, although he had not worked for the museum in six years. This happened because his group life insurance continued for six years without payment of premium, as he qualified for waiver of premium based on the insurer's definition of total disability. Does this happen all the time? No. The insured might have been partially disabled but still unable to perform his job, qualifying him for disability benefits, but ineligible under the waiver of premium.

Health Care Coverage

COBRA

When employees leave their job, under current law they become eligible for continuation of their medical insurance coverage under COBRA for 18 months. If the group long-term disability plan has a conversion option, insured employees have one month to elect a disability conversion policy. They are not eligible to do so if they are already covered by group LTD at a new job.

If the employer has an outside administrator handling COBRA administration, will the employer let the disabled employee maintain his or her status/eligibility as an employee when partially disabled? The COBRA period of eligibility extends from 18 to 29 months if the employee is totally disabled. Before being covered by Medicare, where will the former employee be covered for medical care in the interim? What happens when 18 months of COBRA have expired and they are not yet approved by Social Security (they must be "certified as disabled under Title II of the

Social Security Act, 29 months after the date of termination"); how will their medical bills be paid between the end of 18 months and 29 months? Employee benefit programs can vary significantly from employer to employer and from state to state. The attorney disability advisor can assist with these benefit questions by asking the corporate human resources director and/or the corporation's employee benefits broker/advisor.

Medicare Eligibility

Medicare Part A, which covers hospital care, is free for most people who paid FICA (Federal Insurance Contributions Act) taxes for at least 10 years. Eligibility begins upon reaching age 65. Upon eligibility for SSDI benefits, claimants become eligible for Medicare after 24 months, regardless of age.

Medicare Part B covers outpatient services and doctor visits, with premiums based on income. Disabled claimants may continue to be insured under a working spouse's employer-provided benefit program. In such situations, the Social Security Administration must be notified that a deferral is being sought.

Medicare Part C combines Medicare Parts A and B and may also include Part D, which covers prescription drug costs and may be purchased separately. Private health insurers offer a wide assortment of plans.

If a claimant is still working and covered by their employer's medical plan, they can defer Medicare Part B. Be aware of the following: If claimants plan to defer Part B, they need to notify the Social Security Administration and state that they are seeking a deferral. Without a deferral, premium increase penalties will be imposed for the duration of Medicare coverage.

Electronic Delivery of Employee Benefit Documents

Internet advancements have allowed for quick, efficient electronic delivery of corporate employee benefit programs. Human resources personnel almost automatically communicate via email with their employees, including sharing information regarding their employee benefit programs, without any proof of receipt of the email. At the same time, the majority of group life and disability insurers no longer automatically provide printed booklets to hand deliver to employees as they did in the "old days." Employee benefits advisors have been informed that they would have to pay for printing a client's booklets themselves. Fortunately, the pace of instantaneous communication via modern-day technology has mostly enhanced the communication of employee benefits. Benefit professionals now communicate with their employees by emailing PDFs of employee benefit booklets. For businesses with employees in outlying areas or, especially, residing in other states, the Internet has become the obvious choice for employee benefit communication. We suggest to our employer clients that the safest approach to benefit communication is to deliver summary plan descriptions (SPDs) with a delivery receipt attached.

Note that 90 to 95 percent of enterprises in the United States fall within the category of small businesses. Let's explore the individuals who might be personally responsible for managing and administering their organization's employee benefits—a 25-person law firm's *business manager*, a 15-person museum's *office administrator*, a 9-person consulting firm's *office manager*, a 90-person nonprofit green company's *VP*, and a 40-person manufacturer's corporate *treasurer*. The key point here is that none of these skilled professionals has ever specialized in the administration of employee benefits. Most important for the attorney advisor is consideration of the situation in which employees have become uninsurable while working for their employer and terminate employment without being properly notified of their conversion rights.

To illustrate the importance of proper communication of benefits, consider *Thomas v. Cigna (E.D.N.Y.)*, United States District Court Eastern District of New York 09-CV-5029 (SLT) 02-19-2013. This case references what was determined to be the inappropriate Internet communication of an employee's group life coverage. In this case, *Raymond Thomas, Plaintiff, v. Cigna Group Insurance* et al., *Defendants,* a plan participant had group life insurance through her employer's ERISA. The insured became disabled and stopped working or paying premiums. After she passed away, her beneficiaries filed a claim for her life insurance benefits. The insurer denied the death claim based on the fact that the insured's life insurance was no longer in force. As it turned out, the group life insurance coverage had a waiver of premium benefit for disability. However, the insured had not requested the premium waiver be initiated, so she was no longer covered when she died. The insured's beneficiaries sued the insurer based on the fact that the waiver of premium requirements had not been appropriately communicated to the plan participant due to inadequate delivery of the employer's summary plan description. As the claim was an ERISA claim, the court determined that there was no evidence that the plan administrator had provided the plan participant with an appropriate SPD.

What have we learned from *Thomas v. Cigna (E.D.N.Y.)*? We are reminded that we can expect the proper communication of employee benefits to be scrutinized more frequently in future years. Regardless of whether a corporate employee benefit program is subject to ERISA laws and regulations, employers need sufficient proof that their employees have ready access to all the most recent details of their employee benefit programs, and employees should be aware of what their rights are regarding plan communication.[1]

The U.S. Department of Labor

Employers communicating employee benefit details with their employees online have burdened the court system with cases relative to the issues of proper and appropriate delivery. The U.S. Department of Labor and the Internal Revenue Service's "Guide to Electronic Delivery of Participant Disclosure Materials" clarifies what employers' responsibilities are regarding delivery of plan information.[2]

---

1 Pulled from the author's previously published work: http://www.disabilityservices.com/pdf/THOMASVSCIGNA.pdf.

2 The guide is available, for example, at http://kbpensionservices.com/files/9513/7347/0030/A_Guide_to_Electronic_Delivery_of_Participant_Disclosure_Materials.pdf.

Chapter 10

Disability Insurance Taxation

It is estimated that more than 90 percent of the group LTD plans in existence nationally are "60 percent" plans. There are group LTD programs that insure 66⅔ or 70 percent of income, but they are rare. Actuarial studies have established that at higher benefit levels, the risk increases markedly; hence, the premium percentage increases disproportionately. For example, increasing group LTD from 60 percent to 66⅔ creates an additional 10 percent benefit, yet the added premium can increase by 15 to 20 percent depending on the insurer. The reason is that the insurers can offset LTD benefits with Social Security payments in 60 percent plans. Since the amount beyond 60 percent is not offset by Social Security, it is all pure risk, creating the proportionately higher premium.

The vast majority of the working population insured by 60 percent LTD plans assumes that they are adequately insured. Unfortunately, most recipients do not actually get 60 percent because their benefits are taxable. It is estimated that most 60 percent LTD benefit plans have employer-paid premiums where the employer is taking a tax deduction on their LTD premiums as a business expense. Consider the financial impact to a corporate executive who becomes disabled. If an executive is currently insured to only 60 percent of salary and is in a 30 percent tax bracket, then there is a considerable disability shortfall—the 60 percent taxable LTD benefits are 42 percent after-tax benefits in this tax bracket.

Next, consider an executive earning a $100,000 salary with a $10,000 end-of-year bonus and another $10,000 employer match deposited in a 401(k) plan. The insurable income need for disability purposes should be the executive's entire $120,000 "created income" since the full $120,000 is the total compensation subject to the risk of long-term disability. Insuring a $100,000 salary at 60 percent would be a $60,000 annual disability benefit, whereas insuring a $120,000 "created income" at 60 percent would be a $72,000 annual disability benefit. The difference between insuring at the $120,000 and $100,000 levels is a significant 20 percent. An executive with $120,000 "created income" who is only receiving $60,000 a year in taxable disability benefits ($42,000 after tax) is insured to only 35 percent of his or her "created income."

Benefits are diminished further by the impact of inflation over the duration of a long-term disability. A disability lasting only a few years will quickly diminish a 60 percent benefit considering the impact of taxes alongside inflation. From the point of view of benefit advisors, it is recommended that they evaluate the possibility of (1) increasing benefit levels from 60 to 70 percent, (2) changing the LTD benefit from 60 percent taxable to 60 percent nontaxable benefits, and (3) insuring "created income," not salary alone.

These "shortfall' examples are most relevant when evaluating a client's group LTD program, yet illustrate two key issues for the attorney disability advisor. First, corporate executives need to insure their "created incomes" against the risk of long-term disability. Second, when employers are deducting the LTD premium as a business expense, they can still report the premiums as additional compensation.

Private Letter Ruling: Revenue Ruling 2004-55

When your new client is partially disabled today, he may well continue partially disabled; become totally disabled; or experience some combination of total and partial disability periods. If he is not yet eligible for disability benefits and his employer is paying LTD premiums on his behalf, there may be an opportunity to "create" tax-free benefits when he eventually becomes totally disabled. His employer may be willing to report his monthly LTD premium as additional compensation, thereby potentially creating tax-free LTD benefits when the insured becomes totally disabled. We mention this as an unofficial possibility. We refer to a private letter ruling, Revenue Ruling 2004-55. Private letter rulings refer to a single specific situation in which the Internal Revenue Service (IRS) issues a ruling. At the same time, note that the official IRS regulations have not been changed. There is certainly a reason to expect future rulings will be comparable to the private letter ruling. We are not aware of the existence of adverse consequences relative to this practice. We would rather share the concept with you, warning you of the danger involved, and insist that clients consult their own tax accountant and advisor before acting.

> A private letter ruling is a written determination issued to a taxpayer by an IRS office in response to a written inquiry from an individual or an organization about its status for tax purposes or the tax effects of its acts or transactions. A letter ruling interprets and applies the tax laws to the taxpayer's specific set of facts. (A letter ruling may be revoked or modified at a later date.)[1]

Tax-Favored Disability Insurance

We can establish a general rule for taxation of disability benefits versus the tax deductibility of disability premiums as follows: If an employer pays the disability premiums for employees, deducting the premium as a business expense, then the benefits received when employees are disabled will be considered taxable income. Conversely, if the premium paid is not deducted, then benefits received can be tax-favored.

On January 31, 2003, an IRS private letter ruling clarified what insurance agents and financial advisors have been recommending to their clients for many years. At issue in the letter was the IRS position on a particular employer's proposed amendments to its long-term disability plan. The proposed amendments stated that the employer would pay the LTD premiums for a group of employees,

1 See https://www.irs.gov/irb/2018-01_IRB.

including the amount of each employee's LTD premium, as taxable wages for the year the premiums were paid. This employer would also pay the premium for a second group of employees, but this "group B" would be allowed to make an annual irrevocable election prior to the beginning of each plan year and either (1) have the employer include the individual's LTD premiums as part of taxable wages or (2) have the employer exclude the LTD premium cost as part of taxable wages. In Revenue Ruling 2004-55, the IRS clarified that those employees who become disabled can exclude their LTD benefits from gross income, as they had paid taxes on their LTD premium as if it were compensation. Clearly, such a ruling is important, given the savings it offers to the claimant.

When an LTD program is set up initially as an employer company-paid plan (let's assume it insures to 60% of income), the LTD insurer bases its premium rate on an "employer paid" (or "noncontributory") plan. If the plan is written as "contributory," then the LTD premium rate will be higher. Some insurers add as little as 5 percent to the rate, while others will mark up by as much as 10 to 15 percent. The extra premium is higher because the risk is greater (60% taxable vs. 60% nontaxable benefits). If we assume a 27.65 percent tax rate (15% federal + 5% state + 7.65% FICA), a 60 percent taxable benefit generates a 43.4 percent (60% × 72.35%) after-tax benefit. Obviously, LTD insurance underwriters would attach a different premium rate to insure a 43.4 percent after-tax benefit versus a 60 percent tax-free benefit.

Actuarial studies surveying large numbers of disabled people indicate that the higher the amount of LTD benefit (as a percentage of income), the less likely the disabled person is to return to work. A 60 percent taxable benefit hurts more financially compared to one that is 60 percent tax-free, the latter of which is closer to the claimant's income earned prior to disability. Hence, it makes sense that the LTD premium should be higher when benefits will be nontaxable. Keep in mind that we are not making a universal statement covering all disabled people. Only a small portion of disabled people are tempted to stretch marginal disabilities into total disabilities when benefits are tax-free. Yet this factor still affects an insurer's profitability, and as a result, tax-free disability claims invite a little more scrutiny.

CFO alert: It may be advisable to determine the corporation's maximum financial liability (cost) if every employee uses the tax-favored approach. For example, a business with a payroll of $10 million might have a $30,000 annual LTD premium expense. If every employee participated in the tax-favored program, then the 7.65 percent cost of FICA would be a $2,295 extra cost to the employer this year (plus the moderate cost of workers' compensation and Federal Unemployment Tax Act [FUTA] taxes). This $2,295 extra expense is moderate considering the added benefits of a tax-favored LTD program, particularly for executives in higher-tax brackets. And it is highly unlikely that most employees will elect this option.

Tax Treatment in Various Cases

Disability Insurance Premiums

Premiums paid for a personal disability income policy are not deductible, unless it's a professional corporation, according to Internal Revenue Code (IRC) of 1986 Sections 262 and 265. The premiums do not constitute expenses paid for medical care qualifying for deduction under IRC Section 213.

Benefits

Disability benefits paid to the insured person under an individual policy are nontaxable, according to IRC Section 104(a)(3).

Sole Proprietorship

For disability income insurance:

1. Premiums, when paid by a sole proprietor for his or her own benefit, are personal expenses nondeductible under IRC Section 262.
2. Disability income benefits received by a sole proprietor under an individual policy are nontaxable, according to IRC Section 104(a)(3).

Partnerships

Disability income insurance—benefits and premiums: Partnerships cannot deduct premiums as a business expense (IRC Sections 262 and 265). Benefits are nontaxable to the partners receiving them, according to IRC Section 104(a)(3).

Corporations

Disability income policies—premiums and benefits:

1. Premiums paid by a corporation on a disability income insurance policy are not deductible when the corporation is named as beneficiary of the policy because the premiums are allocable to tax-exempt benefits received by the corporation. (See IRC Section 265.)
2. When the corporation is the owner and beneficiary of a disability income policy insuring its employee, the benefits received by the corporation under the policy are excludable from a corporation's gross income. See IRC Section 104(a)(3).

S Corporations

S corporations (corporations that, in effect, do not pay income tax but rather distribute income and loss among shareholders) are treated as partnerships for tax purposes under IRC Section 1372. A 2 percent shareholder of an S corporation is treated as a partner.

Tax Treatment

Benefits paid to employee, premiums paid by employer:

1. Premiums paid by employers are deductible as business expenses under IRC Section 162.
2. The employer's contribution is excluded from the employee's gross income (IRC Section 106).

3. Benefits received by the employee are taxable, according to IRS Section 105 (a).

Benefits paid to employee, premiums paid by employee and employer:

1. Premiums paid by an employer are deductible as business expenses under IRC Section 162.
2. The employer's contribution is excluded from the employee's gross income (IRC Section 106).
3. The employee-paid portion of the benefits is nontaxable, according to IRC Section 104(a)(3). The employer-paid portion is taxable to the employee, according to IRC Section 105 (a). *Note:* Taxability is controlled by contributions of the employer and employee in the year disability commences, as outlined in IRS Regulation Section 1.105-1(d).

Benefits paid to employee, premiums paid by employee:

1. Premiums paid by the employee are not deductible (IRC Sections 262 and 265). The premiums do not constitute expenses paid for medical care qualifying for deduction under IRC Section 213.
2. Benefits paid to the employee are nontaxable, according to IRC Section 104(a)(3).

Chapter 11

Advising Your Client on Returning to Work: Current Law and Regulations

With lawyers and their clients in mind, this text often focuses on hurdles and personal challenges, but the picture is not totally bleak. One upside is that many people who experience long-term disabilities do return to work. As attorneys, your job is advise these clients on how returning to work will affect their current and future prospects for receiving coverage from their new disability insurer. Lawyers must also help integrate their clients back into the workforce, ensuring that their partial disability does not cause them to face discrimination. And if they do suffer discrimination, lawyers need to know how to advise them on what recourse they have.

Regrettably (yet unsurprisingly), Americans with disabilities experience a disproportionately higher rate of unemployment than Americans without disabilities. The U.S. Department of Labor and White House Council of Economic Advisors have identified the employment levels of people with and without a disability. Based on a 2010–2012 Census Bureau survey, only one-third (32%) of working-age people with disabilities were employed compared to over two-thirds (72.7%) of people without disabilities. Of the people with disabilities seeking employment, 15 percent had not been successful.

Why are so few people with disabilities seeking employment? First, if someone is totally disabled and unemployable, they are naturally not actively seeking employment of any sort. Moreover, a significant portion of America's most seriously disabled are collecting disability benefits through Social Security or a previous employer's group disability program. Yet we can assume that many members of our disabled population would prefer to return to meaningful employment.

Should totally disabled claimants recover to the extent that they can return to the workforce in some capacity, their attorney advisor needs to consider several key points. Most important is the insurer's contractual definition of disability. Are the claimants insured for a residual or partial disability where their benefits could and would be reduced based on percentage of lost income? For example, let's say their group LTD plan insured to 60 percent of lost income and their predisability income was $12,000/month ($144,000 annually). If they returned to work half-time earning $6,000/month, their disability insurer would pay them a prorated benefit upon returning to work at half their predisability earnings.

Another consideration arises when the claimant wants to become insured under a new employer's benefit program. The claimant's disability now becomes a preexisting condition when they become reinsured under a new employer-sponsored group LTD program. Let's assume the new LTD contract has a 3/12 "preex" restriction (not covered for a preexisting restriction in the first 12 months of coverage if treated for that condition within three months of becoming insured). The likelihood that a prior disability will reoccur is high enough that the claimant should be advised about this limitation in her insurance.

Americans with Disabilities Act

Most folks who develop a disability begin to look forward to recovery and returning to an everyday lifestyle to the extent that they can do so. Here is where the attorney advisor needs a clear understanding of the Americans with Disabilities Act (ADA), an employer's responsibilities to disabled employees, and the term "reasonable accommodation." Attorneys assisting disabled claimants need to be able to advise their clients about their legal rights as disabled persons.

Let's first assume that most disability insurance contracts offer both total and partial disability insurance benefits. Although U.S. employers are required to provide workers' compensation insurance for individuals who are injured on the job, they are not required by law to provide short- or long-term disability coverage to their employees. As noted in Chapter 5, six states and territories have sickness laws: New York, New Jersey, California, Hawaii, Rhode Island, and Puerto Rico. These laws offer essentially short-term disability protection that employers in these states are required to provide for employees. Employees are protected by Title I of the ADA and need to understand their rights when they become disabled. (For employers' responsibilities under the ADA, visit https://www.eeoc.gov/facts/ada17.html.)

Reasonable Accommodations for a Disabled Employee

Ever since passage of the ADA in 1990, employers have been held accountable for their responsibilities to disabled employees, as well as the fair treatment of disabled applicants for employment. "No covered entity shall discriminate against a qualified individual with a disability because of the disability of such individual in regard to job application procedures, the hiring, advancement, or discharge of employees, employee compensation, job training, and other terms, conditions, and privileges of employment" [42 U.S.C. § 12112 (a)]. A "qualified individual with a disability" is defined as "an individual with a disability who, with or without reasonable accommodation, can perform the essential functions of the employment position that such individual holds or desires" [42 U.S.C. § 12111 (8)].

The act goes on to explain that "the term 'discriminate' includes . . . not making reasonable accommodations to the known physical or mental limitations of an otherwise qualified individual with a disability who is an applicant or employee, unless such covered entity can demonstrate that the accommodation would impose an undue hardship on the operation of the business of such covered entity" [42 U.S.C. § 12112(b)(5)(A)].

Neither the ADA nor its regulations explicitly define the term "reasonable accommodation," instead merely providing examples of possible accommodations. Thus, the statute declares [42 U.S.C. § 12111(9)]:

The term "reasonable accommodation" may include:

- Making existing facilities used by employees readily accessible to and usable by individuals with disabilities; and
- Job restructuring, part-time or modified work schedules, reassignment to a vacant position, acquisition or modification of equipment or devices, appropriate adjustment or modifications of examinations, training materials or policies, the provision of qualified readers or interpreters, and other similar accommodations for individuals with disabilities.

Employers and courts across the country have been left to interpret these provisions, seemingly on a case-by-case basis. An examination of the resulting case law is advisable for employers facing similar issues. Regulations issued by the Equal Employment Opportunity Commission in implementation of the Rehabilitation Act of 1973, 29 C.F.R § 701 et seq., and court decisions under that act, can be useful tools for deciphering the duties imposed by the ADA. The Rehabilitation Act, the precursor of the ADA, prohibited certain government contractors and recipients of federal funds from discriminating against otherwise qualified disabled individuals.

According to statistics published by the President's Committee on Employment of People with Disabilities, the typical cost to employers for making workplace accommodations for people with disabilities is $200, with more than half of accommodations expenditures totaling $500 or less. Obviously, the potential costs of employment discrimination litigation far exceed those sums.

The Hiring Process

The Equal Employment Opportunity Commission's (EEOC's) Technical Assistance Manual states that recruitment activities may violate the ADA if they screen out potential applicants with disabilities. Employers thus should review their recruiting procedures to ensure that they do not engage in discrimination. While the law does not require employers to launch special activities to recruit people with disabilities, it is recommended that employers expand their outreach efforts to potential sources of qualified individuals with disabilities. In addition, employers are urged to create an environment, or corporate culture, in which applicants and employees with disabilities feel confident they will be given an equal opportunity to compete based on their qualifications. An employer is engaging in unlawful discrimination if it uses qualification standards, employment tests, or other selection criteria that screen out, or tend to screen out, an individual or class of people on the basis of disability.

Benefits, Privileges, and Other Employment Practices

Performance Standards

The ADA does not require that an employer give employees with disabilities special rights with respect to evaluations, discipline, or discharge. Again, the key is equal treatment, so that an employer should not evaluate employees with a disability according to lower standards or discipline them less severely. The EEOC's Technical Assistance Manual states that:

- If a disability affects the person's ability to perform marginal tasks (as opposed to essential functions), then the employer has to provide a reasonable accommodation;
- An employee who needs an accommodation should not be evaluated on the ability to perform without the accommodation and should not be downgraded based on the need for accommodation;
- If an employee with a disability is having performance problems, the employer can ask for medical and other information that is job-related and consistent with business necessity to find out whether the problem is disability-related and whether a reasonable accommodation is needed; and
- If an employer refuses to provide a reasonable accommodation that would not impose an undue hardship,

then the employer cannot discipline or fire an employee whose unsatisfactory performance is due to the failure to accommodate.

Reasonable Accommodations for People with Mental Illness under the ADA

No discussion of reasonable accommodations under the Americans with Disabilities Act would be complete without addressing the issue of people suffering from a cognitive disability. The concept of reasonable accommodation is not new to most business organizations, but they may be concerned about the cost of making reasonable accommodations, the time and energy required to revise job descriptions and duties, and their inexperience working with employees and applicants with mental illness. Likewise, applicants and employees with mental illness bring their own concerns and perspectives to discussion of the ADA's implementation. Although people with mental illness are hopeful that implementation of the law will bring them one step closer to full inclusion in community life, they fear they will take a significant risk if they disclose their illnesses and reveal the need for accommodation in the workplace. Myths and stereotypes about people with mental illness may make some employers concerned about on-the-job safety and their rights with respect to establishing related qualification standards.

Employees and employers should recognize that they can work together to make compliance with the ADA successful with strong cooperation and communication between employers or supervisors and employees in all stages of the employment process. In particular, it is important to approach the formulation of reasonable accommodations as an ongoing process rather than as a one-time solution.

Some people with mental illness find that the irregular and episodic nature of their illness interferes with the steady, regular demands of the workplace from time to time. People with depression, for instance, may face episodes of despair and hopelessness that make it difficult to work. Those with bipolar illness may experience mood shifts from extreme highs to deep lows, which may affect their productivity. Generally, individuals with mental illness have difficulty coping with stress, which may precipitate additional problems in the workplace. Each employee with a mental illness will be affected differently depending on the symptoms, severity, and duration of the illness. This factor underscores the need for individualized determinations of whether an employee's situation can be reasonably accommodated and, if so, what that accommodation will entail.

Maximizing Productivity: Accommodations for Employees with Psychiatric Disabilities

Reasonable accommodations are adjustments to a work setting that make it possible for qualified employees with disabilities to perform the essential functions of their jobs. Not all employees with psychiatric disabilities need accommodations to perform their jobs. For those who do, however, it is important to remember that the process of developing and implementing accommodations is individualized and should begin with input from the employee.

We would urge employers looking to better accommodate an employee returning to work with a psychiatric condition to review the accommodations that can be found at https://www.dol.gov/odep/pubs/fact/psychiatric.htm.

Employer Concerns

The ADA requires employers to make "reasonable" accommodations for employees to be able to return to the workforce. It is helpful to understand the dilemma employers face when contemplating hiring an individual they know is "somewhat" disabled. First, with the cost of providing a complete employee benefit program, including medical, dental, life, and disability insurance, currently costing employers at least 30 cents on every payroll dollar, for a large number of American corporations, employer-sponsored benefits are the number one or number two bottom-line items or expenditures. Although disability and life insurance represent less than 10 percent of the total dollars, my own employee benefits experience tells me that the majority of human resources personnel in the United States do not have a clear understanding of the financial impact of adding an increasing number of group LTD claims to their companies' LTD program. Remember, the vast majority of corporations in the United States have fewer than 50 employees.

A prospective employer may be concerned that a partially disabled employee may impact the stability and cost of their employer-sponsored employee benefit program. Since group medical insurance is the most expensive employee benefit, employers frequently assume that high claims costs will penalize their company's group rates. Employers who offer employer-paid benefits to all employees should understand the "pooling of risk approach" used by group disability insurers. With passage of the Affordable Care Act, the rules governing health insurance should be consistent throughout the states. Most of America's group insurers utilize multiple employer trusts (METs) established specifically for pooling the LTD claims experience of like businesses in order to spread the risk. Businesses that share similar profiles and demographics—white/blue collar, hazardous/nonhazardous occupations, employee mix (number of males vs. number of females), young/middle age, similar industries—will be grouped together. An employer with 30 employees should understand that the cost of a single disability should not impact their costs based on this pooling principle—the cost of a single insured's high claim is pooled with others. There is no reason to not hire someone who is already partially disabled in the hopes of avoiding a long-term disability claim and a subsequent LTD rate increase.

My personal experience has been that, in many situations, someone with a disability may well be a more desirable employee than someone who is not impaired in anyway. Based on my employee benefit background specializing in disability and long-term care coverage, I know that most people with a disability are very appreciative of a job opportunity, and that is why we actively sought out people who were disabled when we were looking for someone to do some telemarketing and customer service work. We hired someone who had been diagnosed with Parkinson's disease several years before. Now that they were familiar with their limitations, they were eager to become productive again. We were grateful and appreciative to have our newest employee representing our organization, and their appreciation for a newfound work opportunity made them a valuable asset to our business.

Social Security's Ticket to Work Program

Americans with disabilities face disproportionately higher rates of unemployment compared to Americans without disabilities, despite increasing emphasis on nondiscrimination, equality, and equal rights. Anyone with a disability should have, to the maximum extent possible, the same opportunities as everyone else. Everyone should have the opportunity to live independently, participate in an active community life, and, especially, be able to engage in productive employment.

The Labor Department/Council of Economic Advisors' Joint Initiative on Employment figures referenced earlier identified a growth opportunity for someone with a disability seeking employment in 2015 and beyond. It was determined that "most job growth is in occupations where computer use is important." In addition, they confirmed that "technology and corporate policies are also creating more possibilities for home-based and other flexible work arrangements that can especially benefit people with disabilities who deal with transportation difficulties and medical concerns."

This is good news for those researching return-to-work opportunities. However, some people collecting Social Security disability benefits are fearful of losing their Social Security benefits if they begin working again. Others are not sure whether they would be able to rejoin the workforce, or they may not know how to go about it. This is why all claimants and their advisors should become familiar with Social Security's Ticket to Work program. This program is free and was designed to prevent the immediate loss of disability benefits and medical insurance. It has been described as a safety net allowing for the opportunity to transition back to the work world. When seeking a job placement service, it is important to make sure it is a certified Social Security Administration (SSA) Employment Network participating in the Ticket to Work program.

The following article from myemploymentoptions.com titled "My Story: Working at Home Can Change Your Life" illustrates the Ticket to Work program's continuing success story.

> I hated the inevitable question, "What do you do for a living?" I didn't want to say that I was on Social Security Disability Insurance (SSDI). I didn't want to tell anyone that I did not have a job. But that was the truth. I had a disability, and it interfered with my ability to work locally.
>
> This was a very hard time for me. I was always a good student, hard worker and a "go-getter." I had always worked since I was a teen. Now, I had too much time on my hands. I missed having a set routine. Moreover, I missed that feeling of being productive and the social interaction.
>
> A few years went by and then I learned the Social Security Administration had created a free return-to-work program for people with disabilities, like me, receiving Social Security Disability Insurance (SSDI) and/or Supplemental Security Income (SSI) benefits. Even though I had not worked in a very long time, I still believed that I had abilities and skills to offer the working world. I just had no idea how to go about getting a job or whether I could handle the "working world" again. Moreover, I was afraid. As much as I needed more money, I simply could not afford to lose my monthly cash or health benefits right away. I needed a chance to "try" working.
>
> However, this Social Security Administration return-to-work program, officially called the Ticket to Work program, was free, which made my ears perk up. They also told me I wouldn't lose my cash benefits or medical care at once. It is a gradual program with a large safety net to allow me to "try" to test the waters of working again and see how I would do.
>
> If I wanted to try it out, all I had to do was contact an employment network (EN) that was certified to handle program participants. I called Employment Options because I liked the name. After I finished all my screenings, they told me I would be a good candidate for working from home.
>
> At first, I didn't think I was cut out for working from home because of my own fears, but then I began to realize what a great deal it was for people with disabilities and their

employers. American companies save on all the overhead, while the employee avoids all the cost and time of commuting. Plus, and perhaps most important, the work-space and work environment [are] already set up with accommodations for a person's particular disability.

My disability is a hidden disability and working from home was my only option. Working from home through the Ticket to Work program has been life changing. I feel I got a second chance at a career because I had the professional help I needed to get a good job that fits my needs.

When I first became a client of Employment Options, I was scared and so many thoughts ran through my head. Could I do this? Should I do this? What about my benefits check? What about my Medicare? The staff helped me fully understand the program so I felt comfortable. My self-confidence gradually improved and I love my first Work at Home position because I felt like I had 'back-up' and support to help me in the job.

I am still a client of the Ticket to Work program and Employment Options today. However, now, I also work for Employment Options and help advocate for the program and the Work At Home services that changed my life. I have been in the program several years and I have grown in my confidence and am gradually working toward self-sufficiency.

Many of the staff like myself receive disability benefits and are in the Ticket to Work program. We share our own stories to help our clients succeed! For those who want to try to work again and receive SSDI/SSI, there is free help for you!

Ticket to Work gave me that cushion to transition back to work, which means now I can answer the question, "What do you for a living?" with a big smile!

Legally Terminating an Employee

In this day and age of numerous state and federal laws protecting employees, especially for health and disability issues, employers are urged to follow very specific legal guidelines if they want to terminate an employee. The process actually starts at the point of hiring under the "Employment at Will" doctrine. If the employer wants to terminate the employee without the possibility of being sued, it is ultimately based on agreeing to the Employment at Will doctrine upon being hired. Both the employee and employer sign a statement specifying that the employee can terminate employment without notice (hopefully with two weeks' notice) for any reason.

Both federal and state laws dictate the limitations on termination of employees. I would first check with a corporate attorney, as well as state and federal laws. In many states, an employer must have "just cause" prior to legally terminating an employee. Employees who believe they should not have been terminated have grounds to file suit against their employer.

Yet another issue that surfaces is the Uniform Commercial Code, which stipulates that "every contract imposes an allegation of good faith in its performance enforcement."

Three Legal Reasons for Terminating an Employee

1. The employee violated a known company rule or rules.
2. The employee is not able to perform the job adequately.
3. The company is reducing its workforce for economic reasons.

The Employee Violated a Known Company Rule or Rules

For an employer to expect a rule to be upheld in the court system, there must be evidence that:

- The rule exists.
- The employee knew it existed.
- That rule was actually violated.
- Another employee or employees had been terminated for this particular infraction.
- Termination was a reasonable punishment for the infraction.

It is expected that the employer is able to prove that the rule was in writing and that the rule had been so displayed that the employee would have been aware of its existence.

The Employee Is Not Able to Perform the Job Adequately

- The employer must be able to prove the employee was incompetent.
- The employer took "reasonable" action to help employees improve performance of their job.
- Before terminating the employee, the employer has documented evidence that the employee had received adequate communication prior to being terminated.

The Company Is Reducing Its Workforce for Economic Reasons

- The employer needs to establish that it is in the best interests of the employer to terminate an employee(s). Note that the Worker Adjustment and Retraining Notification Act of 1988 (WARN) necessitates that employers (especially in any large-scale layoff) give employees at least 60 days' notice of layoff.

Chapter 12

Resources for Claimants

Should anyone ever file disability claims on their own, without a lawyer? I don't advise it, no, but it is possible to file a claim successfully without an attorney, yes.

Filing a disability insurance claim can be a time-consuming, unsettling, and confusing process, particularly the first time. As a claimant, you will need to decide whether to go it alone, without assistance, or to engage the services of a seasoned attorney claims advisor. In this chapter, I offer the information to help you, the disability claimant, make that decision, while also providing guidance to help you file on your own, should you decide to go that route.

The office of the Inspector General for the Social Security Administration (SSA) released a report on August 20, 2010, titled "Disability Impairments on Cases Most Frequently Denied by Disability Termination Services and Subsequently Allowed by Administrative Law Judges," which told a vitally important story. It stated that claimants with a professional advisor assisting them are more likely to have claims that are presented professionally with clear supportive documentation. As a consequence, the SSA is better able to quickly determine the validity of the claim. Professional assistance at the beginning of the Social Security disability insurance process can prevent needless delays for applicants who qualify for benefits.

When you have an attorney, you have someone to communicate with who will guide you through the process. You won't have to devote your time and energy to obtaining forms and communicating with your doctors. Instead, you get to devote all your efforts to dealing with your disability and medical treatments. With legal representation, you can expect to navigate the claims process more quickly and predictably, and also more successfully. And when you have an attorney, you don't have to struggle to become an expert because your attorney is the expert working on your behalf. Moreover, there's a certain pervasive loneliness to filing a claim on your own. With an attorney advisor, you'll be partnering with someone who is totally focused on getting your claim approved.

"Do it right the first time" should be the mantra of anyone filing a disability claim. Seeking legal counsel *after* your claim has already been turned down is still important, but since overturning a claim denial is much more difficult, it is better to invest the effort and lawyer's fees at the outset. Over the past decade, as the denial rate of Social Security disability claims increased to 63 percent, 17 million claims were denied. The ever-increasing number of denials has led to an enormous increase in appeals being filed, overtaxing an already overloaded system, with no relief in sight.

What It Can Be Like to File a Claim without a Lawyer

Imagine you are now disabled. You have mailed your disability claim form to your doctor's office. You remember to call to make sure it was received, and, after a month, you inquire if it was sent to the insurance company. You hear it probably won't go out until the first of next month—the doctor has been away, and there is a paperwork backlog in the office. In the meantime, you have been out of work for going on three months and were expecting benefits to begin with the 91st day of disability.

Several more weeks go by and the bills are really starting to pile up. You move some money from your savings account because you are behind in your mortgage payments. You begin to receive late fees on bills and payments. You are starting to feel very negative about the insurer and the claims process.

You get a phone call from the claims examiner at your disability insurance company who tells you that the company has received your doctor's report and needs to ask you some additional questions. He or she reminds you that the telephone call is being recorded for "quality purposes." You want to be helpful, but you object to the additional details the insurer representative is requesting. He seems to be questioning whether you are even disabled enough to be eligible for benefits. You think to yourself that this isn't going as smoothly as you had expected and hoped. You're worried you might say the wrong thing and jeopardize your claim payments. You remember reading about a federal law (HIPAA) that is supposed to protect your rights and the requirement of confidentiality. You ask the insurance company stranger on the phone about the confidentiality law. He points out that you signed an authorization when you sent in your employee portion of the claim form. Your stomach starts to turn as you think of the implications of your claim being denied. You begin to feel you are in over your head, and your fear is unsettling.

Then you hear that your doctor, who has been your trusted advisor for almost 20 years, has stated you are not disabled enough to be eligible for benefits. Now what? All along, you assumed your physician was an ally. You assumed he understood the duties of your job. Wasn't your doctor the one who said you weren't quite well enough to return to work? You start to feel that the information you and your physician submitted to the insurer is being used against you. And you're right: it is. Once you've made statements to an insurer, you can't take them back. You now realize that you would have been better off to seek an attorney's assistance in filing your claim.

Elements of this story happen to many claimants and can be avoided with the help of an attorney. When you submit a claim, it is important to know up front your likelihood of collecting benefits. An experienced attorney who specializes in filing disability claims will be able to tell you the likelihood of your claim being approved. An attorney will also be able to help you fill out forms and understand the requirements connected to the claims process—and can speak directly with the insurance company and your medical office in your stead. You'll appreciate the guidance and advocacy of a professional advisor who is only interested in your claim being approved.

Self-File Checklist for Claimants without Legal Representation

As you prepare to apply for benefits, make sure to follow these steps:

Make Emotional Allowances for Yourself

Remember, your state of mind will not be the same as it was the day before you became disabled. Your thought processes and decision-making capabilities will be very different. An important factor in your new life, as well as something likely to improve your chances of recovery, is remembering to have enormous compassion for yourself. Most people will never have to face the lifestyle adjustments you will need to make.

Peace of mind is something we should all seek, especially when disabled. The stress of financial pressures, added to not knowing if you will qualify for benefits, can damage your health. It is tragic enough to be facing a life-threatening heart condition without the angst of anxiety and worry about whether or not your claim will be paid. It has been clearly documented that the majority of disabled claimants feel high levels of stress. As the uncertainty continues, it only gets worse. The psychological stressors—pain, medications, doctors' visits, anger, withdrawal, how your spouse is adjusting to your new disability—can be overwhelming.

Keeping these pressures and realities in mind, disability claimants should seek outlets for stress, especially yoga, massage, socializing, talk therapy, relaxing hobbies, or meditation.

Communicate with Your Doctor

In presenting your own claim to your insurer, you must be very careful about your statements regarding the extent of your disabling condition. You will have to communicate extensively with your doctor, possibly explaining to him what language is required and what he is attesting to. You will need to keep track of communications deadlines, as well as perform follow-through on form submissions. You will need to effectively communicate with your claims examiners, and you need to know your rights.

As a disability claimant, you have been under the care of your attending physician or some other medical professional who specializes in treatment of the specific medical or psychological condition that has rendered you disabled. Ask your doctor if she considers you partially or totally disabled. If either is the case, what does she consider your likelihood of recovery? And, most importantly, will she be your ally and attest to your total (or partial) disability? If your doctor is not on the same page as you are, you are unlikely to have success in the claims process.

File Paperwork on Time and Keep Copies

If you are filing an individual disability insurance claim under a policy you purchased on your own, you will need your copy of the original policy. If you cannot locate it, you will need to call the insurance company and request a replacement. You will then need to notify the insurer that you are disabled by registered mail with *return receipt requested.* In your policy, there will be specific criteria as to the timeframe within which you must notify the insurer that you are disabled, the specific time period in which the insurer must provide you with a claim form, as well as the time period within which you must submit your claim form.

If you are filing a disability claim with a group disability insurer under your employer-sponsored, long-term disability plan, you will need a PDF of the certificate booklet with all the policy terms. Even if you have copies of employee booklets describing all your employer-provided benefits, you will need to officially notify your employer via your HR director that you are unable to return to work. Make absolutely sure that you retain a copy of every document submitted relative to your LTD claim in case your claim is denied and you have to file an appeal and/or file suit against the insurer.

Pay careful attention to the deadlines for filing notice of loss/proof of loss and the number of days within which you must file written documentation of your disability.

Review and Correct Your Medical Records

The single most important factor affecting the approval of your disability claim by your disability insurer is preserving the medical records that substantiate your disability relative to the terms of coverage outlined in your disability insurance policy. Although you may never have previously reviewed your medical records, they are yours—they belong to you. If your doctor or her staff is not cooperative, do not let yourself be intimidated. Although insurers' daily demands on your doctor's office can be extreme—making it a challenge for administrative staff to attend to each patient's needs with patience, follow-through, and compassion—you have every right to the staff's cooperation in furnishing you and your insurer the documentation needed to support your rights to benefits.

If you note any error in your medical records, you have every right to ask for correction(s). You should not assume your doctor understands all the daily duties you were performing at your job before you became disabled. Keep in mind that your disability insurance coverage is predicated (more often than not) upon your inability to perform the daily duties of your job at the point of disability. Should you discover anything in your medical records that does not clearly support your claim for benefits (disabled from performing all the material duties of your occupation at the point of disability), then this is your opportunity to pause and discuss the situation with your physician.

You are no longer receiving a regular paycheck based on working full time at your job. You are now disabled, you are no longer medically able to work at your regular occupation full time, and you may never return to the workforce again. It is imperative that you meet with your physician to discuss your need for his absolute, 100 percent cooperation in supporting your disability claim through medical documentation of your disability.

The physician who is attesting to your disability, usually the primary person influencing the insurer's decision to pay your claim, is not an insurance claim professional. Although your doctor may be certifying that your disability will prevent you from performing the duties of your job, he or she may not be aware of exactly what the insurers are looking for. For example, your doctor may not recognize that under certain circumstances (e.g., taking prescribed painkillers for back pain or coronary bypass surgery) you could return to your job, or another job, after your employer makes necessary accommodations to facilitate your return. This is why you must be as educated as possible—regardless of whether you plan to return to work—regarding what benefits you qualify for, including thorough consultation with your lawyer.

Review Your Coverage and Claims, and Answer These Questions

Begin by reviewing the eligibility section of your group LTD booklet to make sure you're presently insured. You may need to double-check with your employer to confirm this fact. If you've been working for your employer for less than one year, you will need to review, and understand, the preexisting restriction clause in your LTD contract. Your disability claim may be handled differently depending on whether you've been insured by your employer's plan for at least a year, especially if your claim is due to a preexisting condition.

Review your policies. If you're unclear about the benefits, call your insurance agent or ask your employer's HR director.

Are you totally disabled? Or are you partially disabled? Is there any lack of clarity about the details of your disability? Review your portion of the claim form. Is there a clear date of disability and a cause? Have you returned to work? Do you plan to return to work? And, if so, when?

Review your employer's statement. Is there a clear job description so that your inability to do the duties of your specific job can be clearly substantiated? Do the dates of disability match your portion of the claim form?

Review your doctor's statement. Does he or she clearly state that your medical condition prevents you from working at your job full time (or part time)? Is there an estimated date when he or she thinks you will be able to return to work? Are his or her dates of disability consistent with your portion of the form and your employer's?

Could you return to work if your workstation were different or if you were moved to a wheelchair-accessible location?

Are you aware that the Americans with Disabilities Act requires that employers provide "reasonable accommodations" for a disabled employee to return to work?

Are you prepared to go through a rehabilitation program, when given the opportunity, if you cannot return to your job? What does your doctor think about this? Are you in agreement with your doctor?

Work with a Disability Claims Agent

If you have an individual disability insurance policy purchased through an insurance agent, call him or her and ask for help. Your agent can be most helpful to you by guiding you through the claims process.

If you are insured through your employer's LTD program, ask the HR director or employee benefits manager how to contact the employer's benefits advisor, who can provide appropriate answers.

Frequently Asked Questions

When should I apply for benefits?
When you and your doctor are certain you will still be disabled beyond the policy elimination (waiting) period.

What does the elimination, or waiting, period refer to?
The number of days that you must be disabled before benefits begin.

What does the term "benefit period" mean?
The number of months or years that long-term benefits are payable.

How do I apply for benefits?
You, the claimant, should ask your employer for an LTD claim form, or, better yet, have your attorney advisor obtain the necessary forms. You need to complete the employee section after your employer has

completed the employer portion. Then, the attending physician who will be attesting to the existence and degree of disability will complete the "attending physician statement."

How long do I have after becoming disabled to file a claim, and how long will it take before I can expect a response?
You have 30 days to file your claim. Insurers must provide written notice of their decision within 45 days of receipt of the claim.

When can I expect to receive my first disability check?
Assuming the disability is valid and the claim is approved, most LTD insurers will send a check out toward the end of the first month of eligibility. For example, if a group LTD plan has a three-month elimination period, the claimant can expect to receive his first check toward the end of the fourth month of disability.

When benefits start, how much income can I expect to receive each month?
Your monthly benefit is shown in your employee booklet or in your group LTD booklet schedule page. In most group LTD contracts, the monthly benefit equals 60 percent of salary, up to a maximum specified limit, offset by benefits payable from other sources (e.g., Social Security, workers' compensation, etc.). If you have an individual policy, the monthly benefit will be shown on the schedule page. If you are partially disabled, your benefit will be based on the percentage of lost income.

Will I be eligible for any supplemental individual policies?
If the disability is job-related, you should be eligible for workers' compensation benefits. You may also be eligible for state cash sickness–disability benefits or other plans. The states (and territories) offering such plans are New York, New Jersey, California, Rhode Island, Hawaii, and Puerto Rico. You or your attorney advisor should also double-check to see if you have elected disability coverage with any of the associations you are enrolled in.

If you have been employed by the government, you may also have disability benefits through civil service, municipal (state, county, and local government) plans, or veterans' benefits.

How does my physician participate in the claims process?

The attending physician's cooperation is vitally important to the LTD claims process. In addition to attesting to your total disability, your physician will need to provide your insurer with all your medical records. This means that both your physician and insurer will have to be familiar with your line of work and the physical demands of the job, as well as any mental or psychological demands. For success, it is critical that the attending physician be your ally in the claims process.

How do I apply for Social Security benefits?

For information on how to apply for Social Security benefits, see, for example, Allan Checkoway, *Getting Paid: An Insider's Guide to Filing Your Long-Term Disability Claim or Appeal* (2010), and Chapters 6 and 7 of this text. If you have group LTD, the insurer will initiate this process. As LTD benefits are offset by Social Security benefits, it is to the insurer's advantage to help the claimant qualify for Social Security, as it is money the insurer will not have to pay. Disability insurers almost always have a skilled team to assist a claimant qualify and file for Social Security disability payments.

Why should I apply for Social Security disability benefits?

When disabled employees who have LTD insurance become eligible for Social Security disability benefits, the insurer coordinates Social Security disability benefits with group benefits.

What if I don't apply for Social Security?

If you do not file a Social Security disability claim, the LTD insurer has the right to offset benefits by what you would have been eligible to collect had you applied, thereby reducing the overall amount you will receive.

Afterword

Disability Protection for Attorneys

When lawyers decide to consider advising clients on filing disability insurance claims, they must envision what it is like to walk in the shoes of these potential clients. What type of disability insurance do *they themselves* own? Efforts to help your client collect long-term disability benefits can be enhanced substantially when you gain an understanding of the psyche and mindset of a client who has become disabled from working at his chosen profession. Similarly, if you own disability insurance yourself, you will have a better perspective on what your disabled client is facing. Like your clients, owning disability insurance will allow you to understand the risks, issues, and consequences of being disabled. Consider the fact that you have invested an enormous amount of time over many years, as well as a significant financial investment in your education, to become a trusted advisor to your clientele. It is time to protect your investment; you cannot afford to inadequately insure your own income against the risk of long-term disability. (This, in a sense, mirrors the practice of investment advisors who invest fully in their own funds.) By investing a small portion of your income in individual disability insurance, you can insure your income with "3 percent dollars." Indeed, a $100,000 income can be insured against the risk of disability for an annual expense of less than $3,000 (dependent upon the age when insured).

Seamless Coverage

Let's first establish some basic criteria for the most liberal disability insurance program an attorney (or anyone) can own. Considering the disability claims paid by the leading disability insurers, we see that there are literally hundreds of causes of long-term disability. Put simply, however, there are five basic claim categories associated with long-term disability:

- Totally disabled only
- Partially disabled only
- Totally disabled, then partially disabled
- Partially disabled, then totally disabled
- Any combination of total and partial disability

Let's evaluate how to accomplish the ambitious objective of providing "seamless" coverage that protects the attorney advisor against any or all of these occurrences.

Total Disability Defined

The heart and soul of any disability contract is the definition of total disability. The most liberal and popular form of coverage is protection that insures one in his or her regular occupation. With a true "own occupation" to age 65 definition of total disability, an insured can expect to receive own occupation income protection benefits even though working in another occupation.

Residual/Partial Disability Defined

Since not everyone becomes totally disabled, disability insurers have developed a benefit that satisfies the needs of insureds who are able to return to work partially disabled. When an insured suffers an income loss of at least 15 to 20 percent and cannot perform one or more important daily duties of his occupation or work, or is unable to work the usual number of business hours, benefits are paid based on the percentage of lost income.

Originally, when insurers developed residual (long-term partial) disability coverage, they typically required a prior period of total disability before residual benefits would be paid. If an insured suffered a gradually debilitating disease, such as multiple sclerosis or Parkinson's, without suffering a prior total disability first, residual benefits would not have been paid. A "zero day" residual disability benefit solved this problem by not requiring any prior days of total disability before partial benefits became payable. Insureds can satisfy their policy waiting period with any combination of total and/or partial disability days.

"Seamless" coverage insures for either total or partial disability, with benefits beginning after any combination of total and/or partial disability days. By combining "zero day" residual disability benefits with an "own occupation" definition of total disability, the most desirable form of seamless disability protection becomes available.

Insuring in a Professional Specialty

Disability insurers have been offering disability policies to medical and legal professionals who perform a specialty since the early 1960s. Physicians practicing a medical specialty (surgeons, radiologists, neurologists, urologists, etc.) should have disability insurance covering them in their own specific medical specialty, not just as a physician, assuming the insurer can be expected to pay benefits for a disability from their specific medical specialty.

The more finite the specific duties of the specialty, the greater the risk of disability. A debilitating back condition or failing vision renders a neurosurgeon totally disabled from his or her primary job. Yes, he can still teach medicine at a local university, or possibly he may be retrained as a radiologist, but he can no longer perform the duties of his medical specialty of neurosurgery. Achieving the ability to practice this specialty is why he went through the added years and expense of an advanced medical education. The take-home point is that everyone performing a specialty should attempt to obtain not just "own occupation" coverage but "specialty" protection in their specific area.

Now that we have identified the value of specialty protection for physicians, let's review the same principles as they apply to the attorney advisor. A simple Internet search shows an impressive total of over two dozen legal specialties. For illustrative purposes, let's discuss the work duties of a tax specialist as compared with a litigator practicing criminal law. The tax specialist's training in financial and tax matters will dictate his or her success. With the criminal litigator, his or her extensive knowledge of criminal law, combined with an influential personality, an impressive aura, and excellent presentation technique, will dictate his impact on the jury and ultimate success. His thought processes must be razor sharp; communication skills and adaptability are other helpful qualities that he may possess.

Next, let's explore examples of some representative causes of disability. A stroke or serious heart attack will greatly impact the full-time litigator, whereas the tax specialist might be more readily able to return to his somewhat less physically demanding work duties, possibly being able to work part-time. As another example, an automobile accident causing the need for a wheelchair will affect different specialties to varying degrees. For instance, "Ironside" played by Raymond Burr, who was a fictional attorney on television confined to a wheelchair, was able to continue his work while disabled.

It is important to note that some state bar associations recognize "specialists" and others do not. In those states that do not certify specialists, it is an ethics violation to promote yourself as one. Remember to refer to the specialty regulations in your particular state.

Historically, disability insurers have generally had good claims experiences among medical and legal specialists. In the drive to maintain and expand their market share within the legal and medical communities, most insurers have utilized "specialty" marketing materials to better gain new clients. This means that at the point of claim the need to prove inability to perform the duties of regular occupation, quite often referring to a specialty or subspecialty, is well established. Promotional marketing materials advertising specialty protection can be valuable documents when filing disability claims if a specific specialty is involved. If the insured owns individual disability coverage, check with the agent or broker to determine if specialty documentation may be needed at the point of claim.

When disability insurers promoted the concept that they would insure medical (and legal) professionals in their specialty, they provided "specialty letters" along with the actual disability policy. The following specialty letter is a representative sample.

SAMPLE SPECIALTY LETTER

____________________ Insurance Company

June 1, 2017

Robert Smith, MD

RE: Policy #

Dear Dr. Smith:

We are pleased to provide you with an explanation that "Own Occupation" means your occupation at the time a disability began with the _________ Insurance Company.

During the "own occupation" period stated in your policy, we will consider you totally disabled if, due to sickness or injury, you are unable to engage in your specialty of _________ (e.g., radiology/orthopedic surgery/cardiology, etc.) provided that was your specialty immediately prior to your disability.

If total disability benefits are payable under your policy, the fact that you could work in some other occupation or specialty would not preclude you from receiving benefits during the own occupation period stated in your policy.

Please note this letter does not alter or liberalize your actual disability policy. Actual determination and payment of benefits will be made in accordance with the provisions of your policy.

Sincerely,

____________________ Insurance Company

Protecting Your Law Firm through Insurance Covering Gross Revenues

According to several disability insurers, attorneys themselves have made substantial increases in claim payments in recent years. Overall, studies show that long-term disability claims for professionals is extending in duration, especially with "own occupation" disability claimants. This may be partly because hard-driving members of the legal profession are susceptible to forms of cognitive stress, alcoholism, and other "burnout" ailments, each of which has a lengthy recovery time.

Attorneys should thus be on the disability alert. Established law practices are often dependent upon the valuable services the principals provide; if a disability occurs, they will be greatly affected. The gross revenues generated from the individual personal services of the firms' attorneys are the financial livelihood of the practice. These gross revenues directly support overhead expenses, and the remaining profits are usually shared between the partners on an equitable basis through the payment of year-end bonuses. Most attorneys insure their incomes against the risk of long-term disability but frequently do not insure their overhead expenses. A Disability Services Group research paper on attorneys covering a seven-year period showed that over this timeframe the respondents' net income increased by 33 percent, while overhead expenses rose by 75 percent. Therefore, insurance for the faster-increasing figure is the form of coverage an attorney is least likely to own.

Let's consider the impact on gross revenues when a significant, revenue-generating senior partner becomes disabled. Substantial fixed budgetary sums are devoted to the overhead expenses of supporting the office needs of the disabled partner. The cost of personnel, professional associates, and office rent all continue at 100 percent, while the disabled professional's contribution to the practice revenue quickly dwindles to zero.

The firm likely does not want to rush into the termination of trusted and trained employees, especially if the timeframe of recovery is unknown. It takes many years of effort to develop a successful professional practice. When an attorney is disabled, the image of being in business must be continued. Clients who repeatedly call and leave messages with a stranger will soon take their business elsewhere. It is critically important to retain the services of a friendly support staff who will continue to maintain professional contact with clients. This gives the disabled attorney the opportunity to recover from his disability and rebuild his portion of the practice. Overhead expense protection allows this to happen.

An attorney's relationship with long-established accounts is based on expertise and trust that is usually developed over a long period of time. The understanding that has been developed ensures customer loyalty. If a partner has a continuing disability, this automatically opens the door to competitive firms and can have a devastating impact on the firm's revenues.

Is it possible that a partner could be replaced during the initial stages of disability? Probably not. Partners' unique talents make them very difficult to replace in the best of circumstances. Would a talented potential replacement consider filling in with the looming possibility of the disabled partner returning to work? Probably not. Let's assume the attorney suffers a heart attack, a leading cause of long-term disability. The Heart Foundation tells us that 250,000 Americans die annually of sudden cardiac death—680 every day of the year—and half of the victims of sudden cardiac death are under the age of 65. Yet, not everyone dies from a first heart attack. Currently, about 7.9 million Americans are alive who have had a heart attack. Many are totally disabled, while others remain partially disabled. Returning to work will be a very distant thought at the point of disability—our attorney is just hopeful that he will recover and live an unimpaired life. After three months of disability, the prognosis has finally improved. However, the patient's physician has already emphasized that 55-hour workweeks will now be a thing of the past. After six months of recovery and careful medical management, the attorney's cardiologist determines that his patient can never return to the pressures of a demanding law practice. Where does this now leave the firm?

Six months elapsed while the healthy partners were hoping for the rehabilitation of their valued colleague and his return to work. Now the process to find a suitable replacement begins. This type of talented individual may be presently employed at another reputable firm. What will it take in time and dollars to find and acquire a competent replacement? Eventually, when a replacement is hired, there will be a lag time of six months or longer to rebuild the firm's revenues. The capital to finance this financial drain will necessarily come from the firm's profits, thereby impacting the entire practice's bottom line.

With this scenario in mind, let's review what can and should be insured with "gross revenue" disability protection.

- Income protection benefits are payable directly to the disabled attorney at up to 70 percent of his predisability earnings.
- Business overhead expense protection provides reimbursement of the disabled attorney's share of the firm's overhead expenses. Expenses can be insured up to 100 percent. Premiums for this coverage are a tax-deductible expense to the firm. (See IRS Publication 535.)

Additional Resources

Department of Defense

"Warrior Care," http://warriorcare.dodlive.mil.

"Wounded, Ill, and/or Injured Compensation and Benefits Handbook," http://warriorcare.dodlive.mil/files/2017/01/DoD-Compensation-Benefits-Handbook_UPDATED-January-2017.pdf.

Department of Justice

"A Guide to Disability Rights Laws," https://www.ada.gov/cguide.htm. *"This guide provides an overview of Federal civil rights laws that ensure equal opportunity for people with disabilities."*

Department of Labor

"Benefit Claims Procedure Regulation FAQs," https://www.dol.gov/agencies/ebsa/about-ebsa/our-activities/resource-center/faqs/benefit-claims-procedure-regulation.

"Compliance Assistance: Group Health and Disability Plans; Benefit Claims Procedure Regulation," December 2012, https://www.dol.gov/sites/default/files/ebsa/about-ebsa/our-activities/resource-center/publications/group-health-and-disability-plans-benefit-claims-procedure-regulation.pdf. *Note the following language: "The Employee Retirement Income Security Act of 1974 (ERISA) is a federal law that sets minimum standards for retirement and health benefit plans in private industry. ERISA does not require any employer to establish a plan. It only requires that those who establish plans must meet certain minimum standards." ERISA covers retirement, health and other welfare benefit plans (e.g., life, disability and apprenticeship plans). Among other things, ERISA provides that those individuals who manage plans (and other fiduciaries) must meet certain standards of conduct. The law also contains detailed provisions for reporting to the government and disclosure to participants. There also are provisions aimed at assuring that plan funds are protected and that participants who qualify receive their benefits."*

"Disability Claims Procedures," adapted from the Labor Department by Lawley Insurance, January 2018, http://www.lawleyinsurance.com/wp-content/uploads/2018/01/Disability-Claims-Procedures.pdf; *concerns rules in effect April 1, 2018.*

"Filing a Claim for Your Health or Disability Benefits," https://www.dol.gov/sites/default/files/ebsa/about-ebsa/our-activities/resource-center/publications/filing-a-claim-for-your-health-or-disability-benefits.pdf.

"Final Rule Strengthens Consumer Protections for Workers Requesting Disability Benefits from ERISA Employee Benefit Plans," fact sheet, December 2016, https://www.dol.gov/sites/default/files/ebsa/about-ebsa/our-activities/resource-center/fact-sheets/final-rule-strengthens-consumer-protections-for-workers-requesting-disability-benefits-from-erisa-employee-benefit-plans_0.pdf.

"Job Accommodation Network (JAN)," https://www.dol.gov/odep/resources/jan.htm.

"Maximizing Productivity: Accommodations for Employees with Psychiatric Disabilities," https://www.dol.gov/odep/pubs/fact/psychiatric.htm.

Department of Veterans Affairs

"Accreditation Frequently Asked Questions," https://www.va.gov/ogc/accred_faqs.asp.

"Applying for Benefits," https://www.benefits.va.gov/BENEFITS/Applying.asp.

"Compensation," https://www.benefits.va.gov/compensation/index.asp. *Includes "Types of Compensation," "Types of Claims," "Claims Process," "Evidence Requirements," "Compensation and Pension Exam," "Effective Dates," "Fully Developed Claims," "Apply," and "Benefit Rates."*

"Directory of Veterans Service Organizations," https://www.va.gov/vso.

eBenefits (tracking claims and appeals), https://www.ebenefits.va.gov/ebenefits/about/feature?feature=compensation-claim-appeal-status.

"Manage Your Representative for VA Claims," https://www.ebenefits.va.gov/ebenefits/vso-search.

"PTSD: National Center for PTSD," https://www.ptsd.va.gov/index.asp.

"Vocational Rehabilitation and Employment," https://www.benefits.va.gov/vocrehab/index.asp.

Equal Employment Opportunity Commission

"The ADA: Your Responsibilities as an Employer," https://www.eeoc.gov/facts/ada17.html.

Hill and Ponton Disability Attorneys

"PTSD Guide," https://www.hillandponton.com/introduction-ptsd-guide/. Includes *"Part 1: What Is PTSD," "Part 2: PTSD Service Connection Flowchart," "Part 3: Compensation and Pension Exams for PTSD," "Part 4: Rating PTSD," "Part 5: Total Disability Based on Individual Unemployability" "Part 6: After the VA Decision—Now What?" and "Part 7: Resources."*

"Social Security Disability Benefits Guide," https://www.hillandponton.com/social-security-disability-benefits-guide.

IRS

"Work Opportunity Tax Credit," https://www.irs.gov/businesses/small-businesses-self-employed/work-opportunity-tax-credit. *The Work Opportunity Credit has been expanded to provide employers with new incentives to hire certain unemployed veterans.*

Law Office of Gordon Gates

"Sample Hearing Brief," http://www.socialsecuritydisabilitylawyer.us/blog/sample-hearing-brief.html. *Also referenced as a footnote in* Chapter 7.

National Archives

"Military Personnel Records," https://www.archives.gov/st-louis/military-personnel. *"This site is provided for those seeking information regarding military personnel, health and medical records stored at [the National Personnel Records Center; NPRC] (MPR)."*

"Veterans' Service Records," https://www.archives.gov/veterans.

National Veterans Legal Services Program

"The American Veterans and Servicemembers Survival Guide," https://www.nvlsp.org/images/products/survivalguide.pdf. *Including* "Chapter 5*: Explaining the VA Claims and Appeals Process."*

PTSD Help Network

"VA Compensation," http://www.ptsdhelp.net/id9.html.

Social Security Administration

"2017 Red Book: A Summary Guide to Employment Supports for Persons with Disabilities under the Social Security Disability Insurance (SSDI) and Supplemental Security Income (SSI) Programs," https://www.ssa.gov/redbook.

"The Appeals Process," https://www.ssa.gov/pubs/EN-05-10041.pdf.

"Disability Benefits," https://www.ssa.gov/benefits/disability.

"Medicare Benefits," http://www.ssa.gov/pgm/medicare.htm; and for Medicare Part D fees, visit https://www.medicare.gov/part-d/costs/premiums/drug-plan-premiums.html.

"Representing Social Security Claimants," https://www.ssa.gov/representation.

"Supplemental Security Income (SSI) Benefits," https://www.ssa.gov/benefits/ssi.

Veterans Today (blog)

"Health," https://www.veteranstoday.com/category/life/medical-and-health. "*Articles on Health and Medical Issues for U.S. Veterans.*"

Vietnam Veterans of America

"VVA's Guide on PTSD," https://vva.org/wp-content/uploads/2014/11/PTSD.pdf.

Appendix A

Excerpt from "ERISA Enforcement of the HIPAA Privacy Rules"

Jamie Lund, https://chicagounbound.uchicago.edu/cgi/viewcontent.cgi?article=5346&context=uclrev.

Heinonline is credited as the source of this content from the public domain.

Autoworker Daniel Duffey, an employee of General Motors Corporation, took advantage of GM's Employee Assistance Program (EAP), which "provides counseling and related services for employees with problems such as those stemming from alcohol and drug abuse." As a participant in the program, Daniel revealed his status as a substance abuser. GM subsequently discharged him. When he filed a grievance protesting the discharge, allegations relating to his participation in the EAP began to circulate, despite previous written assurances of confidentiality.

As Daniel's case illustrates, one way to increase the protection of private health information would be to allow individual civil suits against violators of privacy rules like those established by the Health Information Portability and Accountability Act of 1996 (HIPAA). However, HIPAA itself and the regulations adopted to implement its privacy protection contain no explicit private right of action, and courts have refused to infer a private cause of action under HIPAA for privacy violations.

HIPAA's privacy rules are the primary means of federal regulation of health privacy. The privacy rules were issued by the Secretary of Health and Human Services (HHS) under [the secretary's] rulemaking authority. These rules provide individuals with new rights and regulate the information. Most notably, the rules restrict unauthorized uses and disclosures of information related to nontreatment, nonpayment, and non-health care operations. The privacy rules protect information that is individually identifiable, which is any personally identifying information "created or received by a health care provider that [r]elates to the . . . health or condition of an individual" or to the provision of or payment for health care."

Although HIPAA's principal purpose is to increase access to health care through expanded portability and renewability of insurance, HIPAA also governs the use of individually identifiable health information. The law was passed in 1996.

Notice of Privacy Practices

HIPAA requires ERISA plan sponsors to provide plan participants with documents detailing parties' rights and obligations under HIPAA, including the "privacy notice." Each covered entity that creates or receives protected health information must create and maintain a "Notice of Privacy Practices" detailing potential uses and disclosures of protected health information.

ERISA

Congress enacted ERISA primarily to protect the interests of participants in and beneficiaries of employee benefit welfare plans by establishing standards of conduct, responsibility, and obligation for fiduciaries and by providing appropriate remedies and access to federal courts.

ERISA Enforcement of HIPAA: Should There Be a Cause of Action?

Out of respect for the different roles of the legislature and judiciary, "courts recognize only those statutory causes of action that Congress intended to create." The Supreme Court has held that "the fact that a federal statute has been violated and some person harmed does not automatically give rise to a private cause of action in favor of that person" and that "private rights of action to enforce federal law must be created by Congress." Although ERISA enforcement of HIPAA is arguably more acceptable than an implied cause of action for HIPAA, the courts still will not find a cause of action where Congress intended none to exist. Therefore, whether a court recognizes a private cause of action for privacy-rule violations will depend upon Congress's intent in enacting the two statutes, as manifested in the statutory language and other expressions of intent.

Privacy Notices as Terms of the Plan

Probably the most widely recognized outside source of plan terms is the "summary plan description." Many courts enforce summary plan descriptions even over conflicting terms in actual plan documents. Although some courts seem to place great weight on the fact that summary plan descriptions are required by § 102 of ERISA, "other courts have accepted documents other than summary plan descriptions as containing terms of the plan, so long as those documents are similarly representative. In *Brines v. XTRA Corp*, the Seventh Circuit noted that while informal modifications of ERISA plans are not permitted, prior cases have recognized plan modifications even in the absence of formal documentation. Additionally, since employers often have different plans covering different benefits, informal documentation could arguably constitute a separate and enforceable plan, so long as it does not contradict the written plan.

Appendix B

Excerpt from "Eradicating Discrimination among Individuals with Disabilities: Parity in Employer-Provided Long-Term Disability Benefit Plans"

Andrea K. Short, *Washington and Lee Law Review* 56, no. 4 (1999): 1342–90, https://scholarlycommons.law.wlu.edu/cgi/viewcontent.cgi?article=1572&context=wlulr.

Heinonline is credited as the source of this content from the public domain.

Parity in Long-Term Disability Benefit Levels for Mental and Physical Disabilities

As many as thirty-three million individuals have mental disabilities severe enough to qualify them for protection under the ADA [Americans with Disabilities Act]. The nation's growing awareness of this problem has given momentum to the movement for treating mental disabilities on a par with physical disabilities

Unfortunately, the ADA does not offer an explicit answer as to whether it mandates parity in disability benefits, leaving courts with the task of designing an answer to this question. Thus far, the federal courts of appeals that have faced the issue have refused to interpret Title I as requiring employers to provide equal levels of mental and physical disability benefits.

Case Law on Parity in Long-Term Disability Benefits

The plaintiffs in *Ford v. Schering-Plough Corp., Parker v. Metropolitan Life Insurance, EEOC v. CNA Insurance,* and *Lewis v. Aetna Life Insurance* all filed claims under the ADA alleging that the discrepancy between the levels of mental and physical disability benefits contained in their employer-provided disability insurance plans violated Title I of the ADA. In *Lewis,* the United States District Court for the Eastern District of Virginia held that Title I prohibits an employer from offering individuals with mental disabilities less extensive disability benefits than those offered to individuals with physical disabilities. The other three courts, and the Fourth Circuit in its opinion vacating the District Court's opinion in *Lewis,* however, reached the opposite result and rejected the plaintiffs' substantive parity arguments.

Courts Rejecting the Parity Argument

In *CNA Insurance,* the EEOC [Equal Employment Opportunity Commission] brought suit on behalf of a former employee alleging that the employer's reduction in coverage of mental disabilities violated Title I of the ADA. When the former employee had begun working for the defendant, her long-term disability package covered both mental and physical disabilities from the time of onset until age sixty-five. Subsequently, however, the defendant reduced coverage of mental disabilities to two years, while continuing to cover physical disabilities from the time of onset until age sixty-five. In its suit, the EEOC claimed that this reduction in benefits violated Title I of the ADA by discriminating against those employees who contracted mental disabilities.

In view of this related legislative debate and the absence of explicit language mandating parity, the Seventh Circuit ruled that the defendant's reduction in its coverage of mental disability benefits did not constitute disability-based discrimination because the plan still was available to all employees regardless of disability. Title I of the ADA, the court explained, prohibits an employer from offering individuals with disabilities benefit plans that provide lesser coverage or the same coverage at a higher cost. A plan that offers the same benefit package to all its employees on an equal basis, however, complies with the ADA regardless of what the benefit package includes. Therefore, the court upheld the benefit policy in *CNA Insurance.*

The next court to confront a parity claim was the Court of Appeals for the Sixth Circuit in *Parker v. Metropolitan Life Insurance.* In *Parker,* the Sixth Circuit concluded that the plaintiff was ineligible to sue; nevertheless, the court went on to discuss and reject the substantive merit of plaintiff's parity claim. The Sixth Circuit reasoned that if Congress actually had intended the ADA to mandate parity in insurance, it would not have subsequently needed to pass the Mental Health Parity Act (MHPA). Additionally, the EEOC's interim guidance, which suggests that a lower level of mental health insurance benefits does not necessarily violate the ADA, also persuaded the court to reject the plaintiff's claim.

In addition to this extrajudicial evidence, the court relied on precedent interpreting the Rehabilitation Act as prohibiting only discrimination between individuals with disabilities and those without disabilities. Cases interpreting the Rehabilitation Act uniformly hold that the Act does not recognize distinctions among individuals with different disabilities. Congress must not have intended the ADA, the *Parker* court therefore determined, to eradicate distinctions in disability benefits among individuals with different disabilities. The court concluded that the ADA requires only that an employer offer all its employees the same plan; the fact that the offered plan makes disability-based distinctions is not sufficient to violate the ADA.

The Third Circuit, like its sister circuits, concluded that the ADA does not require a disability insurance plan to cover physical and mental disabilities equally. The court also reasoned that if Congress had intended for the ADA to mandate mental and physical parity in benefit plans, it would have made that evident in the ADA's legislative history. Furthermore, the court placed weight on the fact that Congress passed the MHPA after already having passed the ADA. This fact, according to the court, indicated that the ADA, as currently written, does not require parity between mental and physical insurance benefits. The court concluded that rather than governing the terms of the benefit package, the ADA governs only the means by which the employer offers the benefit plan to individuals with disabilities. Faced with a challenge to the same type of benefit plan as in *Ford,* the United States District Court for the Eastern District of Virginia, in *Lewis v. Aetna Life Insurance Co.,* ruled that a disability benefit plan that provides lesser benefits to recipients who suffer from mental disabilities rather than physical disabilities *does* violate Title I. Although the Fourth Circuit has vacated this opinion, this Note contends that the reasoning that the district court employed in *Lewis,* particularly the application of ADEA precedent, is the proper means of addressing and resolving the issue of parity in disability benefits.

Lewis v. Aetna Life Insurance Co. and *Lewis v. Kmart Corp.*

In *Lewis v. Aetna Life Insurance Co.,* the plaintiff sued his employer after learning that he would lose his employer-provided disability benefits after two years because his benefit plan classified his disability as mental. Lewis alleged that Kmart's disability package violated Title I by discriminating against individuals whose disabilities were mental in nature. After concluding that the plaintiff was eligible to sue under Title I, the Eastern District of Virginia addressed the question of whether discrimination among individuals with disabilities constitutes a violation of the ADA.

Initially, in denying the defendant-employer's motion to dismiss, the *Lewis* court first examined § 12201(c) of the ADA, which is a "safe harbor" provision that limits the statute's substantive protection with regard to insurance benefits. The safe harbor provision permits an employer to offer benefit plans that make disability-based distinctions, but only to the extent that the offeror can demonstrate that it created the distinction based on actual differences in the risk, and therefore the cost, that the disability poses. Essentially, § 12201(c) requires that the distinctions adhere to traditional risk classification principles and not be an attempt to evade the ADA. To fall within the ADA's safe harbor provision, an employer or insurer must draw any disability-based distinction carefully and base the distinction on the estimated cost of covering a particular disability; the safe harbor provision, the court reasoned, does not protect a broad-brush distinction between physical and mental disabilities.

Distinguishing Disability Benefits from Health Insurance Benefits

Employers, and arguably courts, are reluctant to provide mental disability benefits on par with physical disability benefits because they fear that doing so will increase the number and cost of long-term disability claims.

Courts also rely on precedent, legislative history, and agency guidelines addressing health benefits when faced with the question of parity in the context of disability benefits. Congress specifically addressed the issue of parity in health insurance benefits in 1996 by passing the Mental Health Parity Act (MHPA) as an amendment to the Health Insurance Portability Act. The MHPA, however, does not address the issue of parity in disability benefits.

Appendix C

Subjective Symptom Disability Claims: Chronic Fatigue, Fibromyalgia, and Multiple Chemical Sensitivity Syndrome

Rick Lawrence, submitted to the *Life, Health & Disability/ERISA Litigation Conference*, September 23–25, 1998, http://www.cfids-me.org/dicases.html; introductory text by Mary M. Schweitzer, PhD, webmaster.

Heinonline is credited as the source of this content from the public domain.

Editorial Introduction (*Schweitzer*)

The following document showed up in my mailbox; the sender remains anonymous. Consequently, there is no way to guarantee the accuracy of the author attribution or that he is an employee of UNUM Life Insurance Company. I have posted this on the web in the belief that free flows of information are critical to the personal freedom upon which the United States is founded—and essential to the preservation of a free market in the insurance industry (i.e., information symmetry promotes a market solution to the availability and distribution of insurance services, which free market advocates theoretically consider to be a good thing). If anyone can offer corroborating evidence that this document is in fact attributed to the correct author and that the document is unchanged from that which was presented at the conference, I would appreciate it. In the meantime, we thank Rick Lawrence for his research efforts in this extraordinarily useful document and hope that those who make use of this remember to give him proper attribution.

We do warn readers, however, that calling Chronic Fatigue Syndrome, Myalgic Encephalomyelitis, Fibromyalgia, and Multiple Chemical Sensitivity Syndrome "subjective symptom disabilities" can be a bit misleading—as Alzheimer's can be diagnosed without having to perform a brain autopsy, these serious (and overlapping) physical conditions are in no way "subjective" themselves (that is, all in the experience of the patient)—all three produce verifiable physical symptoms that can be recognized by a physician with up-to-date information about these disease syndromes. However, there are no objective tests approved by the CDC or the FDA as "proof" that a patient has any one (or more) of these three disease syndromes. That is not quite the same thing as saying the symptoms are entirely subjective, and the reader must take care not to form the impression that these diseases are diagnosed by patient self-description alone: they are not. To repeat: the problem is that there is no "marker" (such as deterioration of the myelin sheath that appears in the spinal fluid of an M.S. patient) that can "prove" definitively whether or not a patient has CFS, or FMS, or MCSS. The insurance companies are saying, in effect, that until such a marker is found, patients who are sufficiently unfortunate to suffer from these diseases are not insured under regular policies. Those of us who worked for years thinking that we were covered by reputable and honest disability insurance were shocked to find this out, one by one, as claims were denied. The very few who can afford it are taking these cases to court. Because of the ERISA law, we cannot go to a jury of our peers, but must plead our cases before a single appointed judge in one federal court after another. Again, because of ERISA, the standard used to decide whether the claimant was treated "fairly" is not "preponderance of evidence" or "what a reasonable person would assume" from the contract, but rather whether the insurance companies have been operating in an "arbitrary and capricious" manner. More legal legerdemain. This is the background for the following essay.

Note: the issues debated in these courts are not whether or not the particular person really is disabled, but whether the insurance company followed "the rules." The reader can judge for himself/herself. Finally, those of us who are patients and claimants ask that the outside world please refer to the debilitation caused by our conditions (once described by U.S. Asst. Sec. of Health Philip Lee as "disease syndromes") not as "subjective symptom disabilities," a rather awkward phrase that implies that these may "*really*" be psychological illnesses and/or cases of outright fraud, but as "invisible disabilities"—disabilities that may not be clear to the casual external observer, but are quite clear to friends, family, co-workers, employers, and the medical professionals who care for us. The postmodern satire that "everything is subjective" will soon replace Andy Warhol's "fifteen minutes of fame" as the ultimate American experience if these bureaucracies succeed in convincing us that because the experience of health or illness—ultimately, of life itself—is subjective, why then it doesn't exist! One other comment: When reading this, note that the name "Chronic Fatigue Syndrome" first appeared publicly in 1988. It would hardly be surprising, then, that cases would suddenly start "appearing" in the 1990s.

Those of us suffering from ME-CFS, Fibromyalgia, lupus, post-polio syndrome, Gulf War syndrome, rheumatoid arthritis syndrome, connective tissue disorders, neuralgias, and other "hidden illnesses" ask that our representatives in government, and friends in society, step back from the legalism. Ask this basic question: what has happened to our society when a severely disabled person can be left abandoned and impoverished, denied the benefits that were part of their pay while they were able to work, because of the linguistic gamesmanship of the legal community?

To paraphrase: "Justice is the balm that heals the wounds of society." What follows is jurisprudence. But is it justice?

Main Text (*Lawrence*)

The analysis conclusions and/or opinions expressed herein are solely those of the author and are not intended to be, and do not necessarily represent, the views, opinions or positions of UNUM Corporation, its affiliates or subsidiaries, or the policies of the Defense Research Institute, Incorporated.

A. Introduction

The incidence of disability claims based on self-reported conditions has increased dramatically over the last several years. In fact, studies have shown that such claims are among the fastest growing causes of disability in the United States. CNA recently reported that from 1991 to 1996 chronic fatigue syndrome claims increased more than 900%, fibromyalgia, or soft-tissue pain claims, increased 254%, psychiatric-related claims increased 195%, and chronic pain claims increased 100%. Susan, C. Sendra, *Subjective Disabilities a Unique Challenge,* Business Insurance, October 7, 1996, p. 29. Though not strictly limited to disability claims, the State of Washington alone is estimated to have spent as much as $1.7 million in benefits for workers with alleged chemically related illnesses in 1993 and 1994. Sally James, *The Chemically Sensitive Controversy,* Issues of Injury, Vol. 8, No. 3 1994, p. 1. Experience shows that 20% to 40% of back related disability claims are self-reported with no objective evidence to substantiate disability. James R. McMullin, *Confronting the Back-Related DI Claims Challenge,* National Underwriter, February 10, 1997, p. 9.

The self-reported, or subjective, condition is one which cannot be confirmed through objective medical findings. The symptoms of these conditions can be reported to a physician, but are not easily verifiable by standard medical tests or procedures. Generally, the presence and severity of these conditions hinge solely on self-reported symptoms. Self-reported disability claims are difficult to adjudicate because standard, objective medical data indicates that nothing is wrong.

Disability insurance carriers thus face the problem of how to determine when an insured is truly sick; subjective disability claims may be real, but they hold an enormous potential for fraud and abuse. Subjective claims are inherently problematic for disability insurance carriers because "[t]hese types of subjective complaints are easy to make, but almost impossible to refute." *Yeager v. Reliance Standard Life Insurance Company*, 88 F.3d 376, 382 (6th Cir. 1996).

In response to the difficulties that subjective claims present, some carriers are modifying their policies. These changes include self-reported provisions which give a claim examiner the ability to terminate benefit payments after a certain time period has elapsed on claims which are based on subjective or self-reported conditions. While such limitations have been commonplace in group disability policies in regard to mental and nervous claims, these provisions are being applied to a broader array of medical conditions such as: chronic fatigue syndrome; musculoskeletal and connective tissue disorders of the neck and back; fibromyalgia; myofascial pain syndrome; and multiple chemical/environmental sensitivity syndrome. Implementation of these modifications is fairly recent; consequently, the case law interpreting these provisions is still in the early stages of development. Case law does exist, however, that addresses claims based on such subjective conditions. Several of these cases are discussed below.

B. Claims That Are Denied on the Basis of Lack of Objective Medical Findings

There are a number of reported decisions on subjective symptom claims in which the insurer has based its decision denying or terminating disability benefits on the ground that no objective medical evidence supported a finding of total disability. Some courts have upheld these decisions, notwithstanding the lack of an explicit requirement in the policy at issue that a claimant present objective medical evidence supporting a claim for disability. Other courts have held to the contrary. Two cases involving Du Pont's self-insured long-term disability plan provide an interesting comparison of the way in which courts treat this situation, and of the way insurers (or in this case the employer) can approach the problem of subjective claims.

The Du Pont disability plan at issue in these two cases provided in pertinent part: An individual shall be considered 'totally and permanently disabled' if the Board of Benefits and Pensions finds that he is totally disabled by injuries or disease and presumably will be totally and permanently prevented from pursuing any gainful occupation. . . .

Pokol v. E.I. Du Pont De Nemours & Co., Inc., 963 F. Supp. 1361, 1365 (D.N.J. 1997), quoting from the Du Pont Total and Permanent Disability Plan (the "Du Pont Plan").

In *Sansevera v. Du Pont*, 859 F. Supp. 106 (S.D.N.Y. 1994), Du Pont denied the claimant's claim for long-term disability benefits because of his failure to provide objective medical evidence that he was permanently incapacitated by the chronic fatigue syndrome ("CFS") from which he claimed he suffered. *Id.*, at 110.

The court reviewed Du Pont's decision under the arbitrary and capricious standard delineated by *Firestone Tire and Rubber Co. v. Bruch*, 489 U.S. 101, 109 S.Ct. 948, 103 L.Ed. 2d 80 (1989). The court noted that Du Pont defended its denial on the ground that the application for benefits was not supported by objective medical information indicating a permanent impairment. *Id.* at 113. The court found that Du Pont acted arbitrarily and capriciously by ignoring expert opinions regarding the diagnosis and treatment of CFS and by failing to seek the opinion of an independent expert on CFS. *Id.* The court further found that it was unreasonable to require that an applicant demonstrate with medical certainty that a disability will be permanent when: [as] is especially true in the case of an applicant diagnosed with CFS . . . there is currently no method of determining whether a person will ever recover from CFS, nor is there any treatment that has been proven [effective] in overcoming this illness. Because Sansevera has been suffering from CFS from February of 1990 and has not shown any sign of improvement, it is unreasonable to deny him benefits simply because he cannot prove with medical certainty that he will never recover.

Id. at 114-15.

This is an interesting case for a number of reasons. First, notwithstanding the application of the arbitrary and capricious standard, the court appears to have disregarded an express requirement in the Du Pont Plan that a claimant must satisfy before becoming entitled to disability benefits. Specifically, the Du Pont Plan requires that a claimant establish not only that he is totally disabled, but also demonstrate that he is permanently disabled as well. Secondly, the court appears to have disregarded the fact that a reasonable basis for Du Pont's decision existed in the independent medical exams that Du Pont obtained. Courts generally have been reluctant to overturn an insurer's decision when there is a reasonable basis for it. Finally, the court implicitly rejected Du Pont's argument that objective evidence of a disability must be provided before a claimant is entitled to disability benefits. While this aspect of the decision is not surprising, given the lack of any requirement in the plan that a claimant produce objective medical evidence to support his or her claim, as discussed below, just two years after the decision in *Sansevera* the federal district court in *Pokol* held otherwise.

The case of *Pokol v. Du Pont*, 963 F. Supp. 1361 (D.N.J. 1997), provides an interesting counterpoise to *Sansevera*. In *Pokol*, a machine operator filed a claim seeking disability benefits on the basis of fibromyalgia, back and arm pain, cervical symptoms, spondylosis and post-traumatic stress disorder. *Id.* at 1364. Pokol's application was supported by numerous medical reports regarding her physical and psychological health. These reports were reviewed by a member of Du Pont's corporate medical division who concluded that the claimant failed to submit any objective medical information to establish that she was totally and permanently disabled. *Id.* at 1367. Accordingly, Du Pont denied the claim.

Pokol appealed the denial and once again submitted a number of medical reports in support of her application for benefits. Du Pont upheld the denial of the claim. Pokol sued, alleging that Du Pont's denial was arbitrary and capricious. Pokol argued that the failure of the Du Pont Plan to define "objective medical evidence" was a "fatal flaw which requires a finding that the denial of disability benefits was . . . arbitrary and capricious." *Id.* at 1372. Du Pont, in an argument that perhaps should have been made in the *Sansevera* case, or if made, was rejected by the court without comment, contended that since the Du Pont Plan expressly granted discretionary authority to construe the terms and conditions of the Du Pont Plan, interpreting the language "satisfactory medical evidence" to include "objective medical evidence" is neither irrational nor unreasonable. *Id.* The *Pokol* court agreed with Du Pont and went on to find that in light of the absence of objective medical evidence supporting Pokol's claim for disability benefits, Du Pont's decision denying those benefits was neither arbitrary nor capricious. *Id.*

The *Pokol* and *Sansevera* decisions, contrasted with each other, present an interesting conundrum. Notwithstanding consideration of the identical policy language; assertion of disabilities involving subjective symptomatology; presentation of medical opinions that supported the respective positions of Du Pont and the claimant; and application of deferential standards of review in both cases, differing results obtained. This schism points out a fundamental truth of disability litigation: case outcomes are extremely fact and forum sensitive. Perhaps of greatest interest to defense practitioners is the success of Du Pont's argument in *Pokol* within the context of an abuse of discretion standard of review, that a claimant must provide objective medical evidence to support his or her claim of disability, notwithstanding the absence of any such express requirement in the policy.

This argument has succeeded in other subjective disability-based cases. In an unreported decision, *Davis v. U.S. West Inc.* et al., 1996 WL 673148, at *1 (D.Neb. Sept.26, 1996), the claimant presented conflicting medical opinions in support of his disability claim, which asserted everything from no diagnosis to a diagnosis of CFS combined with depression. In *Davis* the United States District Court for the District of Nebraska addressed the issue of whether the long-term disability plan in place on the date of disability ("Plan I"), or the plan in place at the time of the denial of the claim ("Plan III") controlled. Plan I did not contain a requirement that the claimant provide objective medical evidence to support her disability claim. Plan III did contain this requirement. The *Davis* court ultimately concluded that the resolution of this issue was immaterial. It found that U.S. West's claim reviewers and appellate committee always looked for objective medical evidence under either Plan I or Plan III. Thus, claimant's argument that Plan III somehow was designed to limit benefits failed because the objective medical evidence requirement was always in play as a part of the plan. The *Davis* court went on to find that even if Plan I applied, the appellate committee's interpretation of Plan I to require a showing of objective medical evidence was consistent with the Plan's goal of providing sickness disability benefits to individuals who truly merit such benefits. *Id.* at 12. See also *Finster v. Metropolitan Life Insurance Co.*, 927 F. Supp. 201 (N.D. Texas 1996) (summary judgment granted to defendant carrier on ground that plaintiff did not provide adequate, objective medical evidence to support claim that she was disabled as a result of back pain); *Conley v. Pitney Bowes. Inc.*, 1997 WL 580533 (E.D.Mo. 1997) (judgment for defendant after trial on grounds that complaints of subjective back pain were not supported by objective medical findings); *Steinman v. Long Term Disability Plan of the Mav Department Stores Co.*, 863 F. Supp. 994 (E.D.Mo. 1994) (summary judgment granted to defendant plan on ground that claims administrator reasonably found an absence of objective evidence supporting a diagnosis of chemical sensitivity that would form a basis of total disability); *Donato v. Metropolitan Life Insurance Co.*, 19 F.3d 375 (7th Cir. 1994) (denial of claim for disability benefits based on alleged hypersensitivity to common environmental chemicals upheld under arbitrary and capricious standard where insurer reasonably contended that claim was based on questionable medical theory and suspect medical evaluation, testing and documentation).

Acceptance of the need for objective medical evidence to support a subjective symptom claim, however, has not been universal. The unreported decision in *Duncan v. Continental Casualty Co.* 1997 WL88374 (N.D.Cal. 1997) bears out this point. In *Duncan* disability was claimed on the basis of a diagnosis of fibromyalgia, and benefits were denied on the ground that there was no evidence of a medical condition of sufficient severity to support the claim. *Id.* at 1. The United States District Court for the Northern District of California, reviewing the denial under the *de novo* standard, noted that the policy "makes no reference to the 'objective medical evidence' described in defendant's letter denying Duncan's claims, nor does it define the term." *Id.* at 2. The denial letter stated in part:

Objective evidence means medical signs and findings established by medically acceptable diagnostic techniques which show the existence of a medical impairment that results from an anatomical, physiological or psychological abnormality which could reasonably be expected to produce the pain or other symptoms alleged. Subjective complaints alone shall not be considered conclusive evidence of a disability. . . . The attending physician must be able to provide objective medical evidence to support his/her opinion as to why you are not able to perform the duties of your occupation.

Id. at 4. The *Duncan* court stated that Continental cannot exclude a claim for lack of "objective medical evidence" unless the "objective medical evidence" standard was made "clear, plain and conspicuous enough [in the policy] to negate laymen [plaintiff's] objectively reasonable expectations of coverage." *Id.* citing *Saltarelli V. Bob Baker Group Medical Trust* et al., 35 F.3d 382, 387 (9th Cir. 1994). The court further concluded that the denial of Duncan's claim was not sustainable under either the *de novo* or arbitrary and capricious standard. It stated, in pertinent part:

[M]edical conditions that do not give rise to hard laboratory facts or data may still be cognizable claims. In the medical opinion of Duncan's physician, the plaintiff has exhibited symptoms associated with fibromyalgia or CPS [chronic pain syndrome] and has become totally disabled as a result. . . . Continental may not deny Duncan's claim because her physician cannot provide physiological proof where the physical condition is such that physiological proof is not available.

Id. at 5. The purported absence of objective medical evidence as the grounds for the denial of a subjective symptom claim was rejected in another 1997 case. In *Monroe v. Pacific Telesis Group Comprehensive Disability Benefits Plan*, 971 F. Supp. 1310 (C.D.Cal. 1997), the claimant sought disability benefits after being diagnosed by a rheumatologist as having "profound fibromyalgia." The plan had the claimant examined by an internist who concluded that no objective evidence existed to substantiate the claimant's fibromyalgia symptoms. *Id.* at 1312. The plan initially denied the claim based on the internist's assessment and then briefly paid disability benefits on the basis of a psychiatric disability. *Id.* at 1313. Benefits were later denied when another treating physician opined that the claimant's depression was secondary to her fibromyalgia, which might be disabling, but that her depression was not. *Id.* Monroe appealed the denial of her claim and submitted a sleep study which showed that she suffered from a lack of REM sleep. *Id.* The plan upheld its denial.

The *Monroe* court found the denial to be arbitrary and capricious because the plan's examining physician was not a fibromyalgia expert. *Id.* at 1315. In addition, the *Monroe* court felt that there was objective evidence supporting Monroe's claim in the form of the abnormal sleep study performed by the treating physician and the treating physician's notation of certain "trigger points" that caused Monroe to suffer. *Id.* The court further noted that as the treating physician's report was more detailed than that of the plan's examining doctor, the denial was arbitrary and capricious because the plan (1) had given more weight to its doctor's report and (2) had failed to obtain an IME by a rheumatologist as had been urged by the claimant and her treating physician. *Id.*

The above cases highlight one approach that disability carriers sometimes take when dealing with subjective claims: require the claimant to provide objective medical evidence. This, however, is not the only tactic that insurance companies have employed in connection with subjective symptom disabilities as is discussed below.

C. Claims That Are Denied on the Basis of Lack of Definitive Diagnosis

In *Yeager v. Reliance Standard Life Insurance Company.* 88 F.3d 376 (6th Cir. 1996), an industrial nurse filed a claim for disability benefits under a group plan issued by Reliance Standard, claiming that she was disabled as a result of fibromyalgia, chronic low back arthritis, fatigue and carpal tunnel syndrome. The claimant's application was supported by four attending physicians: her primary care physician, a rheumatologist, a neurologist, and a fourth physician whose specialty was not disclosed. *Id.* at 378. Three of these attending physicians opined that claimant was not capable of performing the material duties of her occupation (the opinion of the fourth is unclear). Three of her physicians believed that the probable diagnosis was fibromyalgia. None of these physicians, however, provided a definitive diagnosis of fibromyalgia. The physicians noted a lack of objective findings to support claimant's subjective complaints. *Id.* at 378-79. It is unclear from the decision what medical evidence, if any, was presented by Reliance Standard, which denied the claim on the ground that there was insufficient evidence that plaintiff was totally disabled within the meaning of the group long-term disability insurance policy. *Id.* at 379.

The plan provided that Reliance would pay a monthly benefit if a claimant "is Totally Disabled as a result of a Sickness or Injury covered by [the plan). . . . 'Totally Disabled' and 'Total Disability' mean that as a result of an Injury or Sickness: . . . an insured perform the material duties of his/her regular occupation. . . ." *Id.* at 378. The court reviewed the denial under the arbitrary and capricious standard. The court stated:

The Plan required plaintiff to submit satisfactory proof that she could not perform the material duties of her regular occupation, and defendant had received no medical evidence of any physical condition or anatomic abnormality that would cause plaintiff to be totally disabled. The disabling condition on which plaintiff based her claim for disability benefits is fibromyalgia, but no doctor ever actually definitively diagnosed plaintiff as having this condition. . . . In the absence of any definitive anatomical explanation of plaintiff's symptoms, we cannot find that the administrator's decision to deny benefits was arbitrary and capricious.

Id. at 381-82. Thus, despite the fact that three out of four of plaintiff's treating physicians opined that she was totally disabled, and absent any comment on the medical evidence (if any) presented by Reliance Standard, the *Yeager* court found that the lack of a definitive diagnosis of plaintiff's condition was fatal to her claim. See also *Ellis v. Metropolitan Life Insurance Co.* 126 F.3d 228 (4th Cir. 1997) (denial of claim not arbitrary and capricious despite primary treating physician's diagnosis of a somatic dysfunction where all of treating physicians unable to arrive at a consensus on a diagnosis of the claimant's condition).

Other cases have also turned on the existence of a credible diagnosis. In *Gawrysh v. CNA Insurance Co.*, 1998 WL 329719 (N.D. Ill. 1998), the United States District Court for the Northern District of Illinois, Eastern Division, found CAN's denial of Gawrysh's claim for long-term disability benefits to be arbitrary and capricious. Gawrysh described herself as suffering from chronic fatigue, sinus problems, severe headaches and depression. Her attending physician stated that she suffered from chronic fatigue syndrome, sinusitis with intractable headache, recurrent sinus infections and bronchitis. *Id.* at 1. The CNA claim specialist assigned to Gawrysh's claim obtained her medical records from the attending physician, Dr. Blain, along with a letter from Dr. Blain that explained his diagnosis of chronic fatigue syndrome for Gawrysh. *Id.* Nevertheless, CNA denied the claim stating that the claimant's "maladies did not meet the definition for chronic fatigue syndrome that had been established by the Centers for Disease Control (CDC)." *Id.* at 2. Apparently, CNA believed that the claimant's sinus problems could be the cause of her persistent fatigue. *Id.* CNA also noted that the claimant had three small children and worked in a stressful environment, both of which circumstances might result in fatigue. *Id.* Thus, CNA concluded that there was no objective medical documentation to support Gawrysh's disability claim. *Id.*

Gawrysh appealed CAN's decision and submitted a letter from Dr. Blain which clearly indicated the attending physician's firm belief that the claimant suffered from chronic fatigue syndrome and from chronic sinusitis, the latter condition having required two surgeries. *Id.* In the letter, Dr. Blain also pointed out that Gawrysh had increased antibody levels to the Epstein–Barr virus. On review, CNA found that while Gawrysh might have been disabled for a period due to sinus surgery, there was insufficient objective medical documentation to find her sinus condition to be a source of continual disability. *Id.* The denial was upheld on appeal and Gawrysh's lawsuit followed. The *Gawrysh* court determined that the arbitrary and capricious standard applied in this case and thus that CAN's decision was entitled to great deference on review, provided that it did not: rel[y] on factors which Congress has not intended it to consider, entirely fail to consider an important aspect of the problem, offer an explanation for its decision that runs counter to the evidence before [it], or is so implausible that it could not be ascribed to a difference in view or in the product of [its] expertise.

Id. at 3. The *Gawrysh* court further noted that under the arbitrary and capricious standard it had to consider:

The impartiality of the decision making body, the complexity of the issues, the process afforded the parties, the extent to which decisionmakers utilized the assistance of experts where necessary, and finally the soundness of the fiduciary's ratiocination.

Id. The *Gawrysh* court next stated that the diagnosis of chronic fatigue is not a simple matter. *Id.* It then went on to observe that that no medical test exists for the diagnosis of CFS and that the CDC's protocol requires a physician to rule out other clinically defined causes of chronic fatigue by using a variety of tests. *Id.* The court then noted that CNA believed that Gawrysh's fatigue was caused by sinusitis rather than CFS and it concluded that such reasoning was shortsighted:

CNA did not deny [claimant]'s symptoms existed or had a debilitating effect, but concluded that because the symptoms could not, with complete certainty, be linked to a specific illness, [claimant] was not totally disabled. The uncontroverted evidence indicates that [claimant]'s symptoms were debilitating and were consistent with chronic fatigue syndrome. Rather than punishing [claimant] for the inability of medicine to specifically pinpoint the cause of her debilitating fatigue, CNA should have hired experts or used its own doctors to examine [claimant] to determine the cause and degree of her fatigue.

Id. Thus, the fact that it was unclear whether Gawrysh's fatigue stemmed from CFS or chronic sinusitis was an improper basis for the denial of the view of the court. If CNA doubted the legitimacy of Gawrysh's claims, it should have had outside experts examine her and try to pinpoint the severity and cause of the fatigue. *Id.* at 4. Instead, CNA utilized a claims specialist who apparently had no medical training or experience with issues of fatigue to review Gawrysh's medical records, and that made CAN's claim denial arbitrary and capricious. *Id.*

In *Clausen v. Standard Insurance Co.*, 961 F. Supp. 46 (D.Colo. 1997), the insurer's denial of plaintiff's group long-term disability claim was also found to be arbitrary and capricious. Clausen suffered from hypothyroidism, asthma, lingering viral or flu-like illness, chemical and environmental sensitivities, and pelvic pain.

The attending physician's statement in support of the application related a diagnosis of chronic fatigue syndrome, asthma, myalgias, pudendal nervc irritation and allergy. *Id.* at 1448. After Clausen filed her claim, Standard requested the medical records from all ten of her treating physicians. Standard's medical director reviewed this documentation and questioned the existence of chronic fatigue syndrome and found it "difficult to understand the nature of her impairment." *Id.* at 1449. Thus, Standard scheduled a psychiatric independent medical examination (IME) and internal medicine IME. *Id.*

The psychiatrist concluded that Clausen was not suffering from any psychiatric disorder. *Id.* The internist concluded that there was no evidence of severe, disabling chronic lung disease and that claimant's asthma was very mild. *Id.* at 1449. Thereafter, Standard notified Clausen that it believed there was insufficient objective medical evidence to support her claim, but that it was sending her file to an infectious disease specialist for review. *Id.* The infectious disease specialist, Dr. Edell, concluded that Clausen's complaints were primarily subjective and that there were no laboratory findings or other correlation present to explain her symptomatology. *Id.* at 1450. However, Dr. Edell also stated that Clausen had many of the criteria present that would meet the CDC's definition of chronic fatigue syndrome and that many of the other reports in the file had ruled out other common causes of fatigue. *Id.* Edell thus suggested that Clausen's primary attending physician, Dr. Wright, complete a CFS report. *Id.* Dr. Wright completed the report, and checked off all of the major and minor criteria for CFS, as well as two of three physical criteria. *Id.* Thereafter, Clausen submitted numerous additional records from doctors which concluded that she was disabled as a result of chronic fatigue syndrome. *Id.*

Notwithstanding the receipt of this medical information, Standard's medical director continued to be troubled by the claimant's long history of having numerous somatic complaints, but few objective findings. *Id.* at 1451. While he concluded that the working diagnosis at that point in time should be CFS, he suggested that surveillance be undertaken. *Id.*

The surveillance, conducted over the course of one day, showed Clausen taking a two mile walk with her dog for approximately one-half hour, driving a car and shopping for two hours with her mother and having lunch. *Id.* at 1451-52. At the conclusion of the day of surveillance, the investigators knocked on Clausen's door, informed her that they were assisting Standard Insurance and proceeded to ask her questions about her daily routine. *Id.* at 1452. They obtained a signed statement from her in which she indicated that she took her dog on walks of approximately one mile, three to four times a week and could only drive or sit for one-half hour at a time. *Id.* Standard then requested that Clausen undergo an independent neuropsychological evaluation, the conclusion of which was that from a neuropsychological perspective alone, Clausen was employable. *Id.* Thereafter, Clausen's claim was denied. *Id.*

On appeal, Clausen submitted additional medical records supporting her claim. Standard upheld the denial on grounds that there was "insufficient medical evidence to support Clausen's claim that she suffered a disabling sickness." *Id.* at 1453. Clausen filed suit and the court reviewed the denial under the arbitrary and capricious standard. The court recited the uncontroverted medical evidence that Clausen suffered from CFS and noted that none of the independent examiners to whom Standard referred Clausen disagreed with the CFS diagnosis. *Id.* at 1455-56. The court noted that the reasoning behind Standard's denial was that the medical director believed that the videotape and the report of the neuropsychologist refuted Clausen's subjective statements as to her physical and cognitive impairments. *Id.* at 1456. The medical director maintained that Standard "needed to rely on objective documentation of Clausen's impairment" and that the only such documentation was the videotape and the neuropsychologist's report. *Id.* at 1454. The court disapproved of this approach:

> Standard's attempt to ignore the CFS diagnosis of Clausen's treating physicians and to require, instead, that Clausen provide "objective" evidence of a distinct "physical disease" runs afoul of established law in this circuit.

Id. at 1456. Citing *Sisco v. United States Department of Health and Human Services* 10 F.3d 739 (10th Cir. 1993), the court found that: the lack of 'objective' medical evidence to 'prove' Clausen was disabled by her fatigue or pain cannot constitute substantial evidence that Clausen was not disabled, i.e., that she was capable of full-time work. I now find in addition that neither the surveillance video nor Dr. Thompson's report constitute such evidence. *Id.* at 1457. The court thus found Standard's denial of Clausen's claim to be arbitrary and capricious. *Id.* The court's rationale for its decision focused on the fact that many of Clausen's attending physicians had diagnosed her as having CFS, while none of the physicians who examined Clausen on behalf of Standard or who reviewed Clausen's medical records controverted this diagnosis.

Gawrysh, Clausen, and to a certain extent, *Yeager* highlight an issue that can be a red herring in these subjective disability cases. Claimants, claim administrators, the lawyers who represent these parties and even judges often focus too much attention on the diagnosis of a condition, or the lack thereof. In so doing, these players in the claims/litigation process disregard what is typically the primary concern in a disability case: what restrictions and limitations are caused by claimant's medical condition, and do these restrictions and limitations prevent the claimant from performing the material duties of his or her (or any) occupation.

D. Other Illustrative Subjective Symptom Disability Cases

Another interesting case dealing with a claim for disability based on chronic fatigue syndrome is *Mitchell v. Eastman Kodak Co.*, 113 F.3d 433 (3rd Cir. 1997). In this case, like *Clausen,* the court found that the plan administrator acted arbitrarily and capriciously in requiring the claimant to provide objective medical evidence that he was unable to engage in any substantial gainful work. Mitchell's CFS claim was initially denied by Metropolitan Life Insurance Company (MetLife), the claims administrator under the Kodak group long-term disability plan, on the grounds that Mitchell had failed to "provide objective medical evidence that his condition made him totally and continuously unable to engage in any substantial gainful work for which he was qualified as of June 26, 1989 [the alleged date of his disability]." *Id.* at 436. The denial decision was upheld on appeal and thereafter Mitchell brought an ERISA action to challenge the administrator's decision. Mitchell and Kodak filed cross-motions for summary judgment, both of which were denied, and the matter was remanded to the claims administrator for reconsideration after supplementation of the record. *Id.*.

On remand, Mitchell submitted a letter from his treating physician which explained how the chronic fatigue symptoms prevented him from engaging in any substantial gainful work. Once again, the administrator concluded that Mitchell had failed to provide any objective medical evidence that he was totally disabled as of his alleged date of disability, five years prior to the date of this physician's letter. Mitchell reopened his motion for summary judgment, which the District Court granted after conducting a *de novo* review. *Id.* at 437.

On appeal, the Third Circuit determined that the arbitrary and capricious standard should apply since "the plan in effect at the time of the latest denial decision contained discretionary language." *Id.* at 439. Kodak appears to have focused its appeal on the fact that the record did not contain any explicit doctor's statements that Mitchell was totally disabled as of June 26, 1989. There is no mention in either the Circuit Court or District Court opinions of any independent evaluation or record review by an in-house doctor. The *Mitchell* court found that the undisputed evidence in the claim file showed that as of the date of disability, "Mitchell's chronic and unpredictable fatigue and loss of concentration made it impossible for him to sustain regular paid employment." *Id.* at 440. The court found that while the records lack an explicit statement that Mitchell was totally disabled as of the date of his alleged disability, that alone does not support the administrator's conclusion that Mitchell failed to show total disability as of that date. *Id.* at 441. The court reasoned that what the administrator meant by its stated reason for denial was "that Mitchell failed to submit clinical evidence establishing the etiology of the chronic and unpredictable fatigue and loss of concentration that disabled him from working." *Id.* at 442. It further stated:

Because the disease, although universally recognized as a severe disability, has no known etiology, [citation omitted], it would defeat the legitimate expectations of participants in the Kodak Plan to require those with CFS to make a showing of such etiology as a condition of eligibility for LTD benefits. Thus it was arbitrary and capricious for the administrator to deny Mitchell benefits because of a lack of such clinical evidence of the etiology of his CFS. *Id.* at 443.

A review of the District Court opinion, *Mitchell v. Eastman Kodak Co.*, 910 F. Supp. 1044 (M.D.Pa. 1995), sheds further light on the medical evidence that was presented to the administrator and suggests that if Kodak had focused on the alleged restrictions and limitations caused by claimant's condition, the outcome of the Mitchell case may have been different. First, the District Court noted that Mitchell never offered any evidence or opinions from vocational experts, although it determined that none were necessary because the attending physician's opinion of Mitchell's inability to work due to CFS symptoms accorded with the court's view of the realities of the workplace. *Id.* at 1053-54.

Despite its acceptance the sufficiency of the medical evidence as to the CFS diagnosis, however, the *Mitchell* court took great care to point out that Kodak failed to offer any expert reports or other evidence to counter Mitchell's proof and instead chose to merely argue about its alleged insufficiency. *Id.* at 1054.

The importance of carefully examining and determining the pertinent restrictions and limitations in these subjective symptom disability cases, in other words ascertaining "what the claimant cannot do because of what" is further underscored by the following two cases.

In *Greene v. Metropolitan Life Insurance Co.* 924 F. Supp. 351 (D.R.I. 1996), the claimant filed an application for group long-term disability benefits with MetLife, the policy issuer and claims administrator. Greene asserted that she was totally disabled by chronic fatigue syndrome which was diagnosed by attending physician Armenio. *Id.* at 353. MetLife collected the medical records pertaining to Greene's condition and forwarded them to Dr. Freeman, a medical consultant it hired. Freeman concluded that the information available did not permit an independent confirmation of a CFS diagnosis. MetLife sent this report to Dr. Armenio and requested his comments. He responded that Greene had been responding to gammaguard treatments, but that she had become "completely depleted of energies," and could only work a half a day at most. *Id.* at 355. This response was forwarded to Dr. Freeman, who once again concluded that he could not find any clear physical or psychological limitation of function. *Id.* at 356. MetLife thus denied Greene's claim. Its denial letter stated, in pertinent part, that "the objective evidence submitted does not support the insured's inability to perform each of the material duties of her regular job." *Id.* at 356. Greene appealed the decision and sent additional medical information to MetLife. This information was reviewed and the denial decision upheld. Greene commenced an ERISA action and the court reviewed MetLife's decision under the arbitrary and capricious standard. *Id.* at 357. Greene contended that MetLife acted arbitrarily and capriciously by ignoring the treating physician's observations and diagnosis and by constantly requesting "objective medical evidence" from him when MetLife knew that no diagnostic test exists for CFS. *Id.* at 359. The Greene court stated that "pared to its essence, this case comes down to a choice between the Freeman consulting groups utilized by MetLife and Dr. Armenio." *Id.* The court noted that Greene emphatically contended that the reports prepared by Freeman failed to show that Greene did not suffer from CFS and Armenio's reports did show she suffered from CFS. *Id.* The court also observed that all of the doctors involved in the matter were board certified, at all relevant times, in fields pertinent to the diagnosis and treatment of CFS. Having summarized the essence of the conflicting medical evidence, the court's analysis then shifted to the next logical concern in a disability case, when it stated that: "It is imperative to note that whether or not Greene could perform her job duties was the relevant question in determining her eligibility under the disability plan, not simply being diagnosed with CFS." *Id.* at 360. The court went on to conclude that in a situation such as this where all of the medical experts possess virtually identical information, but their conclusions differ, the applicable "arbitrary and capricious" standard prevents a court from injecting its own judgment into the case to vacate a claim fiduciary's prior determination. *Id.* Accordingly, the court granted MetLife's motion for summary judgment.

In *Renfro v. UNUM Life Insurance Co. of America*, 920 F. Supp. 831 (C.D.Tenn. 1996), the claimant initially filed a claim due to major depression. After the end of the two benefit periods for mental nervous conditions, she asserted that she continued to be totally disabled from multiple causes. *Id.* at 832. Renfro's internist wrote to UNUM in support of her claim indicating that the claimant suffered from arthralgias, myalgias, weakness and other medical problems and that given her allergies and asthma she would be unable to work because she was very sensitive to perfume and other materials common in the work place. *Id.* at 834. After obtaining further records from Renfro's internist, along with records from her chiropractor, allergist and physical therapist, and having these records reviewed by its staff doctors, UNUM denied Renfro's claim on the grounds that nothing in those materials supported disability from a physical standpoint. *Id.* at 835.

Renfro appealed the denial and submitted a letter from a Dr. Furr, a physician who practiced in the areas of chronic fatigue, allergies, and environmental medicine. *Id.* Dr. Furr reported that he had performed testing with various chemicals, as well as referred Renfro to a pulmonologist to confirm that her breathing difficulties were neither psychological nor the product of malingering. *Id.* UNUM upheld its original denial in a letter noting that it had relied on Renfro's internist's assessment that she had the functional capacity to sit for 4 hours, stand for 2 hours, walk for 4 hours and lift up to 25 pounds occasionally, and occasionally bend and stoop. *Id.* at 836. The letter also stated that UNUM's consulting physician had reviewed the claim file and determined that Renfro's pulmonary function test was normal and that her asthma was not debilitating. *Id.*

In follow up to test results submitted by Dr. Furr, UNUM then decided to pay Renfro disability benefits under a reservation of rights, while it continued to investigate the claim. As one of UNUM's staff doctors noted some controversy over whether multiple chemical sensitivity syndrome existed as a legitimate medical syndrome, he recommended that an independent medical examination be performed. *Id.* The IME doctor concluded that Renfro's asthma was mild at best. *Id.* He further observed that the claimant's symptoms could be controlled with aggressive use of an anti-inflammatory drug; at the same time the IME doctor noted that: [claimant] is obviously disabled in that she becomes markedly symptomatic if she leaves her home environment, and thus it would be difficult for her to participate in work outside her home. I do not believe however that this is as a result of a true asthma and may well be functional.

Id. at 837. UNUM upheld its denial of Renfro's claim and she commenced an ERISA action. The *Renfro* court reviewed UNUM's decision under the *de novo* standard. *Id.* at 838. The court then summarized the medical evidence that UNUM had in its claim file. In the *Renfro* court's assessment, the claimant's treating psychiatrist only provided evidence of her mental disability and he disclaimed any expertise concerning allergies. *Id.* Renfro's treating allergist noted diagnoses of several conditions, but did not state that she was disabled due to any of these conditions. *Id.* The court then observed that the opinions of the Renfro's chiropractor and physical therapist could be discounted because (1) neither had the expertise to diagnose an infectious or environmental illness and (2) Renfro had not contended that she was disabled due to any chiropractic or musculoskeletal condition. *Id.* The court also noted that Renfro's internist had suggested that she was disabled due to "very, very severe asthma," but that assessment was contradicted by the results of contemporaneous clinical tests. *Id.* Further, the court commented that while the internist had opined that Renfro's allergies contributed to her disabilities, the allergist who was treating Renfro at that same time did not give a similar opinion. *Id.* at 838. Finally, in the court's view Renfro's pulmonary tests showed only mild obstructive airways disease and the recommended treatment did not indicate that she was disabled. *Id.*

The *Renfro* court then stated its assessment of the case as follows:

As for [Renfro]'s list of the various diagnoses made of her conditions during 1991 through 1993, the issue before the plan administrator was, as it is before this court, whether any condition or combination of conditions suffered by the [claimant] is disabling within the meaning of the applicable plan language. A list of diagnosed conditions, standing alone, does not satisfy the burden of making such a showing of disability. *Id.* Accordingly, the court granted UNUM's motion for summary judgment.

E. Conclusion

A review of the cases that address the denial of disability claims based on subjective symptoms leads to several conclusions. Each case is unique, its outcome highly dependent on the facts and the forum. Some courts have found that denials based on lack of objective medical evidence are not arbitrary and capricious, even in the absence of plan language requiring claimant to produce such evidence. Other courts have overturned "lack of objective evidence" denials. Some courts have found acceptable denials based on lack of a definitive diagnosis. Others have not.

Generally speaking, claims in which the claims administrator or carrier has conducted a thorough review of medical records by an in-house or consulting physician or commissioned an independent medical examination, and arrived at thoughtful and reasonable conclusions resulting therefrom, are more likely to result in a judicial finding favorable to the claims administrator or carrier, in matters governed by ERISA.

Even though conditions such as chronic fatigue syndrome, fibromyalgia, chemical and environmental sensitivity and chronic pain have beguiled and to an extent divided the medical community, courts tend to look with disfavor on claims decisions that are based on conclusory opinions of medical professionals that these subjective conditions don't exist or that a claimant is not suffering from them. However, diagnosis alone does not equal disability. Consequently, it is important to remember that disability occurs when an individual lacks the ability to perform the duties of an occupation. The complexities and difficulties of litigating a subjective condition disability lawsuit can be lessened if the parties and courts maintain their focus on this critical issue

Bibliography

Clausen v. Standard Insurance Co., 961 F. Supp. 46 (D.Colo. 1997)

Conley v. Pitney Bowesm Inc., WL 580533 (E.D.Mo. 1997)

Davis v. U.S. West. Inc., et al., WL 673148 (D.Neb. 1996)

Donato v. Metropolitan Life Insurance Co., 19 F.3d 375 (7th Cir. 1994)

Duncan v. Continental Casualty Co., WL88374 (N.D.Cal. 1997)

Ellis v. Metropolitan Life Insurance Co., 126 F.3d 228 (4th Cir. 1997)

Finster v. Metropolitan Life Insurance Co., 927 F. Supp. 201 (N.D. Texas 1996)

Firestone Tire and Rubber Co. v. Bruch, 489 U.S. 101, 109 S.Ct. 948, 103 L.Ed. 2d 80 (1989)

Gawrysh v. CNA Insurance Co., 1998 WL 329719 (N.D.Ill. 1998)

Greene v. Metropolitan Life Insurance Co., 924 F.Supp. 351 (D.R.I. 1996)

Mitchell v. Eastman Kodak Co., 910 F.Supp. 1044 (M.D.Pa. 1995)

Mitchell v. Eastman Kodak Co., 113 F.3d 433 (3rd Cir. 1997)

Monroe v. Pacific Telesis Group Comprehensive Disability Benefits, Plan 971 F. Supp. 1310 (C.D.Cal. 1997)

Pokol v. E.I. Du Pont De Nemours & Co.. Inc., 963 F. Supp. 1361, 1365 (D.N.J. 1997)

Renfro v. UNUM Life Insurance Co. of America, 920 F. Supp. 831 (E.D.Tenn. 1996)

Saltarelli v. Bob Baker Group Medical Trust et al., 35 F.3d 382, 387 (9th Cir. 1994)

Sansevera v. Du Pont, 859 F. Supp. 106 (S.D.N.Y. 1994)

Sisco v. United States Department of Health and Human Services, 10 F.3d 739 (10th Cir. 1993)

Steinman v. Long Term Disability Plan of the May Department Stores Co., 863 F. Supp. 994 (E.D.Mo. 1994)

Yeager v. Reliance Standard Life Insurance Co., 88 F.3d 376 (6th Cir. 1996)

Sally James, "The Chemically Sensitive Controversy," *Issues of Injury*, Vol. 8, No. 3, 1994.

James R. McMullin, "Confronting the Back-Related DI Claims Challenge," *National Underwriter*, February 10, 1997.

Susan, C. Sendra, "Subjective Disabilities a Unique Challenge," *Business Insurance*, October 7, 1996.

Appendix D

Excerpt from "Law and the Problem of Pain"

Michael Finch, *University of Cincinnati Law Review* 74, no. 2 (Winter 2005): 285–327, https://papers.ssrn.com/sol3/papers.cfm?abstract_id=1143538.

Heinonline is credited as the source of this content from the public domain.

Pain is a universal experience. Its unpleasantness is commonly thought to convey a message of discrete injury or disease. This view, still prevalent in law and clinical medicine, conceives of pain as the central nervous system's immediate response to acute bodily distress. Such acute pain has identifiable origins, occurs through well-known biological mechanisms, and is usually treatable. Yet for an appreciable segment of the world's population, pain is a chronic and pervasive condition having no clear medical meaning. This pain has no discernible relationship to injury or disease, and many critics wonder if it has an organic basis at all.

More than ten percent of the population, predominately women, suffer from chronic pain, and it is often incurable. The resulting personal and social costs are great. Approximately $85 billion to $100 billion are spent annually for the diagnosis and management of chronic pain. Almost half of the Social Security disability disputes pending in federal court involve claims of chronic pain. Damages for "pain and suffering" are often the largest component of personal injury awards and the perennial focus of tort reform.

Despite the prevalence of chronic pain, one question will not go away: Is the pain medically "real"? Pain is a quintessentially subjective symptom, and no practicable tests exist to verify its presence. Under the current medical regime of disease realism, most chronic pain is fragilely classified as a "syndrome" rather than a disease and grouped with a host of controversial illnesses whose legitimacy is still questioned.

The problem of chronic pain is examined by focusing on the most prevalent chronic pain syndrome found in litigation today, fibromyalgia. Fibromyalgia is nothing less than the widespread pain of rheumatism that has distressed humanity throughout recorded history. This pain syndrome has been described as one of the "most controversial conditions in the history of medicine," and it is at the center of the debate about the nature of chronic pain.

Chronic Pain

The concept of fibromyalgia is simple and broad. It refers to widespread bodily pain—an "aching all over" that persists over an extended period of time. For centuries this pain was popularly known as rheumatism. Fibromyalgia is predominately a women's health problem, afflicting women seven to ten times more often than men. This is consistent with the disparate impact of most forms of pain, which women suffer with greater frequency, severity, and duration than men.

The distinguishing symptom of fibromyalgia-persistent, widespread pain-is also the current basis for the disorder's diagnosis. As with much chronic pain, no laboratory test (e.g., a blood test or muscle biopsy) or similar objective evidence exists to confirm a clinical diagnosis of fibromyalgia. The diagnosis ultimately depends on the patient's reporting of subjective symptoms. Using a diagnostic "tender point" test, the examining physician applies pressure to select points distributed over the patient's body and observes the patient's response. A diagnosis of fibromyalgia is confirmed if the patient reports a sufficient number of painful points and her pain has persisted for at least three months.

Despite its controversy, subjective-complaint illness is surprisingly routine in medicine. Many common medical symptoms cannot be objectively verified, including fatigue, dizziness, or nausea. Similarly, many well-recognized disorders lack objective diagnostic tests, including migraine headaches and epilepsy.

Psychosomatic Pain Theory in the Courts

Chronic pain syndrome or "fibromyalgia" was first introduced to the courts in disability litigation. Half of the Social Security disability disputes now pending in federal court involve claims of chronic pain, and no signs indicate that the controversy attending these claims has waned. Courts generally accept that subjective pain can result in disability and that fibromyalgia or chronic pain syndrome is a legitimate illness within the meaning of disability laws. This has been facilitated by congressionally-mandated investigation of the problem of chronic pain, as well as the Social Security Administration's recognition that subjective symptoms can be validated through use of medical signs like the tender point test.

Mental Disorders in Chronic Pain Sufferers

Medical research, however, fails to support the claim that chronic pain, like that associated with fibromyalgia, is primarily the product of depression. First, most fibromyalgia sufferers do not have diagnosable depression. Second, among those who suffer from both depression and fibromyalgia syndrome, many likely have become depressed as a consequence of their chronic pain. A significant amount of psychological disturbance often accompanies chronic medical illness, but to assume that the illness is a product of psychological distress is a mistake.

Appendix E

Subjective Pain Testimony in Disability Determination Proceedings: Can Pain Alone Be Disabling?

Margaret C. Rodgers, *California Western Law Review* 28, no. 1 (1991): 173–211, https://scholarlycommons.law.cwsl.edu/cgi/viewcontent.cgi?article=1380&context=cwlr.

Heinonline is credited as the source of this content from the public domain.

Everyone has suffered pain. Yet, not everyone appears to suffer the same degree or severity of pain. What one person considers unbearable, another may find tolerable. This occurs because each person has an individual pain threshold. As a result, pain cannot be objectively measured; it is purely subjective in nature.

Because pain affects everyone, it is not surprising that physicians consider it to be the complaint they hear most often. Disability insurers, both private and public, view it as an enormous problem. One public insurer, the Social Security Administration (Administration), currently finds its disability insurance program in a state of flux over its attempt to answer the following question: "Because the experience of pain is different for each person, how is it possible to assess pain and determine a severity beyond which one should not be expected to work?"

This Comment will define and explain the confusion surrounding subjective pain testimony in disability determination proceedings, primarily focusing on the problems caused by Congress's approach to such testimony. . . . .

Reacting to a sharp cost increase after the passage of SSI, Congress enacted the Social Security Amendments of 1980 as a way of containing both SSI and SSDI. The main thrust of the 1980 legislation was a requirement that the Administration conduct eligibility reviews every three years. Although the new eligibility review process was originally seen as a promising way to protect taxpayers by "weeding out" those claimants no longer legally disabled, the harsh reality of implementing the process soon became clear: deserving claimants were having their benefits terminated.

In particular, Section 3 of the Reform Act 22 (Section 3) was designed to set forth a consistent and uniform framework for evaluating pain and other symptoms in disability determination proceedings by codifying the Administration's existing policy on pain. For individuals involved in these determination proceedings, Section 3 was the legislation's most promising feature because it provided disability decision makers with the first statutory definition for pain evaluation, and addressed the need for a comprehensive study on the evaluation of pain.

Judicial interpretation of pain, both before and after the enactment of Section 3, has magnified the problem. For example, over the last twenty-five years the Ninth Circuit alone has gone from not requiring objective medical evidence to support a claim of pain in full to requiring fully-supportive objective medical evidence of pain, back to not requiring it, then to requiring it again, and finally to not requiring it. This vacillation reflects the confusion and inconsistency inherent in the Ninth Circuit's approach to pain and serves as a general illustration of the widespread and continuing conflict over pain.

Malingering

The confusion of those persons charged with the responsibility for determining disability based on pain is not surprising. Pain has been referred to as "the great unknown factor" of the disability determination process. And, because there is no objective measuring stick available to measure the degree of pain felt by a particular individual, there is also no way to be objectively certain the individual indeed is suffering. Medical experts have termed those persons who attempt to defraud the Administration by deliberately faking their disability "malingerers." Malingering may be the Administration's greatest fear in relation to its disability program because the government cannot financially afford to promote, even indirectly, such a practice by granting benefits to those persons not truly disabled. Medical experts, however, have concluded that malingering is not a serious threat to the disability determination process because trained health care professionals can identify malingerers early in the disability determination process with medical and psychological tests.

Regulations and Rulings

During the 1980s, the Administration revised some of its regulations and made changes to some of its internal policies to better clarify its pain policy. Its efforts were intended to end the conflict over subjective pain testimony between the Administration and the federal judiciary. These clarifications solidified the Administration's commitment to a disability policy based primarily on objective medical evidence. Thus, the Administration's policy does not permit a finding of disability based solely on the claimant's subjective allegations of pain. Instead, the regulations and internal policies limit consideration of subjective pain testimony to situations in which claimants can show a medical condition reasonably capable of producing their pain:

If you have a physical or mental impairment, you may have symptoms (like pain, shortness of breath, weakness or nervousness). We consider all your symptoms, including pain, and the extent to which signs and laboratory findings confirm these symptoms. The effects of all symptoms, including severe and prolonged pain, must be evaluated on the basis of a medically determinable impairment which can be shown to be the cause of the symptom. We will never find that you are disabled based on your symptoms, including pain, unless medical signs or findings show that there is a medical condition that could be reasonably expected to produce those symptoms.

In 1982, the Administration adopted an "in-house" ruling, Social Security Ruling 82-58 (SSR 82-58), on the evaluation of pain and other symptoms.[161] Similar to 20 C.F.R. section 404.1529, SSR 82-58[162] instructed Administration employees to credit only medically-substantiated pain allegations. SSR 82-58 states in part:

Symptoms such as pain, shortness of breath, weakness, or nervousness are the individual's own perceptions of the effects of a physical or mental impairment(s). Because of their subjective characteristics and the absence of any reliable techniques for measurement, symptoms (especially pain) are difficult to prove, disprove, or quantify. This policy statement emphasizes the need for a sound medical basis to support the overall evaluation of impairment severity and underscores the importance of detailed findings. . . . Symptoms will not have a significant effect on a disability determination or decision unless medical signs or findings show that a medical condition is present that could reasonably be expected to produce the symptoms which are alleged or reported. However, once such a medical condition (e.g., disc disease) is objectively established, the symptoms are still not controlling for purposes of evaluating disability. Clinical and laboratory data and a well-documented medical history must establish findings which may reasonably account for the symptom in a particular impairment. . . . There must be an objective basis to support the overall evaluation of impairment severity. It is not sufficient to merely establish a diagnosis or a source for the symptom.

An individual's statements as to pain or other symptoms shall not alone be conclusive evidence of disability as defined in this section; there must be medical signs and findings, established by medically acceptable clinical or laboratory diagnostic techniques, which show the existence of a medical impairment that results from anatomical, physiological, or psychological abnormalities which could reasonably be expected to produce the pain or other symptoms alleged and which, when considered with all evidence required to be furnished under this paragraph (including statements of the individual or his physician as to the intensity and persistence of such pain or other symptoms which may reasonably be accepted as consistent with the medical signs and findings), would lead to a conclusion that the individual is under a disability. Objective medical evidence of pain or other symptoms established by medically acceptable clinical or laboratory techniques (for example, deteriorating nerve or muscle tissue) must be considered in reaching a conclusion as to whether the individual is under a disability.

In essence, the language mirrored the Administration's policy, thus reaffirming the requirement of objective medical evidence to substantiate pain allegations in full.

The Proposal [223]

This proposal provides for a pain-oriented assessment early in the sequential evaluation process. This early assessment will preclude the evaluation team from rejecting pain claimants' claim for benefits before considering the impact of the pain on the claimants' ability to function.

Under this proposal, a claimant is required to first objectively establish the existence of a physical or mental impairment which could reasonably be expected to produce "some" amount of pain. A claimant could satisfy this requirement by showing physical evidence specifically related to the alleged pain, such as tissue damage or bone deterioration. Alternatively, the claimant could allege pain which is disproportionate to or uncharacteristic of the physical evidence shown. After satisfying either requirement, the claimant must then show behavioral manifestations ordinarily thought to be associated with severe or prolonged pain: a preoccupation with his pain apparent through repeated complaints; a desire and willingness to undergo painful procedures as a way of alleviating the pain; overutilization of the health care system in search of a cure; overreliance on or excessive use of pain medication; audible signs or body language consistent with his complaints such as moaning, limping, bracing himself, grimacing, etc.; and/or other pain-related behaviors which are objectively identifiable such as sleep or eating disorders or sexual dysfunction.

Once the claimant establishes that he suffers from a pain-producing impairment, a functional assessment of the claimant's pain is triggered. This assessment requires the evaluation team to specifically assess the claimant's ability to respond to stimuli present in four categories essential to work productivity: (1) activities of daily living, (2) social functioning, (3) ability to complete tasks, and (4) functional capacity to perform basic work activities. The burden is on claimants to provide the evaluation team with information relevant to this assessment. Such information can come in the form of statements by family, friends, co-workers, employers, and by the claimants themselves.

1. *Activities of Daily Living.* The first category requires consideration of the claimant's ability to effectively deal with life's everyday demands. These demands include ordinary activities such as maintaining personal hygiene, dressing, and feeding oneself, as well as other demanding but necessary activities such as paying bills, taking public transportation, visiting the post office, or using the telephone.
2. *Social Functioning.* The listing's second category requires the evaluation team to assess the claimant's communication and interaction skills in order to determine the claimant's ability to function in a social setting. Assessment of these skills focuses on the claimant's ability to get along with not only his family and friends, but also his landlord, his physician, the grocery store clerk, and the bus driver. For example, persistent social isolation or a history of fighting may demonstrate impaired social functioning due to pain. On the other hand, a desire and willingness to interact with others through participation in group activities likely indicates healthy social skills.
3. *Ability to Complete Tasks.* The third category focuses on the claimant's ability to undertake and complete self-initiated or assigned tasks in a timely manner. Here the evaluation team is concerned with such work-related skills as concentration, persistence, and pace. These skills may be properly measured by assessing the length of time it takes the claimant to complete a work-related task or perform a routine household chore.

4. *Functional Capacity to Perform Basic Work Activities.* The fourth and final category requires consideration of basic work activities. It is important for the evaluation team to consider such exertional activities as sitting, standing, walking, lifting, pulling, pushing, and carrying, as well as those non-exertional requirements demanded by the workplace such as the ability to concentrate, follow directions, report in a timely manner, and get along with both superiors and coworkers.

Case Law

As noted, the Ninth Circuit's recent decision in *Bunnell* reaffirmed the earlier pain standard enunciated in *Cotton.* This standard precludes discrediting subjective pain testimony solely because such testimony is not fully supported by objective medical evidence, is characteristic of many circuit court decisions in this area.

For example, the Tenth Circuit, in *Luna v. Bowen,* drew attention to the issue of subjective pain testimony by addressing the relationship between the medical impairment and the degree of pain alleged. The court explained that by allowing the AU to rely primarily on objective medical evidence to determine whether the claimant's impairment is "reasonably" likely to cause his or her pain, courts place too heavy a burden on claimants to establish a sufficiently tight nexus between the impairment and the severity of the pain alleged. Relying on *Cotton,* the court concluded that after demonstrating the existence of a medical impairment through objective evidence, the claimant is only required to establish a loose relationship between the impairment and his or her pain.

Although facially helpful to claimants, the pain standards articulated in *Bunnell, Luna,* and other decisions are, by themselves, insufficient to correct the unfairness which currently exists within the disability determination process and are inconsistent with congressional intent. . . .

Conclusion

It seems ironic that two of Congress' greatest concerns in enacting the Reform Act, uniformity and fairness, continue to haunt all those involved in the disability determination process. Congress' attempt to placate those concerned over subjective pain testimony by including Section 3 in the statute accomplished little. It is no surprise, therefore, that federal courts, unskilled in the complexities surrounding claimants' subjective complaints of pain, loosely interpreted Section 3 by requiring only a relaxed nexus between an underlying medical condition and the degree of pain alleged. This type of pain policy is in line with the purpose for which the Social Security Act was enacted and should be adopted by Congress in place of the Administration's present policy.

There is no way of knowing the exact number of claimants who have been wrongly denied benefits because of the overly harsh pain policy currently in place. However, continuing to require claimants to provide medically-documented proof of the degree of their pain will most assuredly result in many more legitimately-disabled claimants being denied the benefits they deserve. Congress should pass legislation which adopts *Cotton* and *Luna,* and which is modeled after the Commission's dissenting members' proposal and the Institute's recommendation. New legislation and administrative regulations should (1) eliminate the need for a "reasonable" nexus between the medically substantiated impairment and the degree of pain alleged and (2) include a functional pain-assessment category in the Listing. This will go a long way toward remedying many of the existing problems in the Social Security disability determination process.

Appendix F

Excerpts from "Medical Proof, Social Policy, and Social Security's Medically Centered Definition of Disability"

Franks S. Bloch, *Cornell Law Review* 92, no. 2 (January 2007): 189–234, https://scholarship.law.cornell.edu/cgi/viewcontent.cgi?article=3047&context=clr.

Heinonline is credited as the source of this content from the public domain.

Congress dealt with its concern about an open-ended eligibility criterion by enacting a medically centered definition of disability for social insurance, which it later adopted for federal public assistance benefits as well. This definition limits benefits to persons who can show not only that they are unable to work—a term that the Act partially defines as the ability to engage in "substantial gainful activity"—but also that their inability to work is due to a "medically determinable physical or mental impairment."

The same basic definition remains in place today with statutes, regulations, and court decisions introducing certain modifications over the years. That definition has also carried with it a heavy administrative price. Although disability benefits make up a relatively small number of the total number of Social Security claims—out of approximately 53.5 million current beneficiaries, approximately 11.2 million are receiving benefits based on disability—determining whether disability benefit claimants are disabled consumes the bulk of the administrative resources of the Social Security Administration (SSA).

Clarifying the Medical-Basis Requirement for Pain and Other Subjective Symptoms: Pain Cases and the 1984 Amendments

Although it had been well settled since the 1960s that disability insurance benefits could be awarded based on disabling pain, the requirements for establishing pain-based disability remained unclear through the early 1980s. At one level, the issue was whether pain itself could be a qualifying impairment. Consistent with existing policy, SSA issued regulations in 1980 that included pain, or any other subjective symptom, as a basis for eligibility so long as a medically determinable impairment caused the pain or other symptom. These regulations made sense because the medical causation requirement effectively calls for medical proof of the underlying impairment. However, SSA did not address the more difficult question relating to the second part of the disability assessment: what sort of proof was required to prove that the pain resulting from the medically determined impairment was sufficiently severe to preclude the claimant from engaging in substantial gainful activity? Although a controversial 1982 Social Security Ruling elaborated on this point, the Ruling still failed to distinguish clearly the different proof requirements for causation and severity. As a result, at least for some claims, the Ruling was interpreted as requiring medical proof of severity as well. Litigation ensued, with one of the leading court of appeals decisions on the issue explaining the proper approach as follows: "While the claimant has the burden of proving that the disability results from a medically determinable physical or mental impairment, direct medical evidence of the cause and effect relationship between the impairment and the degree of claimant's subjective complaints need not be produced."

At about the same time, Congress resolved any doubt by enacting what amounts to a special statutory standard for evaluating disability based on pain. Now, the Act directly states that the claimant must provide specific medical proof of a medical impairment that "could reasonably be expected to produce" the degree of pain or other subjective symptom that the claimant alleges keeps him or her from being able to work. SSA implemented the new statutory standard by prescribing a two-step process for evaluating pain-based disability claims. First, the claimant must prove the existence of an underlying medical impairment that "could reasonably be expected to produce" the degree of pain or other symptom that the claimant alleges keeps him or her from being able to work. This, of course, is fully consistent with the medical causation component of the statutory definition of disability. Then, if the claimant can make such a showing, SSA will consider all other evidence in the record to determine if the claimant "is under a disability"—in other words, is unable to engage in substantial gainful activity.

"Medically Acceptable Clinical and Laboratory Diagnostic Techniques"

The Act specifies that a qualifying "physical or mental impairment" must "result [ ] from anatomical, physiological, or psychological abnormalities which are demonstrable by medically acceptable clinical and laboratory diagnostic techniques." SSA regulations implementing this requirement provide that qualifying impairments must be proved with "medical evidence consisting of signs, symptoms, and laboratory findings." The same regulations also specify that a claimant's own statement of his or her symptoms is not itself sufficient proof of these impairments.

Acceptable Medical Sources

SSA regulations recognize the critical importance of establishing a medically determinable physical or mental impairment by distinguishing between "acceptable" and "other" sources of medical proof. Only acceptable sources, mostly licensed physicians and licensed or certified psychologists, are qualified to provide evidence of a medically determinable impairment. Then, once evidence from an acceptable medical source proves the existence of an impairment, SSA looks to other sources to provide evidence of severity, including nurse-practitioners, physicians' assistants, educational and social welfare agency personnel, family, clergy, and neighbors.

This classification of acceptability of medical sources effectively maintains the sanctity of the medical-causation component of the disability standard. Not only must claimants provide medical proof of their impairments, that proof must come from a formally recognized, "acceptable" source. At the same time, this distinction acknowledges that the second part of the standard—severity—is not as clearly tied to medical proof.

Medical Opinions: Treating and Consulting Physicians

As previously mentioned, SSA is statutorily obligated to consider all of the evidence available in a claimant's file before reaching a decision on disability. In furtherance of this mandate, agency regulations provide specific guidelines for evaluating medical opinions. One set of rules, covering consistency and sufficiency, addresses the question of when the record is ready for the claim to be evaluated. Another set of rules explains that SSA should weigh conflicting medical opinions by primarily considering whether the source of the opinion—typically a physician—examined or treated the claimant, the extent to which medical evidence supports the opinion, and whether the opinion conforms to the rest of the record. In appropriate cases, SSA weighs the medical opinions of specialists more heavily than it does those of general practitioners.

Appendix G

Code of Federal Regulations, Social Security Administration "Residual Functional Capacity"

§416.945. Your residual functional capacity.

(a) *General*—(1) *Residual functional capacity assessment.* Your impairment(s), and any related symptoms, such as pain, may cause physical and mental limitations that affect what you can do in a work setting. Your residual functional capacity is the most you can still do despite your limitations. We will assess your residual functional capacity based on all the relevant evidence in your case record. (*See* §416.946.)

(2) *If you have more than one impairment.* We will consider all of your medically determinable impairments of which we are aware, including your medically determinable impairments that are not "severe," as explained in §§416.920(c), 416.921, and 416.923, when we assess your residual functional capacity. (*See* paragraph (e) of this section.)

(3) *Evidence we use to assess your residual functional capacity.* We will assess your residual functional capacity based on all of the relevant medical and other evidence. In general, you are responsible for providing the evidence we will use to make a finding about your residual functional

capacity. (*See* § 416.912(c).) However, before we make a determination that you are not disabled, we are responsible for developing your complete medical history, including arranging for a consultative examination(s) if necessary, and making every reasonable effort to help you get medical reports from your own medical sources. (*See* §§ 416.912(d) through (e).) We will consider any statements about what you can still do that have been provided by medical sources, whether or not they are based on formal medical examinations. (*See* § 416.913.) We will also consider descriptions and observations of your limitations from your impairment(s), including limitations that result from your symptoms, such as pain, provided by you, your family, neighbors, friends, or other persons. (*See* paragraph (e) of this section and § 416.929.)

(4) *What we will consider in assessing residual functional capacity.* When we assess your residual functional capacity, we will consider your ability to meet the physical, mental, sensory, and other requirements of work, as described in paragraphs (b), (c), and (d) of this section.

(5) *How we will use our residual functional capacity assessment.* (i) We will first use our residual functional capacity assessment at step four of the sequential evaluation process to decide if you can do your past relevant work. (*See* §§ 416.920(f) and 416.960(b).)

(ii) If we find that you cannot do your past relevant work, you do not have any past relevant work, or if we use the procedures in § 416.920(h) and § 416.962 does not apply, we will use the same assessment of your residual functional capacity at step five of the sequential evaluation process to decide if you can adjust to any other work that exists in the national economy. (*See* §§ 416.920(g) and 416.966.) At this step, we will not use our assessment of your residual functional capacity alone to decide if you are disabled. We will use the guidelines in §§ 416.960 through 416.969a, and consider our residual functional capacity assessment together with the information about your vocational background to make our disability determination or decision. For our rules on residual functional capacity assessment in deciding whether your disability continues or ends, *see* § 416.994.

(b) *Physical abilities.* When we assess your physical abilities, we first assess the nature and extent of your physical limitations and then determine your residual functional capacity for work activity on a regular and continuing basis. A limited ability to perform certain physical demands of work activity, such as sitting, standing, walking, lifting, carrying, pushing, pulling, or other physical functions (including manipulative or postural functions, such as reaching, handling, stooping or crouching), may reduce your ability to do past work and other work.

(c) *Mental abilities.* When we assess your mental abilities, we first assess the nature and extent of your mental limitations and restrictions and then determine your residual functional capacity for work activity on a regular and continuing basis. A limited ability to carry out certain mental activities, such as limitations in understanding, remembering, and carrying out instructions, and in responding appropriately to supervision, coworkers, and work pressures in a work setting, may reduce your ability to do past work and other work.

(d) *Other abilities affected by impairment(s).* Some medically determinable impairment(s), such as skin impairment(s), epilepsy, impairment(s) of vision, hearing or other senses, and impairment(s) which impose environmental restrictions, may cause limitations and restrictions which affect other work-related abilities. If you have this type of impairment(s), we consider any resulting limitations and restrictions which may reduce your ability to do past work and other work in deciding your residual functional capacity.

(e) *Total limiting effects.* When you have a severe impairment(s), but your symptoms, signs, and laboratory findings do not meet or equal those of a listed impairment in appendix 1 of subpart P of part 404 of this chapter, we will consider the limiting effects of all your impairment(s), even those that are not severe, in determining your residual functional capacity. Pain or other symptoms may cause a limitation of function beyond that which can be determined on the basis of the anatomical, physiological or psychological abnormalities considered alone; e.g., someone with a low back disorder may be fully capable of the physical demands consistent with those of sustained medium work activity, but another person with the same disorder, because of pain, may not be capable of more than the physical demands consistent with those of light work activity on a sustained basis. In assessing the total limiting effects of your impairment(s) and any related symptoms, we will consider all of the medical and nonmedical evidence, including the information described in §416.929(c).

[56 FR 57947, Nov. 14, 1991, as amended at 68 FR 51165, Aug. 26, 2003; 77 FR 10657, Feb. 23, 2012; 77 FR 43495, July 25, 2012]

Appendix H

Acquiescence Ruling 01-1(3): *Sykes v. Apfel*, 228 F.3d 259 (3d Cir. 2000)—Using the Grid Rules[1] as a Framework for Decisionmaking When an Individual's Occupational Base Is Eroded by a Nonexertional Limitation—Titles II and XVI of the Social Security Act.[2]

1 At step 5 of the sequential evaluation process we use the medical-vocational rules that are set out in appendix 2 of subpart P of part 404. In general, the rules in appendix 2 take administrative notice of the existence of numerous, unskilled occupations at exertional levels defined in the regulations, such as "sedentary," "light," and "medium." Based upon a consideration of an individual's residual functional capacity, age, education, and work experience, the rules either direct a conclusion as to whether an individual is disabled at step 5 of the sequential evaluation process or provide a framework to guide our decision at this step. *See* 20 CFR 404.1569a and 416.969a and our preamble to final rules published at 65 FR 17994 (April 6, 2000).

2 Although *Sykes* was a title II case, the same principles apply to title XVI. Therefore, this Ruling applies to both title II and title XVI disability claims.

Issue:

Whether we may apply the Medical-Vocational Guidelines (grid rules) as a framework to deny disability benefits at step 5 of the sequential evaluation process when a claimant has a nonexertional limitation(s) without either: (1) taking or producing vocational evidence, such as testimony from a vocational expert, reference to the *Dictionary of Occupational Titles* (DOT)[3] or other similar evidence; or (2) providing notice of our intention to take official notice of the fact that the particular nonexertional limitation(s) does not significantly erode the occupational job base.

Statute/Regulation/Ruling Citation:

Sections 205(b), 223(d)(2)(A), 1614(a)(3)(B) and 1631(c)(1)(A) of the Social Security Act (42 U.S.C. 405(b), 423(d)(2)(A), 1382c(a)(3)(B)) and 1383(c)(1)(A); 20 CFR 404.1520(f)(1), 404.1566, 404.1569, 404.1569a, 416.920(f)(1), 416.966, 416.969 and 416.969a; 20 CFR Part 404, Subpart P, Appendix 2, section 200.00(e); Social Security Rulings 83-10, 83-12, 83-14, 85-15 and 96-9p.

Circuit:

Third (Delaware, New Jersey, Pennsylvania, and the Virgin Islands). *Sykes v. Apfel*, 228 F.3d 259 (3d Cir. 2000).

Applicability of Ruling:

This Ruling applies to determinations or decisions at all levels of the administrative review process (i.e., initial, reconsideration, Administrative Law Judge (ALJ) hearing and Appeals Council).

---

3 Employment and Training Administration, U.S. Department of Labor, *Dictionary of Occupational Titles* (Fourth Edition, Revised 1991) and its companion publication, *Selected Characteristics of Occupations Defined in the Revised Dictionary of Occupational Titles* (1993).

Description of Case:

Clifton Sykes filed an application for disability insurance benefits after suffering several job-related injuries. After his claim was denied at both the initial and reconsideration levels of the administrative review process, he requested a hearing before an ALJ. The ALJ found that Mr. Sykes had several "severe" impairments and that, because of these impairments, he was unable to do his past relevant work. At least one of these impairments, blindness in the left eye, resulted in a nonexertional limitation. The other severe impairments included the residual effects of a torn rotator cuff, angina and obstructive pulmonary disease. Applying the grid rules in 20 CFR Part 404, Subpart P, Appendix 2 as a framework for decisionmaking without referring to a vocational expert or other evidence, the ALJ concluded that Mr. Sykes was not disabled because he could perform other work existing in the national economy. The ALJ's conclusion was based on his findings that Mr. Sykes had the exertional capability to perform "light" work and that the exclusion of jobs requiring binocular vision did not significantly compromise the "broad base of light work" established under the grid rules.

After the Appeals Council denied Mr. Sykes' request for review of the ALJ's decision, he sought judicial review. Mr. Sykes argued, among other things, that the ALJ erred in relying exclusively on the grid rules to determine whether there were jobs in the national economy that he could perform when his impairments resulted in both exertional and nonexertional limitations. The district court affirmed the ALJ's decision finding that it was supported by substantial evidence. On appeal to the United States Court of Appeals for the Third Circuit, the court reversed the judgment of the district court and remanded the case to us for further proceedings consistent with its decision.

Holding:

After considering the Supreme Court's decision in *Heckler v. Campbell*, 461 U.S. 458 (1983), the court concluded that our "interpretation of 20 CFR Part 404, Subpart P, Appendix 2 section

200.00(e)(2) does not comport with the Social Security Act . . . ." In view of the ALJ's finding that the claimant had a severe nonexertional impairment, the court stated that we cannot establish the existence of other "jobs in the national economy that Sykes can perform by relying on the grids alone, even if [we use] the grids only as a framework instead of to direct a finding of no disability." The court further stated that, "in the absence of a rulemaking establishing the fact of an undiminished occupational base, the Commissioner cannot determine that a claimant's nonexertional impairments do not significantly erode his occupational base under the medical-vocational guidelines [alone]."

The Third Circuit also addressed "the question [of] what additional evidence the Commissioner must present to meet the burden of establishing that there are jobs in the national economy that a claimant with exertional and nonexertional impairments can perform." The court held that the "sort of evidence the Commissioner must present to meet his burden of proof . . . when a claimant has exertional and nonexertional impairments . . . [is] the testimony of a vocational expert or other similar evidence, such as a learned treatise."

As an alternative to producing additional vocational evidence, the court held that we could rely on official administrative notice to establish that a particular nonexertional limitation does not significantly erode a claimant's occupational job base. The court stated that, "official [administrative] notice . . . allows an administrative agency to take notice of technical or scientific facts that are within the agency's area of expertise," in addition to commonly acknowledged facts. Under this alternative, we "would have had to provide Sykes with notice of [our] intent to [take administrative] notice [of the] fact [that the occupational base is not significantly eroded by the nonexertional limitation] and, if Sykes raised a substantial objection, an opportunity to respond. . . ."

The court stated that it was not deciding the issue of "whether Social Security Rulings can serve the same function as the rulemaking upheld in *Campbell*." The court further stated that it need not resolve the issue of whether "the Commissioner can properly refer to a ruling for guidance as to when nonexertional limitations may significantly compromise the range of work that an individual can perform."

Statement as to How *Sykes* Differs from SSA's Interpretation

At step 5 of the sequential evaluation process (or the last step in the sequential evaluation process in continuing disability review claims), we consider the vocational factors of age, education and work experience in conjunction with a claimant's residual functional capacity to determine whether the claimant can do other jobs that exist in significant numbers in the national economy. Section 200.00(e)(2) of 20 CFR Part 404, Subpart P, Appendix 2 provides that, when an individual has an impairment(s) "resulting in both strength [exertional] limitations and [nonstrength] nonexertional limitations," we use the grid rules first to determine whether a finding of disabled is possible based on strength limitations alone. If not, we use the same grid rules reflecting the individual's maximum residual strength capabilities, age, education, and work experience as a framework for consideration of how much the individual's nonexertional limitations further erode the occupational job base. As stated in 20 CFR 404.1569a and 416.969a, the grid rules "provide a framework to guide our decision" in this situation.

SSR 83-14, Capability to do Other Work—The Medical Vocational Rules as a Framework for Evaluating a Combination of Exertional and Nonexertional Impairments, provides that we use the grid rules to determine how the totality of an individual's limitations or restrictions reduces the occupational base of administratively noticed unskilled jobs when a claimant cannot be found disabled based on exertional limitations alone. In those claims where a person comes very close to meeting the criteria of a grid rule directing a finding of not disabled because it is clear that the additional nonexertional limitation(s) has very little effect on the exertional occupational base, we may rely on the framework of the grid rules to support a finding that the person is not disabled without consulting a vocational expert or other vocational resource. On the other hand, an additional nonexertional limitation may substantially reduce a range of work to the extent that an individual is very close to meeting a grid rule which directs a conclusion of disabled. Particular nonexertional limitation(s) may significantly erode or may have very little effect on the occupational base of jobs an individual can perform.

SSRs 96-9 and 83-14 include examples of nonexertional limitation(s) and provide adjudicative guidance on their effects on an individual's occupational job base. Some of the nonexertional limitations described in the SSRs do significantly reduce an individual's occupational job base and would result in a finding of disability. Other nonexertional limitations described in the SSRs do not significantly reduce an individual's occupational job base and would not ordinarily result in a finding of disability if the person's exertional limitations (or "capabilities") would result in a finding of not disabled under the grid rules. Regardless of whether the result is a finding of disability or no disability, we rely on our regulations and the SSRs to provide adjudicative guidance on the effects of particular nonexertional limitations on an individual's occupational job base.

Under our interpretation of 20 CFR 404.1569a, 416.969a and section 200.00(e) of Appendix 2 to Subpart P of Part 404, and of SSR 83-14, we are not required to consult a vocational expert or other vocational resource in all instances in which we decide whether an individual who has a nonexertional limitation(s) is or is not disabled. For instance, we are not always required to consult a vocational expert or other vocational resource to help us determine whether a nonexertional limitation significantly erodes a claimant's occupational base when adjudicative guidance on the effect of the limitation is provided in an SSR.

The Third Circuit concluded that, under *Campbell*, we cannot rely on the framework of our grid rules to deny a claim when a claimant has a nonexertional impairment(s) "without either taking additional vocational evidence . . . or providing notice to the claimant of [our] intention to take official notice of this fact [that the claimant's nonexertional impairment(s) do not significantly erode his or her occupational base] (and providing the claimant with an opportunity to counter the conclusion)." The court held that we cannot establish the existence of other jobs in the national economy that a claimant with a nonexertional limitation "can perform by relying on the grids alone, even if [we] use the grids as a framework instead of to direct a finding of no disability."

Explanation of How SSA Will Apply the *Sykes* Decision within the Circuit

This Ruling applies only to claims in which the claimant resides in Delaware, New Jersey, Pennsylvania or the Virgin Islands at the time of the determination or decision at any level of the administrative review process; i.e., initial, reconsideration, ALJ hearing or Appeals Council review.

In making a disability determination or decision at step 5 of the sequential evaluation process (or the last step in the sequential evaluation process in continuing disability review claims), we cannot use the grid rules exclusively as a framework for decision-making when an individual has a nonexertional limitation(s). Before denying disability benefits at step five when a claimant has a nonexertional limitation(s), we must: (1) take or produce vocational evidence such as from a vocational expert, the DOT or other similar evidence (such as a learned treatise); or (2) provide notice that we intend to take or are taking administrative notice of the fact that the particular nonexertional limitation(s) does not significantly erode the occupational job base, and allow the claimant the opportunity to respond before we deny the claim.

This Ruling does not apply to claims where we rely on an SSR that includes a statement explaining how the particular nonexertional limitation(s) under consideration in the claim being adjudicated affects a claimant's occupational job base. When we rely on such an SSR to support our finding that jobs exist in the national economy that the claimant can do, we will include a citation to the SSR in our determination or decision.

We are considering revising our rules regarding our use of the grid rules as a framework for decisionmaking and may rescind this Ruling once we have made the revision.

Appendix I

Fee Agreements

Social Security Administration, https://www.ssa.gov/representation/fee_agreements.htm

The Fee Agreement Process

A fee agreement is a written statement signed by the claimant and his or her appointed representative specifying the fee the representative expects to charge and collect, and the claimant expects to pay, for services the representative provides in pursuing the claimant's benefit rights in proceedings before the SSA. For the SSA to approve a fee agreement, the representative must submit it before the date of the first favorable determination or decision the SSA makes on a claim after the representative's appointment. If the representative does not submit a fee agreement by that date, the SSA assumes the representative either will file a fee petition or waive a fee. If the representative submits a fee agreement before the date the SSA makes a favorable decision, the SSA will approve the fee agreement at the time of the favorable decision if the statutory conditions for approval are met and no exceptions to the fee agreement process apply. Once the SSA approves the fee agreement, the fee specified in the agreement is the maximum fee the representative may charge and collect for all services in the claim.

The fee agreement and fee petition processes are not interchangeable. However, if a representative elects the fee agreement process but the SSA does not approve the agreement, or if an SSA reviewing official upholds a disapproval of a fee agreement on administrative review, the representative must file a fee petition if he or she wants to charge and collect a fee. The SSA must consider a fee agreement for approval under the fee agreement process through all levels of the administrative appeals process.

The Social Security Act does not require using specific language in a fee agreement. Therefore, representatives may craft their own fee agreement language and SSA will approve the agreement if it meets the statutory conditions of the Act and no exceptions apply.

Representatives may use stamped or photocopied signatures in lieu of their actual signatures on a fee agreement, and may submit a photocopy (or fax) of the original fee agreement. A fee agreement stamped only with a representative's firm's name is not acceptable.

SSA will not disapprove a fee agreement solely because it contains a provision stating that:

- The representative has the right to seek review of the amount that otherwise would be the maximum fee under § 206(a)(2)(A) of the Act.
- The authorized fee does not include any out-of-pocket expenses (e.g., costs involved in obtaining copies of medical reports or state sales tax, etc.).
- The fee agreement applies only to services through a specific level of the administrative appeals process.

For example, the agreement may state that its provisions apply only if the SSA favorably decides the claim(s) at or below the first Administrative Law Judge (ALJ) hearing decision, but that if the claim progresses beyond that level of the administrative appeals process, the representative will request a fee through the fee petition process. If the fee agreement includes this or similar language and the first hearing decision is favorable, the fee agreement applies in that situation, and the ALJ will approve the fee agreement if all the conditions for approval are met and no exceptions apply. If the SSA issucs the first favorable decision after the initial hearing decision (e.g. the Appeals Council issues the favorable decision), the decision maker must disapprove the fee agreement because the representative has not agreed to limit his/her fee to the lesser of 25 percent of past-due benefits or the specified dollar amount (e.g. $6,000). Because the claim progressed beyond the first hearing decision, according to the terms of the fee agreement, the fee agreement no longer applies. The representative may petition for a fee.

- A named third party will pay the representative a fee equal to the lesser of 25 percent of the past-due benefits or the specified dollar amount (e.g., $6,000), and the claimant will have no financial liability for paying the authorized fee.
- The representative will charge interest on the unpaid balance of the authorized fee.
- The representative will share the authorized fee with another person who referred the case.

Conditions for Approval of a Fee Agreement

The following statutory conditions must be met for a representative to obtain the SSA's approval to charge and collect a fee under the fee agreement process:

- The claimant or representative filed the agreement with the SSA before the date the SSA made a favorable decision. In concurrent titles II and XVI claims, the date of the favorable decision under the first title decided is controlling for both titles.
- The claimant, the claimant's legal guardian or representative payee, and representative both signed the agreement. If the claimant is legally incompetent or under age 18, a court-appointed representative or the person responsible

for the claimant's care may sign the fee agreement. For example, a mother may sign an application for title XVI benefits, an appointment of representative form, and a fee agreement on behalf of her child.

- Will be approved if all other factors are met.

Exceptions to the Fee Agreement Process

In certain situations approval of a fee agreement is administratively unfeasible, either because it could lead to authorization of fees in excess of the statutory limit under the fee agreement process, or could otherwise cause inequity for a claimant or a representative. Therefore, the SSA will not approve a fee agreement for purposes of authorizing a representative's fee in the following situations:

- The claimant appointed more than one representative associated in a firm, partnership, or legal corporation, and all did not sign a single fee agreement. This rule applies in all cases except when the representative(s) who did not sign the fee agreement waived charging and collecting a fee. The SSA must have received the waiver(s) before the date of the favorable decision.

A "single fee agreement" is defined as one agreement signed by all parties to the agreement. Therefore, if the claimant appoints a representative after submitting a fee agreement, the representative must sign onto the first agreement or the claimant and representative must submit an amended agreement signed by all.

- The claimant appointed representatives who are not members of a single firm, partnership, or legal corporation. This rule applies in all cases except when the claimant and the appointed representative(s) from a single firm, partnership, or legal corporation signed the fee agreement, and any other appointed representative(s) waived charging and collecting a fee. SSA must have received the waiver before the date of the favorable decision.

- The claimant discharged a representative, or a representative withdrew from the case, before SSA favorably decided the claim and the former representative did not waive charging and collecting a fee.
- The representative died before SSA issued the favorable decision.
- A State court declared the claimant legally incompetent and the claimant's legal guardian did not sign the fee agreement.

Information to Include in a Fee Agreement

- The Social Security Act (the Act) does not require using specific language in a fee agreement. Therefore, representatives may craft their own fee agreement language and SSA will approve the agreement if it meets the statutory conditions of the Act and no exceptions apply.
- SSA has written fee agreement model language that complies with the statutory conditions for approval of a fee agreement. However, because a fee agreement is a contract between a representative and his or her client, each fee agreement is unique, may appear in any form, and may include provisions in addition to the fee. For example, a fee agreement may contain additional provisions for payment of out-of-pocket expenses for medical reports, interest on an unpaid balance of an authorized fee, or for establishing a trust or escrow account, etc.
- Representatives may use stamped or photocopied signatures in lieu of their actual signatures on a fee agreement, and may submit a photocopy (or fax) of the original fee agreement. A fee agreement stamped only with a representative's firm's name is not acceptable.

Provisions That Will Not Prevent SSA's Approval of a Fee Agreement

SSA will not disapprove a fee agreement solely because it contains a provision stating that:

- The representative has the right to seek review of the amount that otherwise would be the maximum fee under § 206(a)(2)(A) of the Act.
- The authorized fee does not include any out-of-pocket expenses (e.g., costs involved in obtaining copies of medical reports or state sales tax, etc.).
- The fee agreement applies only to services through a specific level of the administrative appeals process. For example, the agreement may state that its provisions apply only if SSA favorably decides the claim(s) at or below the first Administrative Law Judge (ALJ) hearing decision, but that if the claim progresses beyond that level of the administrative appeals process, the representative will request a fee through the fee petition process. If the fee agreement includes this or similar language and the first hearing decision is favorable, the fee agreement applies in that situation and the ALJ will approve the fee agreement if all the conditions for approval are met and no exceptions apply. If SSA issues the first favorable decision after the initial hearing decision, e.g., the Appeals Council issues the favorable decision, the decision maker must disapprove the fee agreement because the representative has not agreed to limit his/her fee to the lesser of 25 percent of past-due benefits or the specified dollar amount (e.g., $6,000). Because the claim progressed beyond the first hearing decision, according to the terms of the fee agreement, the fee agreement no longer applies. The representative may petition for a fee.
- A named third party will pay the representative a fee equal to the lesser of 25 percent of the past-due benefits or the specified dollar amount (e.g., $6,000), and the claimant will have no financial liability for paying the authorized fee.

- The representative will charge interest on the unpaid balance of the authorized fee.
- The representative will share the authorized fee with another person who referred the case.

Provisions That Will Cause SSA to Disapprove a Fee Agreement

The following are examples of provisions that are inconsistent with the statutory condition that the fee specified in the agreement does not exceed the lesser of 25 percent of the past-due benefits or the specified dollar amount (e.g., $6,000). SSA will disapprove a fee agreement containing a provision stating that:

- The claimant will pay a minimum fee. For example, the fee agreement calls for a fee equal to 25 percent of the past-due benefits or the specified dollar amount (e.g., $6,000), or at least $1,500.
- If 25 percent of the past-due benefits exceeds the specified dollar amount (e.g., $6,000), the representative receives a fee equal to the specified dollar amount and retains the right to petition for an additional fee. (Representatives retain the right to request administrative review under the fee agreement process; however, they may not substitute the fee petition process for the fee agreement process once SSA issues a favorable decision.)

Appendix J

Attorney Fee Agreements for Disability Claims: What Is a Fair and Legal Agreement?

Ken Casanova

Individuals with disabilities must often seek the assistance of an attorney either to obtain or keep disability benefits to which they are entitled. A fee agreement is a contract between the individual and the attorney in which the attorney sets the fee and other charges for his or her services.

Sometimes, a client will question whether the total amount of money an attorney is asking for is fair or unfair. *How can an individual determine if the fee or other charges are reasonable, proper, and legal given the particulars of his or her case?*

In some rare instances the client knows that the fee the attorney is asking for is clearly excessive and unfair, sometimes even outrageous. Yet the client may feel desperate: the disability insurance company is wrongly trying to deny or terminate his or her rightful disability benefits, and a knowledgeable lawyer is promising to help obtain or maintain the benefits.

However, the attorney is asking for more money than would, by any stretch of the imagination, be fair for the amount of work that would be done by the attorney. Often finding a disability lawyer is difficult, the client doesn't know where else to turn, and there may be tremendous pressure to make a decision quickly.

So the disabled person can be in a terrible conflict: sign an agreement against his or her better judgment, or perhaps go without help and lose the disability benefits. What should the person do? *If he or she has already signed an unfair or excessive agreement, what can be done to terminate the agreement?*

The Three Types of Fees

An attorney is entitled to a fee for the legal services he or she provides. The attorney may also be entitled to charge for certain other legal costs. The fee is generally charged in one of three ways:

1. A flat fee of a fixed amount
2. A fee charged at an hourly rate
3. A contingent fee

A flat fee would cover the entire fee for the attorney's work.

A contingency fee, by contrast, is normally a fixed percentage of the total award of monies, if and only if an award is obtained. The lawyer cannot charge a fee if he fails to obtain monies for the client. The attorney is taking a risk, and therefore may claim a larger sum than he or she might normally obtain at an hourly rate. The contingent fee is designed to allow people to obtain legal services they might never be able to afford should they lose the case.

Sometimes, a lawyer may fairly charge, if agreed to with the full knowledge of the client, a fee using more than one of these methods: for example, a contingent fee with the addition of a limited flat fee or hourly charge should the case be lost. Most often, however, a lawyer charges by only one of the three methods.

But how is a client to know whether what a particular lawyer charges for a disability case is the fee normally charged by most lawyers, or is in itself fair and legal?

People with Myalgic Encephalomyelitis/Chronic Fatigue Syndrome (ME/CFS) in particular often lack the energy to go "comparison shopping," and in any event not all disability lawyers are even familiar with ME/CFS.

Social Security Fee Agreements

Most disabled individuals seek one of two forms of disability insurance: (1) Social Security disability or (2) private disability insurance through an employer. Often a person will be applying for both types of insurance, since private disability policies usually require the person, if eligible, also to apply for Social Security.

Fortunately, attorney fee agreements for Social Security benefits are regulated by Social Security. Generally, attorneys use contingency fee agreements in Social Security cases. A lawyer using this type of agreement is allowed, by law, only to charge 25 percent of a person's *retroactive benefits*, up to a maximum of $6,000. *[Ed. Note: The maximum dollar amount may have increased after 2015.]*

A lawyer may successfully petition Social Security for more than the maximum if he or she can document a valid reason for an increased fee. A lawyer may additionally charge reasonable expenses in addition to the fee.

Employee Disability Policies

More complicated and problematic are fee agreements in private disability insurance cases. These cases usually consist of an insurance company attempting to deny an application for benefits; or a company trying to terminate benefits that are already being paid.

Often an insurance company ignores the individual's legitimate disability and intentionally attempts to deny benefits on a false or dubious pretext. At this point the disabled person needs an experienced lawyer to stand up to the insurance company. The lawyer may be able to pressure the insurance company by asserting the client's contractual rights through one or more letters, by utilizing appeal procedures, or when these options fail, by suing the insurance company.

Often in these cases there is not as significant an accumulation of retroactive benefits as occurs in Social Security cases. Hence, it may be more difficult for a lawyer to obtain his fee by taking a percentage of the retroactive benefits on a contingency basis.

Several other possibilities exist for obtaining a fair fee. One would be an hourly fee; the drawback here would be that most people would not be able to afford more than a few hours of the lawyer's work, and cases which go to trial would entail many, many hours of the lawyer's billable time. Beyond several hours of such time, most people would only be able to afford a lawyer's time if they actually succeed in winning their benefits. So this sets up an intrinsic need for some type of contingency agreement.

Monthly vs. Lump Sums

Generally, disability benefits are paid monthly as a percentage of the person's former salary for as long as the person continues to be disabled. Sometimes, the benefits can be paid, instead, in one lump-sum payment. This type of payment may be preferred by the insurance company and will not be to the benefit of the disabled person. One does not know how long s/he may be disabled with ME/CFS, FM or other chronic illness. Benefits may be needed for many years.

A lump-sum payment is a one-time payment and as a total benefit might only cover an equivalent of 5 years of monthly payments. A person should be very cautious in deciding to take a lump-sum payment. However, sometimes one is forced to decide whether to take a lump sum or possibly face an insurance company's threat to limit or terminate monthly benefits.

In other types of lump-sum payment cases (such as auto insurance cases), a lawyer will take the case on a contingency basis. This is perfectly possible in a disability lump-sum case. Different lawyers will charge different percentages—often from 25 percent to 40 percent. One should determine the average rate and not pay a higher fee than what most lawyers charge.

Again, however, be careful of a lawyer pressuring you to take a lump sum as a way of collecting his fee if you would be better served by collecting monthly payments for as long as you are disabled.

The Worst Case

Now I am coming to the most excessive fee payments that patients with ME/CFS might be asked to pay.

Because of the practical difficulties of collecting a contingency on retroactive monthly benefits, *there may be some lawyers who seek to collect what may be an unfair and clearly excessive fee by attempting to take a percentage of the individual's actual ongoing monthly benefits for as long as he or she continues receiving benefits. The lawyer may try to take a percentage of the person's monthly income into the indefinite future, perhaps for 10 or 20 years.*

Such a fee agreement might require a person to pay a percentage, say 10 to 40 percent of a person's past, present and future monthly benefits. Think about it. If a person receives a check for $1,000 a month, and the lawyer takes 25 percent, that's $250 a month or $3,000 per year. If the person were on disability for 10 years, this would be $30,000 or for 20 years, $60,000. And who can afford to have 25 percent of their monthly income drained off to an attorney for what may be many years?

Is such an agreement fair or legal?

In Massachusetts, attorney fee agreements are legally governed by the Massachusetts Supreme Judicial Court Rule 3:07, 1.5, "Fees." The rule on the legality of an agreement reads: *"A lawyer shall not enter into an agreement for, charge, or collect an illegal or clearly excessive fee."* Among the factors to be considered in determining whether the fee is clearly excessive are the following:

1. *The time and labor required,* the novelty and difficulty of the questions involved, and the skill required to perform the legal service properly . . .
2. The fee *customarily* charged in the locality for similar legal services . . .
3. The *amount involved and the results obtained* . . .
4. Whether the fee is fixed or contingent.

A fee must bear a relationship to the amount of work reasonably performed by an attorney on a case. Although a contingency agreement rewards the attorney for taking a risk, the actual amount obtained must not be "clearly excessive": the fee must bear some relationship to the actual work performed by the attorney. Any agreement which attaches a percentage of a person's future benefits indefinitely in exchange for a fixed amount of a lawyer's time raises a serious question of excessiveness and enforceability.

Moreover, the amount of work the attorney actually performed must be reasonable, given the nature of the case. (In other words, if most attorneys take 20 hours to complete a case, a lawyer probably cannot bill 100 hours, even if he actually works that many hours.)

For instance, in the example above, a contingency in which the attorney attempts to collect 25 percent of a disabled person's monthly check indefinitely into the future ($30,000–$60,000) for doing only 20 hours work is most likely to be found by a Court to be clearly excessive, and therefore the agreement would not be enforceable.

Moreover, according to the Massachusetts Supreme Judicial Court [SJC] decision, *In the Matter of Fordham, 1996*, the Court cited case law which holds that the above factors for evaluating excessiveness are to be evaluated by the standard of "a lawyer of ordinary prudence."

Additionally, the decision holds that the "*test . . . .is whether the fee 'charged' is clearly excessive, not whether the fee is accepted as valid or acquiesced in by the client.*"

This means that the client cannot be held to a clearly excessive fee agreement even if he or she signs it. The SJC rule holds that fees "must be reasonable to be enforceable against a client."

Other Matters to Be Wary Of

An attorney may attempt to obtain monies unfairly in another way. One such way is to deceptively obtain a fee by claiming unreasonable charges for certain expenses such as "overhead," "disbursements," etc.

If the amount charged in an agreement clearly has no reasonable relation to such expenses, then it may be an attempt to collect a flat fee deceptively. Relatively large amounts for such "expenses" may really be fees which normally should be applied to hourly rates. For instance, if a lawyer asks for several thousand dollars as a "retainer" or "initial payment," the lawyer must take from this amount only what he earns hourly—he generally must return any unearned amount. All charges in an agreement must be explained fully; there must be no deception.

As explained above, the mixing of hourly rates, contingency fees, and flat fees is potentially permissible—but make sure that the attorney justifies in terms of work to be performed any agreement which calls for both a contingency percentage and a substantial flat fee. Remember, an excessive fee is defined as one which bears no reasonable relation to the justifiable work performed on a case.

No matter what the fee arrangement, always ask for an actual accounting of the time the lawyer spends on your case. Determine if the total charges of hourly work bear a reasonable relationship to the fee; also check to be sure you are paid any refund from your retainer for hours not worked.

In my opinion, *you should avoid signing* an agreement which you believe to be clearly excessive.

And *avoid signing* an agreement in which you sign away a portion of your monthly income for an indefinite future. The lawyer could be obtaining an undefined excessive amount for what might be a fairly limited number hours worked.

It is more reasonable if your case has to go to Court to agree with your attorney to pay a *fixed dollar amount* as a contingency fee only if your case is won. The contingency would probably reflect both the lawyer's expected work time as well as a dollar amount for the contingent risk. You then could make partial payments from your benefits for a period of time necessary to pay off that amount. Perhaps some other contingent fee could be arranged; but remember such a contingency should be a fixed dollar amount having some relation to the amount of work actually performed.

If you believe an agreement you have already signed is clearly excessive and therefore unenforceable, you can go to the *Massachusetts Board of Bar Overseers and make a complaint.*

The Board can terminate any improper agreement and discipline the attorney. The address of the Board is: Board of Bar Overseers, Office of the Bar Counsel, 75 Federal St., Boston, MA 02110, 617-728-8750.

Don't continue to pay an unjustified amount of money for the legal services you obtained.

(This article is not providing legal advice; if the reader has a specific legal question, s/he should seek competent counsel.)

About the Author

Allan Checkoway, RHU, has worked in employee benefits services and health care insurance for over 35 years, helping both employers and people with disabilities. He is one of the leading authors of books and articles on topics related to disability insurance, including *Disability Income: A How To Guide* (R & R Newkirk), *Disability Income Insurance* (Kaplan Publishing), and *ElderCare Survival Kit* (ElderCare Publishing). His articles have been featured in the *Wall Street Journal, Legal Economics, Lawyers Weekly,* and many other professional trade journals. He has also been awarded the National Association of Health Underwriters Norma Medill Award for Journalism.

Allan is the principal of Disability Services Group, a full-service employee benefits firm that offers a complete portfolio of life, short-, and long-term disability, medical, dental, and long-term care insurance coverage. With his firm, he has helped corporations purchase the most beneficial disability programs for their employees and created the Disability Counseling Service to help disabled employees file long-term disability claims. Disability Services Group also created *Getting Paid,* a resource manual on filing disability claims and appeals, and *I'm Disabled . . . Now What?,* a guide to lifestyle changes, to help seniors and those with disabilities enjoy more independent and enriched lifestyles.

A past president of the Disability Insurance Training Council, as well as past regional vice president of the National Association of Health Underwriters, Allan is a frequent speaker at professional association meetings and educational conferences.

Write to Allan Checkoway, Publisher, c/o ElderCare Publishing, 389 Boston Post Road, Sudbury, MA 01776, or send an email to allan@eldercaresurvival.com.

Table of Cases

Index

R

S